# Radical Change

# Radical Change

The Death of the American Dream

Cornucopia or Armegeddon

Abundance

Unemployment

Inequality

DANIEL SULLIVAN

ISBN: 0692439145
ISBN 13: 9780692439142
Library of Congress Control Number: 2015906856
Curtis Hollow Publishers, Brookline MA

# In Memoriam

During the final phase of the completion of this book, my beloved wife, Susan Marie Sullivan, died after a long and courageous battle with a rare form of bone cancer. Her treatment, though ultimately not successful, benefited greatly from advances in DNA-designed chemotherapy drugs. Those drugs were based, in large part, on the research conducted at the Broad Center in Cambridge, Massachusetts. While breakthrough advances in the past decade have furthered our understanding of how the human body functions, we are still a long way from discovering a cure for cancer. Yet the development of new technologies is rapidly accelerating progress toward that goal.

My wife's death reminded me that despite the potential dark side of some of the technologies discussed in this book, the science of the future will create far better, healthier, longer and more rewarding lives for our children and grandchildren, for which we should be very grateful.

# TABLE OF CONTENTS

# Acknowledgments

To my three beautiful daughters, Rebecca, Anna and Kristen, who were the inspiration for me to begin to write this book, and to my deceased wife Susan, whose grace and beauty in very difficult times were the inspiration for me to finish it. During the course of writing this book, although my wife died, my life was enriched by the birth of three grand-children. This reminds me that life is a constant process of renewal -- a message that hopefully this book conveys.

Also, to Margaret Kelner, my assistant and editor, who was there from the beginning -- unflappable in the face of endless revisions -- whose quiet encouragement and determination pushed the book forward.

**Radical Change:** A fundamental acceleration of change in the world causing a paradigm shift in our relationship with humanity, machines, artificial intelligence, the earth and the universe.

Daniel Sullivan, author, 2015


**Cornucopia:** An abundant overflowing supply; an inexhaustible horn of plenty.

*Merriam Webster*


**Armageddon:** The place where the final battle will be fought between the forces of good and evil; the battlefield of Megiddo, the war to end all wars; thereafter, God will set up His kingdom.

Revelations 16:16

# Introduction

Technology has always inspired science fiction, but new technologies often overtake the vision of the science fiction writers of the prior generation. We go to the bottom of the seas in vessels far beyond the imagination of Jules Verne, we examine our bodies with MRI and brainwave imaging devices far more precise than the x-ray vision of Superman, and we have smartphones far more sophisticated than the one Dick Tracy used. The previous generation of science fiction writers got the concepts right, but new technologies, when they arrived, were better and often far more creative.

Isaac Asimov envisioned robots that looked and acted human. This challenge to science has proven to be much more difficult than first anticipated, so we do not yet have robots that perform as well as those described in *I Robot*.[1] But Asimov's robots did not possess most of the astounding powers of the Internet. And while robotic development has been slow, it has recently begun to accelerate dramatically, so we are only a generation away from robots that will be very lifelike. Since the early and innocent predictions of the future of robotic behavior, there has been a great deal of scientific progress in the artificial intelligence that empowered those robots.

These advances have inspired a new generation of science fiction movies that predict a far more terrifying future relationship with robots. Movies such as James Cameron's *The Terminator* and Joss Whedon's

---

1  Isaac Asimov, *I Robot* (Gnome Press, 1950).

*Avengers: The Age of Ultron* warn us that the advances in artificial intelligence may not be a benign development.

If science fiction writers continue to be relatively reliable soothsayers of our future, there is real cause for concern. In fact, these visionaries may fall far short in their predictions. No science fiction writer predicted the over one million applications of the Internet, until technology created them, and this is just the beginning. Are the world's great writers losing their vision of the future? Not really. New technologies are now advancing so fast that we cannot keep up with the possibilities they empower; not even our best science fiction writers can.

Today, many predict that artificial intelligence (AI) will become so super intelligent that it will come to dominate the human race.[2] Others predict that bots, created by nanotechnology, will escape our control and swarm all over us like "grey goo." These are not the musings of science fiction writers; they are the well-considered opinions of brilliant, well-regarded physicists, mathematicians and scientists from a plethora of disciplines.

More recently, less futuristic observers from disciplines such as economics are beginning to focus on what advancing technologies may do to our collective economic well-being, long before a superhuman form of AI may escape the genie's bottle and attempt to enslave or annihilate all of us. The reality of the worldwide failure to economically recover from the Great Recession of 2008, our current stubborn unemployment and wage stagnation, the serious decline of America's middle class and the spectacular increase in worldwide economic inequality are now

---

2 The term artificial intelligence (AI) has taken on many divergent meanings as this technology has made astounding advances in the past few decades. It can now signify the intelligence of the self-adjusting braking systems in our automobiles, the algorithmic trading programs that dominate our stock markets, IBM Watson's triumph over brilliant contestants in the game of "Jeopardy," or the futuristic advanced artificial super intelligence (ASI) such as Hal in the movie *2001*. Later chapters address the meaningful differences in each of these stages of AI, but for now the term AI will be used to include only the common smart devices we now incorporate into our daily lives and the more advanced intelligence displayed by applications such as IBM Watson. Futuristic applications of an advanced AI more intelligent than humankind will be referred to as ASI.

established facts. A growing number of experts and an even more persuasive growing body of evidence indicate that exponentially advancing technologies may be a significant part of the cause of these very troubling trends and that these forces will worsen in the relatively near future.

Since 1970 wages for working Americans have stagnated and the middle class has declined dramatically. Following the Great Recession of 2008, millions of middle-income Americans suffered from the loss of jobs that supported their middle-class lifestyle and faced foreclosures on their homes, which were often their nest eggs for retirement. For many of these individuals and families, there is little hope of meaningful reemployment and a restoration of their former dreams of the golden years. Their plight is mirrored in the struggles of young Americans seeking to obtain a decent education and to enter the workforce with a sense of optimism for the future, not a back-breaking load of student debt. In fact, only the very rich have participated in any meaningful way in the economic recovery of our country. Thomas Piketty, an economist at the London School of Economics, and Emmanuel Saez, an economist at the University of California, Berkeley, both acknowledged experts in income and wealth distribution, estimate that 95 percent of all of the growth in income that occurred in the recovery from the Great Recession (2009-2013) went to the 1 percent comprising our wealthiest Americans.[3]

In *The Second Machine Age*,[4] Erik Brynjolfsson and Andrew McAfee argue that technology today has become so proficient that it is destroying more jobs than it is creating and that this is contributing to serious unemployment, wage stagnation and growing inequality in the world. Given that the previous two hundred years of economic history disprove this point, it

3 Thomas Piketty and Emmanuel Saez, "Income Inequality in the United States, 1913-1998," *Quarterly Journal of Economics*, 2003, update 2013, Excel format, January 2015; Estelle Sommeiller and Mark Price, "The Increasingly Unequal States of America: Income Inequality by State, 1917 to 2012," Economic Policy Institute, http://epi.org/publication/income-inequality-by-state-1917-2012.

4 Erik Brynjolfsson and Andrew McAfee, *The Second Machine Age: Work, Progress, and Prosperity in a Time of Brilliant Technologies* (W.W. Norton & Company, Inc., 2014).

has been a hard sell. However, there is a growing sense that something is very different about today's economic hardships, especially the economic plight of the American middle class. The reversal of fortune suffered by the American middle class since approximately 1970 has created for many the stark realization that the fundamental assumptions upon which the American Dream historically has been based are now no longer valid.

One great legacy of technological progress during the Industrial Revolution was the creation of a true middle class in American society inspired by the American Dream -- if you worked hard enough and dreamed big enough, you could achieve, if not great wealth, at least economic prosperity and/or sufficiency. "The streets are paved with gold!" falsely rang out in Ireland and throughout Europe. This was a nation of great opportunities -- a democratic melting pot. Although the streets were not paved with gold, they were paved with golden opportunities. The middle class was a democracy open to most who wished to work hard, to seek an education, and to ensure that, if not their generation, then certainly their children had the opportunity to succeed. Often this required parents to postpone or sacrifice their own prosperity and remain in poverty. It was a dream with lots of inequality due to racial, gender, ethnic and religious intolerance and discrimination, which should never be forgotten or dismissed, but even these problems began to be addressed by the end of the Industrial Revolution.

The promise of the American Dream has always been one of our country's greatest strengths. It has provided the incentive for generations of Americans to work hard and take the economic risks necessary to build businesses, create jobs and improve their lives. On a more fundamental level it has provided the social inspiration that has created a society where people of very different racial, ethnic, religious and economic backgrounds have shared a common hope and commitment to the ideal that through hard work would come the reward of providing a better life and a greater opportunity for the next generation. The deep-seated belief that our nation encouraged and nurtured the social mobility that follows from economic advancement drew Americans together, proud to be patriotic citizens of the greatest country on earth. Until recently, the success that the power of the American Dream promised made our economy and the opportunities it offered for social advancement the envy of the world. Based on the trends of recent history and the characteristics of the development and proliferation of some of the new, astoundingly powerful technologies discussed later in this book, there is real concern that these basic assumptions have been seriously compromised and that, therefore, we are witnessing the death of the American Dream.

Brynjolfsson and McAfee were some of the first to explore the effects of the incredible growth of AI on our current adverse economic conditions. These predictions of the *economic* effects of advancing technologies are in many ways profoundly more threatening than the message of the current genre of science fiction movies because they are not based on the premise that in the future there will be mind-bending breakthrough advances in science. These threats to our everyday welfare are very real, based on *today's* technologies. In fact, many of the effects of these threats are already occurring all around us. These early manifestations are but the tip of the technological iceberg that is coming toward us -- and there will be an enormous impact long before our upcoming existential battle with a form of advanced artificial super intelligence (ASI). There will be no blockbuster movies such as *The Terminator* or *Avengers* made about these developments, because they will appear too mundane for Hollywood. However, for working-class Americans, these developments are very troubling. Worse, it will be very hard to appreciate the full extent of this debacle until it may be too late. The principal objective of this book is to examine the current debate about the role of advancing technology in our economy in the next few decades. This laypersons guide will attempt to separate the chaff from the wheat, as well as the prurient and sensational or politically motivated from the clear and present danger regarding these issues.

There are two certainties in our future. First, as a society, some of us will enjoy a Cornucopia of abundance beyond the wildest dreams of our forebears. Second, this abundance will come at a very high price for many others. On the way, there will be a great deal of uncertainty and discomfort, and within this promise will lie the seeds of Armageddon.

I am not a physicist nor a mathematician, nor am I an expert in computer science, the Internet or AI. My only experience with high-tech was in representing the Massachusetts Institute of Technology (MIT) for almost twenty years, principally in the planning and development of Kendall Square in Cambridge, Massachusetts. Kendall Square is now recognized as one of the world's greatest centers for life sciences, AI, computer science, DNA research and other high-tech developments. My best qualification for writing this book may be that I have three wonderful daughters in their mid-thirties and three grandchildren, who were born while I was writing this book. I grew up in a generation that felt an obligation to leave the world a better place for its children and grandchildren. This concept is the underlying message of this book, and it is my motivation for writing it.

As an attorney, I often saw the dark side of things. It is said that "A great lawyer should have the imagination of a small child left alone in a dark room." With musings such as these, I have often worried about how my generation is going to meet its obligations to its children. About three years ago, I read a book by Ray Kurzweil entitled *The Singularity Is Near* (2005).[5] Ray Kurzweil is an inventor and visionary and one of the key participants in a debate that may literally determine the future of humanity.

What did Ray have to say?

- He will live long enough for science to solve the issues of aging and he will become immortal and transmute himself into a form of ASI. Think of the movie *Her* with a different ending.
- AI will continue to grow exponentially, so that within the next thirty years computer intelligence will far exceed the sum of all human intelligence on earth (i.e., the Singularity).

---

5 Raymond Kurzweil, *The Singularity Is Near: When Humans Transcend Biology* (Penguin Books, New York City, NY, 2006).

- To accomplish these objectives, we will need to find other sources of matter beyond silicon chips -- such as rocks -- with which to build computers. According to Ray, a 2.2 lb. rock contains the theoretical capacity to compute trillions of times more powerfully than the human brain.

Ray also has his worries:

- The speed of light may eventually limit how fast computers can calculate. Even more worrisome is that there is just so much matter in the *reachable* (my term) universe that we can use to build new computers. Given how much capacity there is in a 2.2 lb. rock, I can live with this "limit," but Ray is a very big thinker.
- I sense that Ray is also concerned that a growing number of experts in AI and related fields are becoming skeptical (and many alarmed) with the possibility that the astounding growth of AI will not turn out okay for us. If this view begins to prevail, the relative freedom from scrutiny and the continued massive funding for the unfettered development of AI might face stiff resistance. This could literally be a life-threatening event for Ray's aspirations of immortality.

All of this information and more is found in the approximately six hundred pages of *The Singularity Is Near*. Unfortunately, Ray only devotes a few pages to describe why all this is going to turn out to be just fine, versus the remainder of the book, in which he brilliantly analyzes why these forces of change are already at work, are exponentially accelerating and are irreversible. Now, if you had bet against Ray over his career, you would be cashed-out by the house by now, so I take some comfort in Ray's optimism about our future. However, I have very high standards for my obligations to my children and grandchildren. So since finishing Ray's book, I have spent my retirement immersed in this subject.

After all of this effort, I am not certain where we are headed, but one thing is certain: This debate is based on solid facts and observations from the past and present and a very thoughtful and informed consideration of the foreseeable future. The participants in this debate are not unhinged wackos seeking recognition with sensational but unfounded predictions of the future. For the most part, they are very serious people, well recognized and respected in their respective fields as geniuses.

Given the stakes involved, it is disturbing that this discussion is being undertaken by only a very limited spectrum of individuals, albeit extremely well qualified and intellectually brilliant ones. This group consists mainly of physicists, mathematicians, futurists, ethicists, and, more recently, economists. This is not a discussion that should be limited to any one or a few disciplines no matter how qualified or brilliant its participants may be. The forces of technological change are already transforming our daily lives and will dramatically affect the economic legacy we will leave for our children long before there is the threat of a confrontation with a form of ASI.

The conclusions in this book represent an assessment of what is known, what is foreseeable, and what is forecasted for the uncertain near future, referred to here as the Near Horizon (2035). There is also a brief and modest attempt to provide a glimpse into what we may expect by the Far Horizon (2055). This is only a period of forty years, and yet it is as far out into the future as our present uncertainty allows because technology and its applications are moving forward very rapidly.

When I began to write this book, I had no idea what a challenge it would be -- but I was ready. My nickname (often used behind my back) at my former law firm was Sometimes Wrong -- but Never Uncertain. To prepare myself for writing this book, I went to Staples to replenish my supply of cassettes for my Dictaphone, which I had taken with me from my former employer, Goulston and Storrs in Boston, Massachusetts. (Goulston first learned of their generosity here.) At the store, I asked the nice, very earnest young man (Bill) where Staples kept the cassettes for Dictaphones. An unpleasant silence fell until he asked, "What is a

Dictaphone?" Bill was very cordial. He ignored my embarrassment and helped me buy a brand new digital recorder with twenty tracks and many other high-tech features that he breathlessly expounded upon. I took it home, could not operate it, and settled for using Dragon on my laptop, which worked only a little better. In hindsight, there were many lessons from this incident that could have benefited me in writing this book, but I didn't know what I didn't know. After completing this book, I now realize how much could have been learned from that simple trip to Staples.

It is fair to say that we all feel the world is changing; it always has been. But what if I were to convince you that we are now entering a period when the rate of change in our lives and in America and the world is beginning to accelerate exponentially, unlike in any other period in history. And what if I could convince you that this rate of change will bring with it an untold abundance for many, but with it will come the real danger of terrible conflict, unemployment, inequality, dislocation and political and economic upheaval on a scale never witnessed before -- and perhaps, ultimately, not a Cornucopia of abundance but economic and/or existential Armageddon? That change -- that force -- is Radical Change.

At its most fundamental level, this discussion must begin with a basic recognition that humans are hard-wired not to feel good about change. It is the irony of evolution that while it has created us (intelligent humans) through 3.7 billion years of unrelenting evolutionary change, it also has instilled in us an inherent fear and distrust of change. For us, as living entities, certainly in the near term, fear and distrust of change is very good because change is full of danger and uncertainty. In fact, if any organism (humans or any other species) did not fear change, uncertainty and danger, that species would not do very well surviving in this harsh world. But whether we like it or not, change is inevitable, irreversible and amoral in its effects. Modern Homo sapiens have struggled with the challenges of change for, at least, the last two hundred thousand years (this is a very conservative starting point), and yet, in our daily lives change makes us feel very uncomfortable.

Due to forces described later, the rate of change in the twenty-first century will accelerate rapidly. These forces will affect our lives in more and more apparent ways and will rapidly create a paradigm shift[6] in our most fundamental assumptions and approaches to one another and to our place in society, the world and the universe, if not in our lifetimes, then certainly in the lifetimes of our children and our grandchildren. For those of us with real lives, such as soccer moms or professionals, who are constantly on the move 24/7, armed with smartphones, iPads, and iPods to keep us on top of things, and for the unemployed, the struggling middle class and the very wealthy, we really do not want, nor do we have the time, to explore the dark side of anything. For this we have the daily news. But now may be the only time when humanity can make a difference in the type of world our children, and certainly their children, will inherit.

"Okay, Chicken Little -- out you go before you get someone upset!" The purpose of this book is to get a lot of people upset, which may be the only salvation we have. I wish it were as Winston Churchill once scathingly told an adversary in the House of Commons: "[You] are not a wolf in sheep's clothing, you are but a sheep in sheep's clothing!" This wolf is real and indisputable in my view. The only uncertainty is how the story will end or, perhaps more correctly stated, how and when it will continue to unfold, and whom it will benefit and whom it will decimate.

"Okay, so who or what is the wolf?" For lack of a better definition, it is technological progress!

"Whew! For a minute there you had me concerned, but obviously you need to get a life! Technology is good! Just a minute, someone's calling on my iPhone." Yes, technology is very, very good. By any unbiased, objective standard or measure, our lives are better today in the

---

6 Thomas Kuhn, *The Structure of Scientific Revolutions* (Chicago: University of Chicago Press, 1962). A classic paradigm shift is the effect of Einstein's theory of special relativity on the previously unchallenged law of Newtonian mechanics. Paradigm shifts in science are extremely well described in this seminal book. One important point made in Kuhn's work is that once you enter a paradigm shift, you can never go back to your previous approaches and assumptions.

United States and in the world (even in the underdeveloped nations of the world) than ever before. New biological advances in health care and aging; genetic advances in disease prevention and cures, organ regeneration and transplants, and altered agricultural products; and computer advances in AI, robotics, telecommunications, etc. are creating standards of living beyond our parents' wildest imaginations. Our everyday lives have been forever transformed by the laptop, the Internet and the interconnectivity of telecommunications. There is no turning back! If you do not believe that, put your laptop and your smartphone in your dresser drawer for about a week and let me know how it turns out.

"So, where's the rub?" The rub is that the promise of technology may be an enchanting song of the Sirens of Titan beguiling us onto the rocks of Scylla and Charybdis.

"Really, since you've retired you've had way too much time to yourself." The problem is that some of the most brilliant minds in the world, those most familiar with the drivers of Radical Change, are in chilling agreement on one fundamental premise: We are experiencing the beginning of technological developments that are occurring much more rapidly today than ever before because they are the inevitable result of the exponential growth of computer capacity that began at least sixty years ago.[7] Where those experts disagree is on the question of how fast and profound the manifestation of this acceleration of change will become and how this change will alter civilization as we now know it. What is truly amazing about this challenge is that it has received so little attention to date. Perhaps this is because, unlike prior revolutions in human development, whether it was the Age of Agriculture or the Industrial Revolution, this revolution is emerging very rapidly, and it has not yet made itself fully apparent. But it will, and when it does, it will dramatically transform our lives at a rate of change that the world has never before experienced.

---

7 Actually, there is a robust group of scientists and writers who feel we are running out of good ideas. I will examine what supports this dangerous misconception later in this book.

If we are to come out of this well, we will need to work hard as a team and engage in some social engineering that many may feel has already failed and been discarded or discredited. There are a few principles in Part Five of this book that may serve to guide us. There may also be many other ways for us to overcome the great challenge we will confront prior to the Far Horizon, but before we can hope to take meaningful action, we have to recognize the nature of the threat and find the collective will to act decisively. This is the principal purpose of this book. In facing this challenge, we should be guided by the timeless words of one of our greatest leaders. Speaking on radio to a dispirited and divided nation still in the grips of the Great Depression, Franklin D. Roosevelt challenged all Americans:

> The only thing we have to fear is... fear itself... nameless, unreasoning, unjustified terror which paralyzes needed effort to convert retreat to advance. ... A host of unemployed citizens face the grim problem of existence, and an equally great number toil with little return.

He challenged an equally divided Congress to join in this monumental effort:

> But in the event that the Congress shall fail to follow [this] course of action... I shall... wage a war against the emergency as great as the power that would be given me were we, in fact, invaded by a foreign foe.[8]

The analogy of comparing the effort required to win the battle with advancing technologies to the historic struggles in the Great Depression or the invasion by a "foreign foe" is not a grandiose attempt to grab the reader's attention. We are in a war of our own making; the casualties are not yet painfully obvious, the enemy is not clearly defined, and it

---

8 Franklin D. Roosevelt, on taking the Oath of Office, March 4, 1933.

comes bearing great gifts, but the ultimate stakes are no less relevant to the quality of the civilization that we shall leave for our children and grandchildren.

One thing is certain: Our future and the future of our children shall be filled with far greater abundance, more meaningful, happier and longer lives than we can ever imagine, more growing pains than we will wish to bear and more daunting challenges to our intellect, personal values and spirit than we have ever experienced. It is the objective of this book to quicken our awareness of these issues, to explain in simple lay-persons terms how serious the stakes are and to suggest some very basic issues that need immediate attention so that we will be able effectively to participate in and, hopefully, guide our destiny. These seem to be sensational and perhaps even irresponsible statements! Especially from an author who cannot claim great expertise in any of the fields of science that lie at the core of understanding this debate.

But if you have children or know someone who does, bear with me with an open mind for a few hours.

# Part One

The Power of Radical Change

# Chapter One

## LESSONS FROM THE PAST:
### Plus Ça Change, Plus C'est la Même Chose

For almost two centuries, this has been an amusing and intuitive observation of the nature of the human experience. Throughout the Industrial Revolution, new inventions were considered marvels and sources of amusement and fright. Women, dogs and, discretely, men were horrified when Model T Fords roared through. The Chicago World's Fair in 1893 marked one of the greatest exhibitions of new technology ever before assembled, and the world was enchanted and, literally, electrified.

We and our ancestors have all held a sense of nostalgia about the past mixed with a sense of wonderment and awe over how much the world has changed in our lifetimes. This nostalgic remembrance of times past has persisted for generations, and yet, until recently, there has continued to be this feeling that even though everything was changing, things remained pretty much the same. So what is different today? Change is inevitable, and it has been with us since the beginning of creation. But what if in the future change were to occur so rapidly that it literally caused a paradigm shift in how we live in this world and how we are able to predict and prepare for the foreseeable future (i.e., Radical Change)?

This book is premised on the belief that we have already entered into an era of Radical Change. This rate of change is being powered by forces beyond our past experience and is now approaching the limits of our comprehension and control. These forces will pervasively alter our relationship with one another, our world and the universe, causing a paradigm shift in our assumptions and approaches to our lives and the society in which we live. To understand the full implications of living through a period driven by the force of Radical Change, we must first go back and review some basic lessons from history. This may seem to be contradictory, but some lessons from history remain timeless. Being guided by certain truths from history while experiencing a paradigm shift is not a contradiction, because to understand the forces causing this paradigm shift it is important to understand how we got here. The forces now propelling Radical Change did not emerge in a vacuum. They are the inevitable evolution of the technologies from our past.

Attempting to summarize the entire development of human civilization is beyond my ability and anyone's attention span. But I must begin by establishing the proper context for this discussion. Fortunately there are a number of previous books on this subject that have meticulously gone back into human history to establish the course of the evolution of civilization that has led us to the present day. At the risk of oversimplification, I will brutally shorten this history to try to capture the most salient characteristics and trends that will help us to understand why the future within our lifetimes will look very different from our past.[9]

Historically, the species most closely related to present-day human beings, Homo sapiens, first emerged in Africa approximately two hundred thousand years ago.[10] About fifty thousand years later early Homo sapiens began the long walk to every part of the earth. Life was short and brutish. At this time, Homo sapiens lived by hunting and gathering. In some parts of the world, early technologies started to emerge. Stone

9 For those of you who are intellectually appalled at such a resolution of these immensely important and complex historical and intellectual issues, you are invited to begin by reviewing the following references, which support this summary: Bill Bryson, *A Short History of Nearly Everything* (Broadway Books, 2003); and K. Eric Drexler, *Radical Abundance, How a Revolution in Nanotechnology Will Change Civilization* (Perseus Books Group, 2013).

10 This is a very rough estimate, since an early species of Homo sapiens roamed the earth at least one million years ago.

tools and fire began to appear around 100,000 BC. These primitive technologies changed the way Homo sapiens subsisted. But despite these changes, Homo sapiens continued to survive solely as hunter-gatherers until around 20,000 BC. However, the Age of the Hunter-Gatherer did not end at this time, nor did it end in all parts of the world at the same time. In fact, the hunter-gatherer form of subsistence still continues essentially unchanged in a few very isolated regions of the world even today.

Around twenty thousand years ago, Homo sapiens began to discover the benefits of farming, and slowly, over many continents and many centuries, hunter-gatherers began to cultivate food. This dramatically changed the way in which humans lived. It was the first time humans could remain in one locale because agriculture required settling in one place. It was the beginning of the Age of Agriculture. This brought greater abundance, security, and a more socialized civilization. During this age, humans began to settle in larger and larger groups, and new technologies were developed that enabled the building of structures in wood and stone, the creation of irrigation systems to improve the growth of crops, and the transportation of goods by such inventions as the wheel in approximately 4,000 BC. At the same time, laws to regulate human behavior and commerce and early forms of government, both benevolent and not so benevolent, were established. Later in the Age of Agriculture, humans pursued more advanced skills in cartography and navigation and weaponry, which allowed previously distinct civilizations to trade, communicate, go to war and pulverize each other, or otherwise interfere in one another's business.

Historians differ slightly as to when the Age of Agriculture first began to give way to the Industrial Revolution. For the purpose of setting the context of this book, I will conclude that the Industrial Revolution began in the more advanced civilizations on earth toward the early part of the eighteenth century. This ushered in a period of slightly more than two hundred years of unparalleled development of significant technologies that radically changed the way in which humans lived, worked, loved and otherwise maintained and amused themselves. Progress was still seemingly slow and was certainly not felt equally in all parts of the world nor even in all parts of any nation. It is important to point out that this was the first time historians referred to a new era as a revolution. This choice of terminology provides a profound insight into this era because, compared to previous ages, in many ways it unfolded at a rate that was considered revolutionary. During this relatively brief period, there were enormous advances in many technologies, best characterized by the invention of the steam engine, which was first developed by Thomas Newcomen in 1712 and first patented as an engine by James Watt in 1781. Although invented in 1712, it took over eight decades of tinkering (some by Watt) for it to work well, but when it did, the rest was history.[11] Steam engines soon became not only the symbol of the Industrial Revolution but also its backbone. The steam engine revolutionized how goods were moved, how products were manufactured and essentially how life was powered. It spelled the end of the role of the workhorse and the beginning of a period of massive dislocation of the world's poor, whether by immigration to other countries (symbolized in the United States by the main entryway for immigrants, Ellis Island) or dislocation within countries (the movement of farmers to the slums of the burgeoning cities). The changing economic power in the world caused by these technologically driven forces also played a very important part in wars of liberation and conquest. America was freed from British rule and taxation by the American Revolution and was nearly divided by the Civil War. Despite hardships and bloodshed, the Industrial Revolution provided opportunities for many to obtain, if not great wealth, at least economic security, and the great middle class of America was born. It was a revolution and not just an evolution into a new era -- it was the Industrial Revolution.

While historians have not yet agreed on the date that marks the end of the Industrial Revolution, most feel we have moved into a new era that

---

11 There is a lesson here regarding the time often required to successfully roll out a new technology to the point where it has a major impact on society. It is also an early example of the fact that the first use of a new technology often proves to be the least important of its ultimate applications.

will not and cannot be defined by the traditional markers or metrics of the Industrial Revolution. For the purposes of this book, I will set the end of this era to be in the middle part of the twentieth century. At about this time the great intellectual and economic forces that characterized the previous era fundamentally began to shift, transformed by forces far different than those that forged the past. This era lasted for approximately two hundred plus years. Like previous eras, it did not end everywhere in the world or even in any one nation at one time.

Many writers have attempted to compare the nature and degree of change that occurred in each of these ages but the conclusions ultimately become very subjective. What is undeniable is that the time period encompassing each age has sharply declined from the distant past to the present, yet the magnitude of transformation *within* each age has remained very dramatic. The Age of the Hunter-Gatherer lasted about two hundred thousand years, the Age of Agriculture lasted for approximately twenty thousand years and the Industrial Revolution lasted approximately two hundred years. There is a definite pattern here -- one we should not cavalierly dismiss. No matter how you measure the degree of the transformation in civilization from age to age, the rate of evolution of history has dramatically accelerated. We should anticipate that, due to the forces of Radical Change, this accelerating pace of history will continue during our lifetimes and on into the future.[12]

Despite this historical evidence, most of us still hold on to the belief that the world has not changed a great deal in our lifetimes. It is a comforting thought providing both a security for our future and a warm and comfortable sense of loss and nostalgia for our past. These are understandable feelings, but they may divert our attention from the challenge of the new technologies of the future. The pace of change in the next

---

12 This comparison of the acceleration of change between ages could be made much more dramatic if we began the Age of the Hunter-Gatherer as the date on which the first evidence of early ancestors of Homo sapiens appeared on earth, well over three to five million years ago. On an evolutionary basis, we could even conceive of a starting point for another era of evolution beginning with the origin of life nearly 3.7 billion years ago.

forty years to the Far Horizon will create virtually as much upheaval in our lives as was experienced in the entire period of the Industrial Revolution. With this change will ultimately come the undeniable conclusion that *Plus Ça Change, Plus C'est la Même Chose* is no longer a lesson *from* the past; it will be a lesson *of* the past!

# Chapter Two

## TECHNOLOGICAL PROGRESS:
### The Good, the Bad and the Ugly

The development of new technologies has always been the prime driver of the rate of change in our world and the defining hallmark of each era. In the Age of the Hunter-Gatherer, it was the creation of the first stone tools and the use of fire. In the Age of Agriculture, it was the inventions of the wheel, written language and the printing press. In the Industrial Revolution it was the inventions of the steam engine, light bulb, telegraph and telephone. In the period from the end of the twentieth century to today, it may be the invention of computers, the Internet, or the digitization of just about everything. Change in every era has, however, not been driven by one or even a few new inventions, but by many technological developments and breakthroughs, taken together. Therefore, to forecast our future, we should not focus on what may be invented but on the more fundamental issue of how technology itself develops and transforms our world. To gain a better insight into this process, I will again examine some lessons from the past, but this time the relatively recent past -- the Industrial Revolution.

During the Industrial Revolution there were dramatic technological advances in the fields of transportation, mass production of goods, education, health care, physics, chemistry and engineering and, at the end of this era, the birth of computers. It was a revolution in which new technologies not only advanced the quality of life, but also caused tremendous job dislocation, redistribution of income and the creation of weapons of mass destruction -- such as nuclear weaponry and chemical and biological forms of warfare. Many observers of history remarked that during this period life was dramatically changing, and indeed for many, particularly those fortunate enough to live in the developed nations of the world, life was indeed changing rapidly. The age-old Malthusian struggle of population growth versus the ability of the world to feed and shelter its inhabitants seemed almost solved, and we landed on the moon. Standards of living and health care rose dramatically, and even in the underdeveloped world there were major advances in the essentials for life, health, sanitation, clean water, nutrition and democracy.

But despite these enormous improvements in the quality of life, not everyone shared equally in the bounty. In fact, one could argue that the discrepancies in the quality of life between the citizens of the very poorest nations and the fortunate few who benefited from the discoveries of the new age became progressively more disparate. What is, however, undeniable is that a new class of economically well off but not aristocratic individuals arose through the centralization and industrialization of business, commerce, etc. in many nations. This was a form of democracy and even individuals who remained essentially unskilled began to see hope that through their own efforts they could work their way out of poverty into the developing middle and upper classes in their respective societies.[13]

The American Dream, long before it was so beautifully articulated by Reverend Martin Luther King Jr., was coming true for many. At the same time, we should remember that many civilizations were, and still are, dealing with a lack of the basic essentials of life. This inequality

---

13 For an extremely thorough and well-documented dissertation on this subject, see Thomas Piketty, *Capitalism in the Twenty-First Century* (Harvard University Press, 2014).

marked the Industrial Revolution as significantly as the abundance it provided for so many.[14]

Despite the hope and promise of the Industrial Revolution, in reality there were many Winners and many Losers. For generations farmers had experienced hardship and uncertainty, but with life on a farm came a deep-rooted sense of pride and dignity and the security of being self-sufficient. New technologies forced many of these farmers and their families to move to the burgeoning urban slums that marked the nineteenth and a good part of the twentieth centuries. There the farmers, including (unfortunately) many of their very young children, found unskilled jobs in the factories and many more supporting jobs in the slums in which they were forced to live. Whether the farmers' quality of life became better or worse is a subjective value judgment, but certainly the possibility of a far better life became a viable dream and a reality for many.

Perhaps nothing captures the concept of Winners and Losers better than the fate of the workhorse. In the Age of Agriculture and at the beginning of the Industrial Revolution, the workhorse was essential. Horses provided the power at the center of all activities. They were the means that produced and transported the basic food, clothing and shelter for agricultural societies and provided the power to usher in the Industrial Revolution. With the invention of the steam engine, however, the fate of the workhorse was sealed. The steam engine did not just compete with horses, the steam engine eliminated the functions that a horse could perform. Machines could do more work, more powerfully, with much less maintenance and risk of loss and much more cheaply than a workhorse could perform, no matter how badly it was treated. A friend of mine who grew up in the corn fields of Iowa in the 1940s and 1950s told me of the saying, "Horse strong but tractor smart." The steam

---

14 Even for the very privileged, life had its brutish moments. In the eighteenth century the lifestyles of the kings of France included cold castles, terrible toilet facilities, no toothpaste and little health care. When health care was available, it was often more fatal than the disease. By the Age of the Robber Barons in the nineteenth and early twentieth centuries, things had gotten much better, but by today's standards a long weekend at the Breakers in Newport, Rhode Island, summer home to Cornelius Vanderbilt, would not be considered to be a weekend in the lap of luxury.

engine was an equal-opportunity destroyer of jobs. In addition to horses, it also eliminated many jobs of hard manual labor. This struggle was best captured by the powerful description of the battle of John Henry -- "a steel driving man" -- against a steam hammer. The story grabbed the attention of an America giddy with the power of its new inventions. In this apocryphal story, John Henry was alleged to have beaten the steam engine, but, like the workhorse, he expired in the process.

Another invention of the Industrial Revolution bears mention. In 1794 Eli Whitney patented the cotton gin. Almost overnight, it transformed the way fabric was produced and immediately displaced thousands of workers in the cotton mills of the nineteenth century. Not surprisingly, many of the skilled and unskilled workers in those mills were not happy with this result. Between 1811 and 1813 a British mill worker, Ned Ludd, led a group of unemployed workers on a short, violent rampage, damaging a small number of the new machines.[15] The uprising was quickly and brutally suppressed by the British Army, but forever after, those who have held strongly felt views adverse to the introduction of new technologies that threaten the status quo have been referred to as Luddites.

There are certain lessons to be learned from examining how new technologies transformed life during the Industrial Revolution. These lessons will not be abrogated in the paradigm shift of Radical Change. Some of the most pertinent of these lessons are as follows:

- Technology creates wonderful advancements in many aspects of the human condition (economic, educational, health, longevity, leisure, democracy, etc.).
- Technology creates tremendous dislocation and changes in markets, human relationships, opportunities and income and wealth distribution.

15 In 1812 the British Parliament made "machine breaking" a capital offense (the equivalent of homicide). This might have been the unwitting beginning of a now growing debate on whether machines (i.e., computers/AI) should be accorded fundamental human rights.

- Technology is amoral -- it creates tools because they can be created. When new technologies are created, they often produce great benefits, but technology is an amoral force that can, especially in the hands of people with ill intentions, cause great evil. When left alone, it can still get us into a lot of trouble.
- Technology relentlessly moves forward, but as it does it creates powerful forces that attempt to protect the status quo from these economic, religious, moral, ethical and political changes.
- Technology builds upon the past and constantly accelerates its impact on society.

These are admittedly very basic observations, but because they are so basic, they may be some of the few fundamental principles that we can look to for guidance as we plot our course forward.

Because the major focus of this book is on the effects of advancing technology on employment and economic equality, I will examine some of the lessons of the Industrial Revolution on these issues in more detail. One inevitable consequence of technological improvement in the Industrial Revolution was the destruction of jobs. We prefer to use the euphemism *replacement* because during this period new technologies created many more rewarding jobs than they destroyed. But technology replaces workers, not jobs -- ask the workers. We assert, somewhat naively, that technology replaces jobs because it creates so many new ones. But if it is your job that has been eliminated and made obsolete, it does not make a new job just for you. Because technology has advanced the quality of life so dramatically we are extremely reluctant to examine the adverse consequences that arise from technological advancement. All experts agree that during the Industrial Revolution new technologies created more new jobs than they eliminated. To understand whether this will be true in our future, we need to appreciate certain characteristics of job creation in this era. First, the overwhelming majority of the new jobs created by the technologies of the Industrial Revolution required relatively unskilled, cheap labor. If farmers were forced to leave the farm where they had planned on making a hard but honest living, they moved to the city. There, farmers found relatively unskilled work in factories and support-services jobs that arose such as shopkeepers, policemen, firemen, bartenders and government bureaucrats. It was an age in which everyone believed that the rising tide floated all boats, but for some they seemed either stuck in the mudflats or they did not sail off happily into the sunset. This came to be referred to as the "price of progress."

A second lesson from the Industrial Revolution receives much less attention. As technologies become more and more sophisticated in the twenty-first century, this lesson may become very painful, but it will be essential in understanding where to anticipate future job "replacement" by advancing technologies. Many of the jobs that were destroyed by unskilled labor in the era of the Industrial Revolution had previously been performed by *skilled* labor. For example, the production of silver bowls, shoes, shirts, plows and rifles, etc. had been the province of the guilds of Europe and *skilled* shopkeepers in America. By breaking down complicated tasks into very small repeating ones, the machines of the Industrial Revolution were able to destroy many otherwise skilled professions. Today we have lost touch with the implications of this early form of technological development. This strongly influences our assumption that new technologies will replace *only* unskilled jobs in the future, but historically, this was never the case.

To appreciate how technology will affect our future economy I must reexamine an almost universally accepted theory of economics. This theory has remained virtually unchanged since the beginning of the Industrial Revolution. In a very simplified version, it postulates:

- Technology leads to greater productivity of workers, thereby allowing fewer workers to produce the same number of goods or services.
- Greater productivity leads to a lowering of the prices of goods and services.

- Lower cost of goods and services creates greater demand for more goods and services (but not necessarily the same goods and services).
- Greater demand for goods and services creates more jobs (but not the same jobs, nor do the new jobs necessarily require the same levels of education or skills of the workers who held the former jobs).

Economists have expanded, modified and complicated this economic theory in a mountain of erudite learning, but at its heart it is very simple and it has worked very well in predicting the growth of new and expanding markets and the replacement of jobs not only in America but also the world for, at least, the last two hundred years. So what could go wrong with the continuing reliance on this "holy grail" of economics? The problem is that this is not a law. It may be a brilliant observation that works as long as you do not change the approaches and the assumptions upon which it is based (i.e., the paradigms). However, if technology is now evolving more rapidly than ever before in history, and if we are entering a paradigm shift, this theory needs to be reexamined with a jaundiced eye.

From the very beginning of the reign of this economic theory, a few experts had reservations. One of those who harbored serious concerns about the short-term effects of this theory and who also foresaw a longer-term problem with the dislocation of workers it predicted is particularly noteworthy because he was one of the greatest economists of all time, John Maynard Keynes.

In 1930 Keynes published a collection of his papers in a seminal work, *Essays in Persuasion*.[16] The collection closes with a paper entitled "Economic Possibilities for Our Grandchildren," in which Keynes states that the purpose of this essay is:

---

16 John Maynard Keynes, *Essays in Persuasion* (Classic House Books, US publication, 2009). The US publisher claims (with a great deal of expert support) that *Essays in Persuasion* is one of the one hundred greatest books ever written.

not to examine the present or the near future... [but to] take wings into the future.... What can we reasonably expect the level of economic life to be a hundred years hence? What are the economic possibilities for our grandchildren? (p. 194)

Keynes states that in his view, until approximately 1700, "almost everything that really matters... was already known to man." But all that changed. In Keynes' words, "We are living, then, in an unsatisfactory age of immensely rapid transition."

Keynes goes on to write, with an almost eerie prescience, that:

the increase of technical efficiency has been taking place faster than we can deal with the problem of labour absorption. ... We are being afflicted with a new disease of which some readers may not yet have heard the name, but of which they will hear a great deal in the years to come -- namely, technological unemployment. This means unemployment due to our discovery of means of economising the use of labour outrunning the pace at which we can find new uses for labour.

However, Keynes concludes that "this is only a temporary phase of maladjustment," and he predicts that "the standard of living in progressive countries one hundred years hence" may help to solve what he refers to as "the economic problem" – the battle to eke out a life of mere subsistence.[17] Keynes foresaw both the short and the long-term effects of technological progress. He concluded that in the long term, technological progress would lead to the formation of a large leisure

---

17 A number of economists have referred to Keynes as the source of the concept of "technological unemployment" but dismiss or minimize the importance of his insight because Keynes believed this to be only a "temporary phase." Keynes should be forgiven for not predicting the development of the astounding technologies of the twenty-first century and the *enormous* challenges these technologies pose in terms of the minimum qualifications for these "new uses for labour." The long-term implications of "technological unemployment" will be addressed in more detail in Chapter Twenty.

class. This was the legacy to be left to his grandchildren "within one hundred years." We have not seen the development of the leisure class that Keynes predicted, although the work week has decreased a bit for most of us. We are, instead, experiencing the problem of technological unemployment. In 2030 we shall pass the one hundred years forecasted by Keynes. If Radical Change disrupts the operation of traditional economic theory, as Keynes predicted, we are in for a lot of problems, because the leisure class he foresaw in a hundred years will not be a gilded aristocracy but a large and permanent class of unemployed and largely unemployable people left behind in the wake of all this progress.

In 1900 agriculture accounted for approximately 45 percent of all employment in the United States. By 1950, this was down to approximately 10 percent, and by 2000 agriculture accounted for less than 2 percent of the American workforce. The transition of farmers and their families to the urban slums was harsh, but it was dismissed as the inevitable growing pains of change -- the price of progress. In January 2013, Oxford University published a report on the future of job loss in America in the next twenty years.[18] After meticulously reviewing a staggering amount of information on job classifications and using conservative assumptions about the growth of technological capacity in the future, the Oxford Report concluded that over 47 percent of current employment opportunities were jobs that technology could replace in ten to twenty years. That is about the same percentage of change in employment that occurred in agriculture in one hundred years during the Industrial Revolution. What would have been the effect on the growing pains of America if that transition had occurred in not one hundred years but in ten to twenty? And what if the transition to the new economic opportunities of the future requires a dramatic transformation of the skills required to

---

18 Carl Frey and Michael Osborne, *The Future of Employment: How Susceptible Are Jobs to Computerization?*, Oxford University Engineering and Science Department (Oxford University, Oxford, September 17, 2013).

qualify for these opportunities? This is not a question but a challenge. The answer to this challenge may come from understanding what is radically different in the forces creating change in society today compared to those forces that shaped the progress of the Industrial Revolution.

# Chapter Three

## RADICAL CHANGE:
### Moore's Law

Many forces contribute to the rate of change in the world. One force that is radically different today is the exploding force of computer capacity and the technologies that this capacity most directly impacts, particularly AI. Virtually all experts agree that computer capability is expanding exponentially (i.e., at least doubling every two years) and has done so for over sixty years. Based on current research and development efforts, most experts believe this growth will continue for, at least, ten more years. These same experts are, however, in serious disagreement as to the extent to which growing computer technology will shape our future.

To understand the rate of growth in the power of computers, we need to go back in time to 1965 and to the office of Professor Gordon Moore, then employed at Fairchild Semiconductor in Palo Alto, California. Professor Moore is widely regarded as one of the pioneers in the history of modern computers and was at the epicenter of computer development for many years. Among his many achievements, Moore was the cofounder of Intel. In 1965 Moore postulated, based on his wealth of experience with computers, that the capacity of computers to store information on a single chip and for the same cost would double every twelve months. While at Intel, Moore subsequently conservatively revised his estimate to every two years. The capacity to store information is only one component (an extremely important one) in computer capacity. Other important factors include speed of calculation, energy consumption, heat dispersion and what may prove to be the most fundamental and important element, the efficiency of the programs that run computers. Moore did not predict this, but, in fact, *every* element of computer capacity has increased on approximately this same exponential doubling curve.

As a result, many commentators and experts have now bastardized the reference to Moore's law, using this term to encompass all elements of the growth of computer capacity. Also to simplify the math many experts define the period of doubling as every two years, although objective measurements of the growth of computer capacity since 1950 support a rate of growth that doubles closer to every eighteen months. For most purposes in this book, we will adopt the common usage of the term Moore's law and the more conservative assumption of two years as the time of doubling.[19]

This astounding increase in computer capacity has been the result of literally thousands of improvements to every aspect of computers, from the size of the switches, to the speed of calculations and improvements in the basic architecture and software programs that drive computers. Some of the advances were the result of breakthrough technological developments such as the use of silicon chips and integrated circuits, and others were only marginal improvements considered singly, but taken together they have accomplished the unthinkable, a sustained doubling of capacity, at least every two years, creating over sixty years of exponential growth.

---

19 Over the course of sixty years, this seemingly modest change in the assumption of the time of doubling (i.e., from eighteen to twenty-four months) results in a mind-numbing difference in predicted computer capacity. It is the difference between thirty and forty doublings, which results in one thousand times more computer capacity. In Chapter Four, which explores the fundamental nature of all exponential growth curves, the significance of the magnitude of this difference becomes even more apparent. Regardless of the assumption you choose, in 2015 we have a virtually incomprehensible amount of computer capacity, as predicted by Moore.

In relying upon Moore's law to forecast the future, we must be cognizant of its limitations. Moore's law is not a law of science. Laws of science, such as the laws of gravity or thermodynamics, are used to accurately predict future events or outcomes with certainty, except under extreme circumstances and conditions.[20] Moore's law is just an observation, a brilliant insight into the future, but not an iron-clad guarantee of the growth of computer capacity. We also need to remain cognizant of the fact that vastly increased computer capacity, at least over short periods of time, does not change the world in which we live. This lag time in the impact of increasing computer power has created a dangerously false sense of security that things are just about the same. As a result, we tend to diminish the importance of what we may someday regret, the inevitable consequences of an explosion of computer intelligence.

Most experts believe that computer capacity cannot go on doubling indefinitely. Moore himself stated that the doubling of capacity would inevitably slow down. Since 1965 the general consensus has been that this slowdown would occur within the next ten years or so. Fifty-plus years later, many experts, including many of those at Intel, still one of the leaders in computer development, continue to hold this same belief (at least ten more years). The only thing that changes is the year in which this slowdown is predicted to begin.[21] Despite these perennial forecasts, since 1950 there has been an almost uncanny steady exponential growth of computer capacity through periods of war, recession, intense funding of computer research and computer winters of neglect of focus and funding. This rate of growth is demonstrated by Chart 3.1 (a), "Exponential Growth: 1965-2015" and Chart 3.1 (b), "Exponential Growth: 1965-1990."

---

20 For the purposes of your everyday life, such as walking around up on a slanted roof or fiddling with a hot stove, you can forget this clarification.

21 As this book was about to be published, Moore's law celebrated its fiftieth birthday. The event was marked by the predictable outpouring of news articles proclaiming the demise of this remarkably long run. These articles reminded me of the famous observation by Mark Twain: "The rumors of my death have been greatly exaggerated."

Chart 3.1 (a)

### Exponential Growth: 1965-2015
### (doubling every two years)

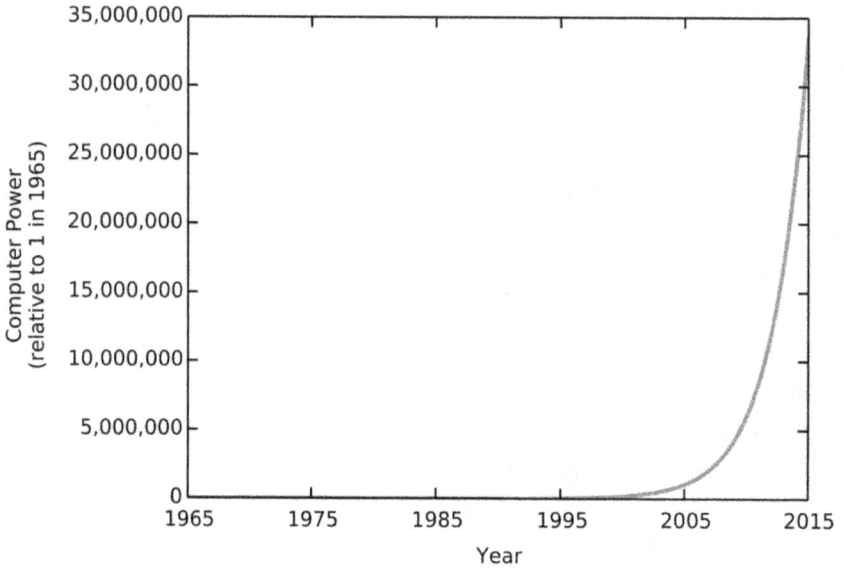

Chart 3.1 (b)

### Exponential Growth: 1965-1990
### (doubling every two years)

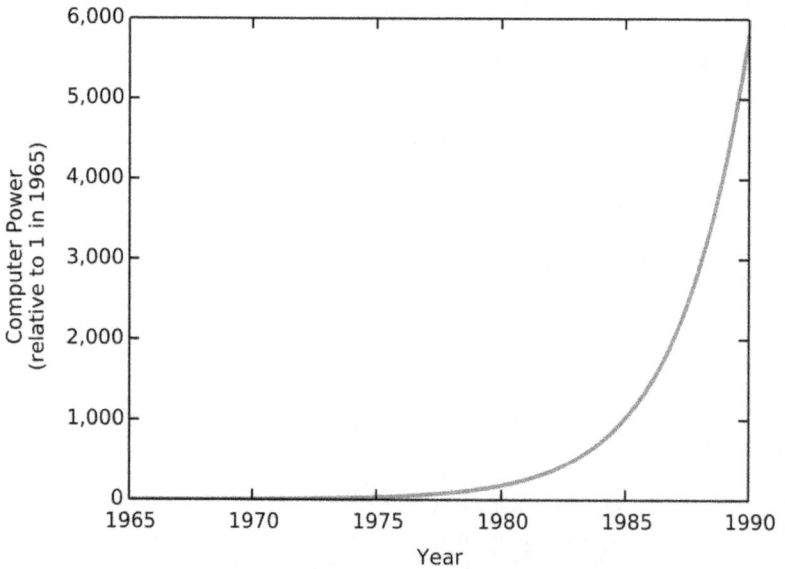

Due to the scale of Chart 3.1 (a) (1 to 35,000,000 units of computer power), there appears to be virtually no growth in computer power from the year 1965 to the year 2000. During this period computer capacity was actually developing very rapidly, but on a scale where the first delineation is 5,000,000 units the curve on the chart appears flat. By changing just the scale of measurement, this dramatic rate of growth becomes apparent. Chart 3.1 (b) analyzes the period 1965-1990 but utilizes a much reduced scale of delineating the rate of growth of computer power (1 to 6,000 units of computer power). The assumptions regarding the rate of growth are the same for both charts, only the frame of reference has been changed. Chart 3.1 (b) demonstrates that computer capacity during this thirty-five year period increased at an astounding, almost unimaginable rate.

Common sense, the law of diminishing returns and the fate of the lemmings strongly reinforce the opinion of most experts that this growth rate of exponential doubling has to slow down soon. However, almost sixty-five years of incontrovertible historic evidence and a small band of futurists such as Ray Kurzweil support a contrary view. In *The Age of Intelligent Machines* (1990), *The Singularity is Near* (2005) and *How to Create a Mind* (2012),[22] Kurzweil persuasively argues that computer capacity has passed and will continue to pass through a series of paradigms in its development, causing "measures of information [to] follow predictable and exponential trajectories, belying conventional wisdom." Kurzweil would probably agree that Moore's law is not a *law* of science, but he argues that the growth of computer capacity it predicts is driven by inexorable forces of technology that lead to the same result. The future may very well prove him to be correct, once again. If he is right, the power of computers will rapidly exceed the capacity of the human brain well before the age of the Near Horizon.[23]

---

22 Ray Kurzweil, *The Age of Intelligent Machines* (MIT Press, 1990); *The Singularity Is Near* (Viking Books, 2005); *How to Create a Mind: The Secret of Human Thought Revealed* (Viking Press, 2012).

23 The term "capacity of the human brain" in this context refers to the capacity to make calculations, not the ability to think like a human.

The earliest predictions of the demise of the growth of computer capacity were based in part on the fundamental limitations of the vacuum tubes that were the core components of all early computers. Vacuum tubes required a great deal of energy, they gave off a resulting great deal of heat, and the laws of physics placed absolute limits on how much they could be miniaturized. What happened? Scientists saw this coming and invented the silicon chip. Since then, the chip has been sliced and diced and placed in three-dimensional arrays, etc., but silicon is also running out of juice for future improvement. Today the gates in the most advanced silicon chips are just seven microns wide. That is the width of about five to ten atoms. They can't get much smaller. The fundamental laws of science will, therefore, ultimately create the same fate for the silicon chip as they did for the vacuum tube.

In 2015 there is another generation of computers under development. One promising development is the quantum computer. Unlike classical computers, which operate with algorithms with bits that flip between "one" and "zero," quantum computers use quantum bits, "quibits," which exist solely at the subatomic (quantum) scale. At this scale, matter acts very differently and the laws of science as we have previously understood them do not apply, so a quibit can exist as a "one" and a "zero" at the same time. Also if you link subatomic particles in a certain manner, changing the characteristics of one particle will simultaneously change the characteristics of the other particle even if they are miles apart. This phenomenon is known as *entanglement* and seems to defy Einstein's prediction of the limits of the speed of light.[24]

How do quantum computers work? No one knows -- even Geordie Rose, the president of Canadian-based D Wave (the world's leader in quantum computing), isn't really certain. What is certain is that there is enough promise in this technology to draw multimillion-dollar investments from diverse interests such as the CIA, the US Department of Defense, Google and Amazon. Will this be the basis of the next generation of computers, as silicon was to the vacuum tube? Maybe not, but this

---

24 Kurzweil may be right about this one as well.

is only one potential breakthrough in technologies now under development. Kurzweil would call these technological advances *paradigm events.* Other research efforts are examining radically new ways to program computers to better mimic the function of the human brain. Recent breakthroughs have led many experts to predict that the next paradigm event will occur in this area of computer development. Historically, programming a computer to do even a simple task, such as picking up a rubber ball, with instructions of "one" or "zero" is even more complicated than it sounds, yet any three-year-old can play with a ball. This inherent limitation of current algorithmic programs has been partially overcome only by the blunt-force approach of science -- applying massive computer power to utilize extraordinarily complex operating instructions (algorithms) to perform simple functions such as "Pick up a rubber ball." Because this format for programs has been a fundamental characteristic of computers since the beginning, many experts have myopically looked for improvement solely by tinkering with the efficacy of the use of the basic "one"/"zero" technology. This approach is akin to the methods of previous experts who devoted their careers to refining the technology of vacuum tubes and more recently silicon chips as the only way to create more computer capacity. This is odd because for many years, science has known that a much more effective way for a computer to operate exists, the way a brain, especially a human brain, processes information. I will explore this field of research loosely termed "deep learning" in greater detail later in this book, but for now it is sufficient to simply highlight one recent scientific breakthrough that has occurred in this field of research and development.

For years, it has been known that the brain functions by electronic impulses passing between synapses in neurons in the brain. Science has also known that, while in some ways similar to the "one"/"zero" calculations between the gates of silicon chips, the brain's use of the synapses is much more efficient. Recently new fields of research in how to mimic the brain's efficiency to improve computer programming have begun to show real promise. On August 7, 2014, IBM unveiled a new type of computer chip that is designed on the basis of "the wrinkled layer of the human brain." Not surprisingly, IBM named the chip Synapse. In laboratory tests, it has recognized cars, people and bicycles one hundred times faster and with, at least, ten thousand times less energy than conventional chips. IBM engineers are now engaged in efforts to link thousands of these chips together in a revolutionary new form of supercomputer.[25]

There are literally hundreds of other potential breakthrough approaches to advancing computer capacity now underway. According to Kurzweil, one or more of these approaches will inevitably result in another paradigm event in the development of computer capacity. If this is so, we should be very careful of what we wish for. Advanced computer capacity, AI, is not a benign technology. Massive advances in this capability will bring wonderful results, but as is the case with many technologies, with these remarkable advances can come some often unintended and potentially disastrous consequences.

Even if the experts working on developing advanced computer technologies do not achieve further breakthrough technologies, the growth rate of computer capacity will only diminish, it will not stop. And we are sitting on a mountain of current capacity that is only beginning to be utilized to create technologies that will dramatically alter our world. It is clear from the literature that most experts in this field have consistently underestimated the continuing rate of growth of the power of computers and, more importantly, the resulting growing capabilities of many technologies that are driven by exponentially advancing computer power, capacity and speed. Given the amount of thoughtful analysis that has been undertaken in this field, this seems to be a very curious oversight. The answer may lie in the simple fact that the long-term effects of a sustained doubling of any sum every eighteen to twenty-four months result in astronomical sums that are counterintuitive to our human experience. Except for a very few well-trained mathematicians, physicists and

---

25 "IBM Chip Processes Data Similar to the Way Your Brain Does," *MIT Technology Review,* August 13, 2014.

futurists, the rest of us, including many brilliant economists, politicians and business leaders, dismiss this progression with a shrug: "Yeah, it's growing really fast." We cannot afford to harbor this cavalier attitude about the growth of this technology. The remainder of this chapter and Chapters Four and Five will address why.

Consider just one aspect of the effects of Moore's law. In just the past two years, more *additional* computer capacity has been developed than had previously ever existed. The application of this capacity will take years to implement, but inevitably it will be applied. Even if some of the experts are correct and computer capacity stops growing in ten years, we will experience five more doublings of our current level of computational power. This is thirty-two times the capacity that existed in 2015 and over one thousand times the computer capacity that existed in 2005. The amount of computer capacity (AI) that will exist by 2025 will be so staggering that virtually all of the consequences that are forecast in this book to occur before we reach the Near Horizon will be not only achievable but also inevitable. This is the essence of the challenge in understanding the force of Radical Change upon our lives in the future. We have no prior experience with anything that even approaches this phenomenon. To appreciate the impact of this technology on our lives, we must *fully* understand how dynamic and potentially unstable this force may very soon become.

Gaining a true appreciation and understanding of the impact of this phenomenon is harder than you might think. Many commentators begin by using some everyday applications of sustained exponential doubling of a sum. These anecdotes may provide a layperson with some feel for how unsettling the results of this process are.

As an avid golfer, I have chosen a story about a golf wager. Player A and Player B play golf every Sunday afternoon for the same stakes: a $5 wager to the winner of the first nine holes, the second nine holes, and for the best combined score (i.e., $15 in total). One Sunday, Player A suggests they change the wager and play the first hole for a penny and double the wager on each succeeding hole, so two cents for the second hole, four cents for the third hole and eight cents for the fourth hole, etc." Player B is very suspicious of Player A's motives because Player A generally wins and likes to take his money. But at a penny a hole, why back out? So Player B agrees. At the ninth hole the two friends are playing for $2.56 for that single hole. Player B begins to relax: "How bad can this get?"

Fast forward to the eighteenth hole, for which the two of them are now playing for over $1,300, for just that single hole. Player B is glad it is over. Had they agreed to play the front nine holes again after lunch, the stakes for just the twenty-seventh hole would have been over $670,000. Even Donald Trump would not want to play that game. Had they agreed to play the final nine holes, the thirty-sixth hole would have been for approximately $340 million. Yes, that starts with a big *M*! Most experts agree that Moore's law as applied to computer capacity has led to more than thirty-six doublings since the birth of computers. So are you now beginning to get a feel for what exponential change in computer growth really means?

Having discussed a number of anecdotes of a similar nature with friends and experts, I have a sense that people who feel they appreciate the results of exponential change do so only to a very limited degree. Anecdotes about wagers on golf are more likely to provoke laughter than understanding. The immensity of this rate of growth is simply beyond our human experience. We are ingrained to think linearly, not exponentially. Recently, in a conversation with an old buddy from college, we discussed exponential change. Until his retirement a couple of years ago, Barry was a leading partner at one of the five largest accounting firms in the world. In our conversation, I casually asked Barry if he understood exponential change. Asking a retired partner in one of the world's greatest accounting firms whether he truly appreciates the nature of exponential change could be considered insulting. Fortunately, since Barry is over six feet two and weighs over three hundred pounds, we were on the telephone. He was one thousand miles away. I got the answer I was expecting: "It grows really fast!" Yes, I agreed, but how fast? We then proceeded to discuss the golf wager. After about four holes, I asked Barry what the stakes would be after thirty-six holes. Barry wasn't buying it!

He hemmed and hawed but finally blurted out, "Well, probably around $17,000." As we know, the answer is over $340 million. Barry was off by a factor of twenty thousand magnitudes. Ask yourself, on what other topic could two reasonably intelligent human beings agree on most conclusions but begin with a misunderstanding of the fundamental facts by an order of magnitude of over twenty thousand?[26]

In considering the effects of technology on our future, we cannot afford to misjudge its driving force by a magnitude of twenty thousand. In fact, we can't misjudge this challenge at all, we need to get it right the first time. The following two chapters will explore in more detail the basic nature of all exponential curves. This is not simply a math lesson. The characteristics of an exponential growth rate of computer capacity must be fully understood if we are going to forecast and hopefully control this technology in the future. The first of these characteristics has been addressed in part in this chapter: Sustained exponential doubling quickly produces astronomical sums in relatively short periods of time. A second characteristic is much more subtle -- at the beginning of an exponential rate of growth (i.e., the one-penny, two-pennies and four-pennies stage), not much seems to be happening, but once the sums start to become significant the result explodes astronomically. As a result, even at the early stage of a technology undergoing rapid exponential change, a momentary delay in understanding the effects of its rate of growth, especially one with potentially harmful applications such as AI, may give it a head start that can never be overtaken. This predicament was captured brilliantly in Walt Disney's classic, *The Sorcerer's Apprentice*. The lazy apprentice uses a spell to double the mops cleaning the Sorcerer's chambers only to learn to his horror that this has created way *too* many mops. The result is comical, befitting a children's fable. The implications of the force of Radical Change created by the exponential doubling of computer capacity are far more frightening than those in the Disney saga and, unfortunately, they are also far more real and menacing.

---

26 A few pundits might suggest Obamacare.

# Chapter Four

---

## EXPONENTIAL CHANGE:
### Fast -- "Really" Fast

"No Eric, things are going to be really different! No, no, I mean *really* different!" This is a part of a purported conversation in 1986 between Mark Miller (Project Xanadu) and K. Eric Drexler, the father of nano-technology and author of one of the seminal works about the future, *Radical Abundance*,[27] Miller was attempting to describe to Drexler how fast computer computation had become. Based on actual, objective, quantified measurements, between 1986 and 2015 computer capacity, per dollar, had doubled approximately twenty additional times and had become about one million times more powerful than the technology that confounded Miller and Drexler in 1986.[28] If two leading experts in the field of computers struggled to appreciate the rate of growth of the power of computers back in 1986, it is understandable why most laypeople today do not appreciate this phenomenon. The failure of not only laypeople but even many experts in multiple fields

---

27 K. Eric Drexler, *Radical Abundance* (Public Affairs, a member of the Perseus Books Group, 2013).

28 This conclusion is based on verified measurements of the growth of computer capacity that support a doubling every eighteen months, rather than the assumption in most of the literature of a doubling every two years.

to appreciate or, even worse, to disregard the accelerating rate of the development of the power of computers (AI) may be one of the most egregious and painful misjudgments of our generation. AI is not a technology such as electricity, solar power or robotic-driven automobiles, which captures the human imagination with a promise of essentially only halcyon results. It is a technology much more akin to the mixed blessings of nuclear energy or genetic research, except that some of the potential applications of advanced AI may be far more sinister and potentially harmful. Also, unlike the development of technologies in these other fields, these technologies have been growing exponentially for a long time and are projected to continue to do so. The phenomenal rate of growth of the power of computers has occurred even though we have not created an equivalent to the concentrated effort of the Manhattan Project, which drove the development of the atomic bomb. The technological breakthroughs in computers are the result of the combined effort and investment in many fields of technology and from hundreds of thousands of sometimes seemingly unrelated efforts around the world, but together these efforts dwarf the magnitude of the Manhattan Project.

To describe the rapid, virtually incomprehensible growth of the power of computers, many experts have referred to well-known everyday applications of modern computers. For example, the smartphone in your pocket and/or the 2012 Sony PlayStation has as much computer capacity as any of the world's multimillion-dollar supercomputers of the mid-1990s. These examples (and there are many more) get people's attention, but they aren't very helpful in understanding how dramatically this advancing computer capacity will affect our future. In fact, our everyday experience with computers tells us otherwise. Anyone who has tried to use Siri knows that she is not very smart. I was recently reminded of these limitations when I attempted to use Siri on my iPhone 5. The conversation went something like this:

Dan: *"Siri, give me the names of Italian restaurants in Brookline, Massachusetts."*

Siri: *"I do not have maps of Syria, Donald."*

Dan: *(raising my voice slightly, and with my Irish temper beginning to show) "Siri! I want the names of Italian restaurants in Brookline, Massachusetts!"*

Siri: *"This is your problem, Donald, not mine."*

Dan: *(Then I was really pissed. Not only did she have my name wrong, but she also had an attitude! So I let her have it.) "Goddammit, Siri, I want the names of Italian restaurants in Brookline, Massachusetts."*

Siri: *"There is no reason to curse me, Donald."*

Dan: *(Exasperated, I suggested to my wife, "Honey, let's go to our favorite Italian restaurant on Beacon Street." And for good measure, I decided to set Siri straight.) "Siri, my name is Dan, not Donald."*

Siri: *"I understand, Dan not Donald."*

Dan: *("Damn, I hate those twenty-something Apple engineers!")*

These experiences confirm the commonly held belief that nothing extraordinary is occurring in the development of AI, so assertions based on objective measurements of computer capacity are not very persuasive.

Another approach to make people aware of how powerful computers have become is to describe computational power in objective, quantitative terms of computer capacity. Since 1993 the fastest computers in the world have been ranked by a peer-approved objective method termed the LINPACK Benchmark. Each year, the LINPACK ratings are published in the TOP500 List. In 1994 the top spot was held by Fujitsu's Numerical Wind Tunnel supercomputer with a peak capacity of 1.7 gigaflops per second. (A gigaflop is a trillion ($10^9$) transactions.)[29] By 2008 the fastest supercomputer was the IBM Roadrunner with a computational speed of 1.2 petraflops per second (this is $10^{15}$). This is a one-thousand-fold increase in computer power in less than fifteen years. In 2013 the world's fastest computer was China's Tranhe-2 with a capacity of 33.8 petraflops per second. Government agencies in China and India, as well as Intel, have all announced plans to develop the first supercomputer to reach the exaflop level ($10^{18}$, one quintillion flops, or one thousand times faster than a petraflop) by 2018. This capacity will far exceed the computational capacity of the human brain.[30]

Describing computer capacity using these objective standards sounds very scientific and impressive, but it is virtually meaningless to all but a few humans on the planet. How much is one quintillion? If it were measured in Ping Pong balls stacked side by side, it would reach from the earth to the moon ten billion times with a lot of spare Ping Pong balls left over. Does that help? These numbers are, pardon the pun, astronomical and almost incomprehensible. Similar magnitudes of numbers could be used to describe how many stars there are in the universe or atoms in a tablespoon of water. But in this context the numbers are not just incomprehensible, they are inconsequential. Who, but for a few geek physicists, really cares how many atoms are in a tablespoonful of water? This is *not* the case when these numbers describe computer power. Today, and certainly on our journey to the Near Horizon, the driver of the growth of particularly knowledge-based technologies is computer capacity. As this capacity doubles exponentially, it will create not just the possibility of inventing great

---

29 What is a flop? It is a floating point operations per second. This is the basic computation that measures the capacity of all computers.

30 This is solely a measure of capacity, not an indication that this computer will be able to think like a human.

new technologies and vastly advanced AI -- it will literally force the development of such technologies. Because computers and AI have become so central to the growth of new technologies, the promise of Cornucopia or the risk of Armageddon, based upon applications of these technologies, cannot be understood until one *fully* comprehends how powerful computers have become, and how much more powerful computers will become in the *very* near future.

Obviously, increases in computer capacity alone do not cause change, at least not immediately. I will explore the relationship between the growth of computer capacity and the development of knowledge, creative inventions and applied transformative technologies (ATT) in the world today and tomorrow in the following chapters. But for now, I will remain focused on the engine for all this change.

Understanding sustained exponential change is difficult because in our daily lives we have never actually experienced this sensation -- well, almost never. One reason for this phenomenon is that by its very nature exponential change cannot be maintained for more than short durations.[31] In the real world, we have simple studies of exponential growth -- for example, in the breeding habits of lemmings and rabbits. These studies all conclude that after short periods of dramatic change, there is a near total collapse. But computer capacity will not collapse; it may slow down dramatically or it may even flatten, but by then we will have one hell of a lot of computer capacity. We already do. So I have attempted to find an everyday example of the sensation of exponential change that a layperson could get her arms around.

An experience in college may be as close as I will ever come to this feeling. One very cold evening in the dead of winter, Woody, a friend on the ski team, and I decided to alleviate our boredom by "borrowing" a toboggan from the priests (we attended a Vermont Catholic college). We took it down the college's twenty-meter ski jump. That is about the

---

31 The growth of computer capacity and an increasing number of knowledge-based technologies (such as DNA sequencing) that are directly driven by computer capacity seem to be the exceptions that prove the rule.

height of a six-story building. Yes, there was some alcohol involved. The first few seconds into the ride were exhilarating beyond description, and this may be as close to the feeling of exponential change as I will ever know. Unfortunately the law of gravity prevailed, and Woody and I and the toboggan crashed to earth, splintering the toboggan neatly down the middle. Fortunately for me, Woody was in the front of the toboggan. Since I am hopeful that you have not shared this experience, I came up with another example -- a roller coaster. While riding a roller coaster, there is that moment when you approach the summit. At this point, the world seems normal, level and sane. Then, breathtakingly, the roller coaster begins to descend with what seems to be a horrific rate of acceleration -- you feel yourself pushed back into the seat, gulping for air and terrified, and, depending on your basic disposition, you either yell "Holy shit!!!" or some other form of off-color remark or "Yahoo!!!". This may be as close to the feeling of exponential change as we will get, at least for a while.

So much for the feeling we are after. This is a serious book. So I will examine exponential growth from a more scientific perspective. Chart 4.1, "Exponential versus Linear Growth: Exponential Growth of Computer Power (upper line) versus 3 Percent Annual Growth (lower line)," plots the rate of exponential growth doubling every two years (the upper line) versus linear change (the lower line). The lower line represents an increase of approximately 3 percent a year, which is about the average economic growth rate of the world's economy over the past one hundred years.[32]

At the end of fifteen years things on the exponential curve are getting interesting, but if you take this curve out twenty years it is an eye-opener! This chart demonstrates the basic characteristics of all exponential curves. To correctly judge our future, we must be very cognizant of these attributes because the radical improvement of computational

32 Thomas Piketty, *Capital in the Twenty-First Century* (Belknap Press, Harvard University Press, 2014). Similar to the problem with Chart 3.1 (a), the rate of economic change at 3 percent annually appears flat. It is not, but on the scale of 1 to 35,000,000 the growth is inconsequential.

Chart 4.1 **Exponential versus Linear Growth**

Exponential Growth of Computer Power (red)
versus
3% Annual Growth (green)

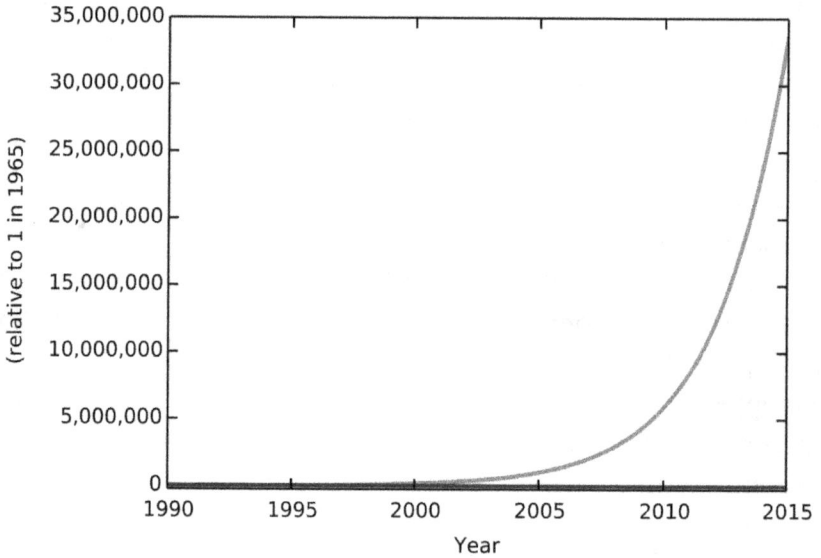

power will follow this curve. Exponential curves all start with extremely small beginnings -- think of doubling a penny five or six times (i.e., sixty-four cents). The initial amount does not change remarkably in the first few doublings. In fact, at the beginning of an exponential curve, the difference between the upper line and the lower line is negligible. This is sometimes referred to as the *flat stage* of an exponential curve. However, after eight to ten doublings (twenty years), the exponential curve begins to accelerate, and the difference between the upper line and the lower line becomes, at first, apparent, and then staggering. As the curves move forward, the exponential curve begins to skyrocket, not unlike the feeling when entering the "Holy shit!" moment of a roller coaster. This stage of exponential change is often referred to as the *knee* of an exponential curve.[33] Most computer experts agree that the development of computer capacity is well into the knee of an exponential curve. These experts do not, however, agree on how quickly things in our world will change once we enter this knee. It almost doesn't matter, because if we are describing phenomena that will occur in the lifetimes of our children or their children, the "Holy shit!" moment is out there even if the experts are off by a decade or two. Once you climb the knee of the exponential curve, the "Holy shit!" acceleration is upon you.

Even when you have absorbed the anecdotes and reviewed the objective measurements of computer capacity, it is very difficult to relate to what Chart 4.1 may portend for your everyday life in the future. In fact, it is so counter-intuitive and unwieldy that it is virtually impossible to absorb, even if you are a mathematician, a physicist or an economist. As a result, some of the writers in these fields have plotted exponential change on a logarithmic scale,[34] as shown on Chart 4.2, "Logarithmic Scale: Exponential Growth of Computer Power (upper line) versus 3 Percent Annual Growth (lower line)." On a logarithmic scale, the demarcations on the vertical side of the chart increase by a factor of ten

---

33 The term *knee* comes from the shape of the curve at this stage.

34 Eric Brynjolfsson and Andrew McAfee, *The Second Machine Age: Work, Progress, and Prosperity in a Time of Brilliant Technologies* (W.W. Norton & Company, 2014).

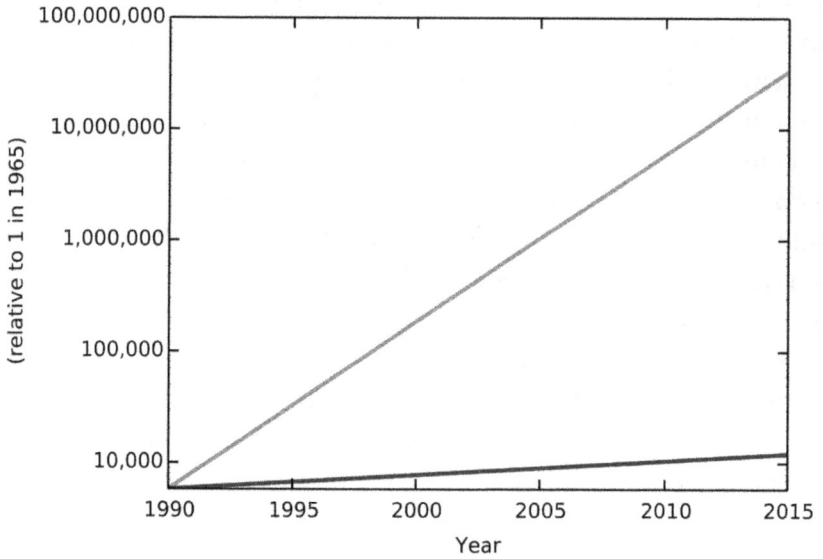

Chart 4.2       **Logarithmic Scale**

Exponential Growth of Computer Power (red)
versus
3% Annual Growth (green)

for each calibration. Logarithmic charts are used to measure a number of phenomena such as sound. Measured logarithmically, one hundred and ten decibels is ten times louder than one hundred decibels, not 10 percent greater. As you can see, this makes the chart easier to analyze for certain purposes, but for the layperson, the appreciation of how fast the change is occurring is totally lost. The lines on this chart are representative of *linear*, not exponential, acceleration, which is at the heart of the problem in understanding the force of Radical Change. Since the point of this book is to raise your level of concern, I will stick with Chart 4.1. Both charts are accurate, but Chart 4.1 more graphically portrays what is *actually* occurring over a sustained period of exponential change. On Chart 4.2 (the logarithmic chart), there will *never* be a "Holy shit!" moment. On Chart 4.1, it is only a question of time.

As stated earlier, most laypeople intuitively feel that the almost vertical acceleration shown on the curve of exponential change can't go on very long. Something has to give. Most experts, with the exception of Kurzweil and an incredibly loyal and devoted following, believe that the growth of computer capacity for the same price will ultimately *begin* to flatten out. But with the accumulated amount of computer capacity that exists today, even without major technological breakthroughs, we will go out to a point where even Kurzweil really won't give a damn.[35]

At the risk of being accused of claiming to be a mathematician, Chart 4.3: "Exponential Growth of Computer Capacity," places a value on the amount of computer power that had been developed by 1950. This was approximately the end of the era of warehouses full of vacuum tubes. These computers could out-calculate humans, but they were primitive. This computer capacity has been given a value of one.

---

35 Actually, this may not be true. Ray is a very big thinker. Even the speed of light is a limit on Ray's imagination that he is unwilling to accept. Ray believes that within his lifetime, technology will continue to push longevity out to the date when we will discover the secret to eternal life. I am no Kurzweil, but I have a related interest in technology. I hope that golf technologies will continue to develop and improve my golf game faster than it deteriorates due to my aging. So far, technology has accomplished a lot for my game, but not enough to keep my handicap from increasing exponentially. I wish Ray Kurzweil better luck.

| Chart 4.3 | | | |
|---|---|---|---|
| **Exponential Growth of Computer Capacity** | | | |
| | **Years** | **Doubling**<br>**(every two years)** | **Value/Units** |
| 1950 | | | One |
| 1990 | 40 | 20 | one million |
| 2010 | 60 | 30 | one billion |
| 2030 | 80 | 40 | one trillion |

The values through 2015 are substantiated measurements of computer capacity, such as those measured by LINPACK.[36] Based on assumptions supported by most experts in the field of computer development, the calculations to the year 2030 as shown on Chart 4.3 are very realistic, in fact, conservative.

By examining this chart, you can see why this book is entitled "Radical Change." By 1990 (twenty doublings) computer capacity for the same price was one million units more powerful than in 1950. By 2010 it was one billion times more powerful. By 2030 it is forecasted to be one trillion times more powerful. These numbers *are* nearly incomprehensible, but they are not the product of science fiction. The numbers through 2010 are based on objective measurements of computers that have already been developed.

Many experts have dismissed the importance of the power of existing computer capacity because the world does not yet seem radically altered by its existence. The answer is actually very simple. Most of our current computer power just got here. As this book will explore in detail later, it will take time for computer capabilities to be applied to create transformative technologies, but the course of our future driven by this force is no longer a question of *if*; it is solely a question of *how soon and how far.* From 2015 to 2020 (a period of five years) the growth in computer capacity is projected to grow by ten billion units of capacity. This is about ten thousand times the entire growth of computer capacity from 1950 to 1990. If you either do not believe the astronomical numbers in this chapter, or you are intrigued -- please go to ExponentialGrowthCalculator.com and play with one of the free exponential calculators found there. It will confirm these mind-boggling results.

There are two important lessons to be gained from this chapter. The first lesson is that the nature of the curve of an exponential rate

---

36 As discussed earlier, the actual measurements support a shorter period than two years for each doubling.

of growth helps to explain why the force for change created by grow-ing computer capacity is not more apparent today. We as a society are just emerging from the flat stage of the exponential curve. The sec-ond lesson is more unsettling. We already have an amazing amount of computer capacity at work creating new technologies that will radically transform our world, *but* an astoundingly greater amount is coming *very* soon.

At this point, you are probably asking yourself, "If the world or the United States or even just New York City is experiencing Radical Change (the roller-coaster sensation), why isn't it clearer and more apparent to everyone? Certainly, our experiences with roller coast-ers at Busch Gardens and Disney World conclusively establish that if an exponential rate of change occurs (the "Holy shit" moment on the roller coaster), you will know it. This complacency is the great-est stumbling block to recognizing how precarious our relationship with the power of computers and computer intelligence has already become.

We have faced similar paradoxes before. During the 1940s, many experts in astronomy believed that alien intelligent life forms must exist somewhere in the universe. These experts postulated that the universe should be filled with millions if not billions of such intelligent forms of life. There was one huge problem with all of these theories. Despite years of effort, no one had successfully confirmed the existence of a sin-gle such alien being.[37] One day, while sitting at a luncheon with friends, Enrico Fermi, one of the world's greatest astrophysicists, exclaimed totally out of the blue, "So where is everybody?" The same could be said of Radical Change. If computer intelligence is driving Radical Change, and if it has been growing exponentially for over sixty years, why are its effects not more apparent in our world today? This is not a hypotheti-cal question. Our nearly unshakable confidence that things are pretty

---

37 This is not to offend the growing number of people who firmly believe in the exis-tence of UFOs, but so far, the established scientific community has not embraced this idea.

much the same today as they were in the past seriously hinders our ability to appreciate how and why Radical Change will influence our world tomorrow.

As described earlier in this chapter, one reason for this puzzle arises from the very nature of the curve (namely, the flat stage of exponential growth), but there are other reasons as well. Change has no objective standard of measure. Unlike speed, temperature, or the growth of computer capacity, there are no objective, scientific standards to quantify change. A few experts have somewhat arbitrarily identified major technological developments in the history of civilization (such as the invention of the printing press and/or the steam engine) to delineate how fast things are changing. This approach is, however, very subjective. Other experts have attempted to equate change with economic progress measured by any one of a number of traditional economic standards, such as the gross national product and/or individual productivity over time. But even if reliable long-term statistics of these concepts existed (which they do not),[38] statistics on economic wellbeing measure (imperfectly) only one dimension of change in our world.

Despite these well-intentioned efforts, we do not have an objective, widely acceptable standard or metric with which to quantify rates of change in the world over any meaningful period. We cannot even agree on what are the most pertinent aspects of our civilization that should be used as the benchmarks for determining whether or how fast our civilization is changing. Lacking objective forms of measurement to quantify change, we fall back on what we feel is different about our current situation from our memories of yesteryear. We are now the 24/7 society with smartphones, laptops and social networks like Facebook and Twitter to keep us plugged in. We sense things are

---

38 The recent meticulous work of Thomas Piketty may be the exception. See Piketty's book *Capitalism in the Twenty-First Century* (Belknap Press, Harvard University Press, 2014).

changing rapidly, but they do not seem exponentially faster, not even in New York City.[39]

While thinking about the problem of judging the rate of change in the world by using only our own current frame of reference, I was reminded of a family vacation to Conway, New Hampshire when I was ten. We rode the Cog Railway to the summit of Mount Washington, the highest peak in eastern North America. It is also one of the coldest places on earth. The construction of the railway was completed in 1869 and was considered, at the time of its construction, to be one of the engineering marvels of the era. The Cog Railway operates by rotating a giant cog that literally pulls the railcars up the slope of the mountain at a steepness that defies the laws of gravity. After twenty minutes of an exciting, soot-filled ride, we approached the halfway station to take on water for the locomotive. We were all encouraged by the conductor to stay aboard the train. Exhibiting a trait that would later mark my legal career, I decided to jump out onto the platform. I did, and promptly fell on my ass. The reason? In the twenty minutes of riding the Cog Railway, my inner ear had adjusted to the slope and told me it was normal. Once I stepped on the objectively flat platform of the halfway station, reality, namely the law of gravity, set in hard.

Why is this anecdote relevant? Because we are all riding on planet earth on the ascending curve of Radical Change. The rate of change in our world is accelerating, but so far we remain essentially on the flat stage of exponential change. To the extent we have experienced change, we have acclimated to it as it has quickened, but objectively it has not moved very much. This sense of changing expectations is demonstrated by the figures depicted in Chart 4.4, "Exponential Growth: Three Generations of Experience. Exponential Growth of Computer Power (upper line) versus Applied Transformative Technologies (lower line) "

Two aspects of Chart 4.4 are important to emphasize. First, no matter how much increased computer capacity directly empowers the rapid development of a new technology, there will be a lag between the time

---

39 The taxicabs in New York City may be an exception to this rule.

that a technology is first invented and the time that it will be developed into a widely utilized application that will transform our lives (applied transformative technologies, ATT). The factors affecting the length of this lag time will be discussed in later chapters, but for now the important point is to be cognizant of the fact that this period of transformation is inevitable and that for many technologies the transition period may be very long.

The upper line on Chart 4.4 demonstrates the same exponential rate of growth as was shown on the previous charts. The lower line assumes that technologies that will transform the way we live will double every twenty years. Admittedly, this is a totally arbitrary assumption, but whether the rate of doubling is every ten years or every thirty years, it leads to the same obvious conclusion: No matter how fast computational power advances, it will take a significant period of time for this capability to transform the world with ATT.

Figure One on Chart 4.4 represents my generation, born at the beginning of exponential change (1945). My early experience was on the flat stage of the curve. By 2015, I've seen a lot, including the birth and aging of the now generation. Things seem to be happening faster, but "it is no big deal." I am not at all prepared for the ride ahead.

Figure Two represents my children's generation (1985). They were born into a world that was just about to enter the knee of exponential change. During their childhood and young adulthood, the curve has experienced some upward movement, but to them, "it was no big deal." They are not ready for the ride ahead either. Figure Three represents the generation of my grandchildren. They were born in 2014 and 2015, now entering the knee of exponential change. For them, every experience in their lives will be rapidly changing. But as Andy Garcia said in the movie *Oceans 11*, "[They were] born ready." The rate of change in the world is now accelerating rapidly, but they have no prior form of reference to appreciate this fact.

By 2015, I'm outdated, technologically handicapped and a duck out of water! On the other hand, my daughters feel that things are

Chart 4.4

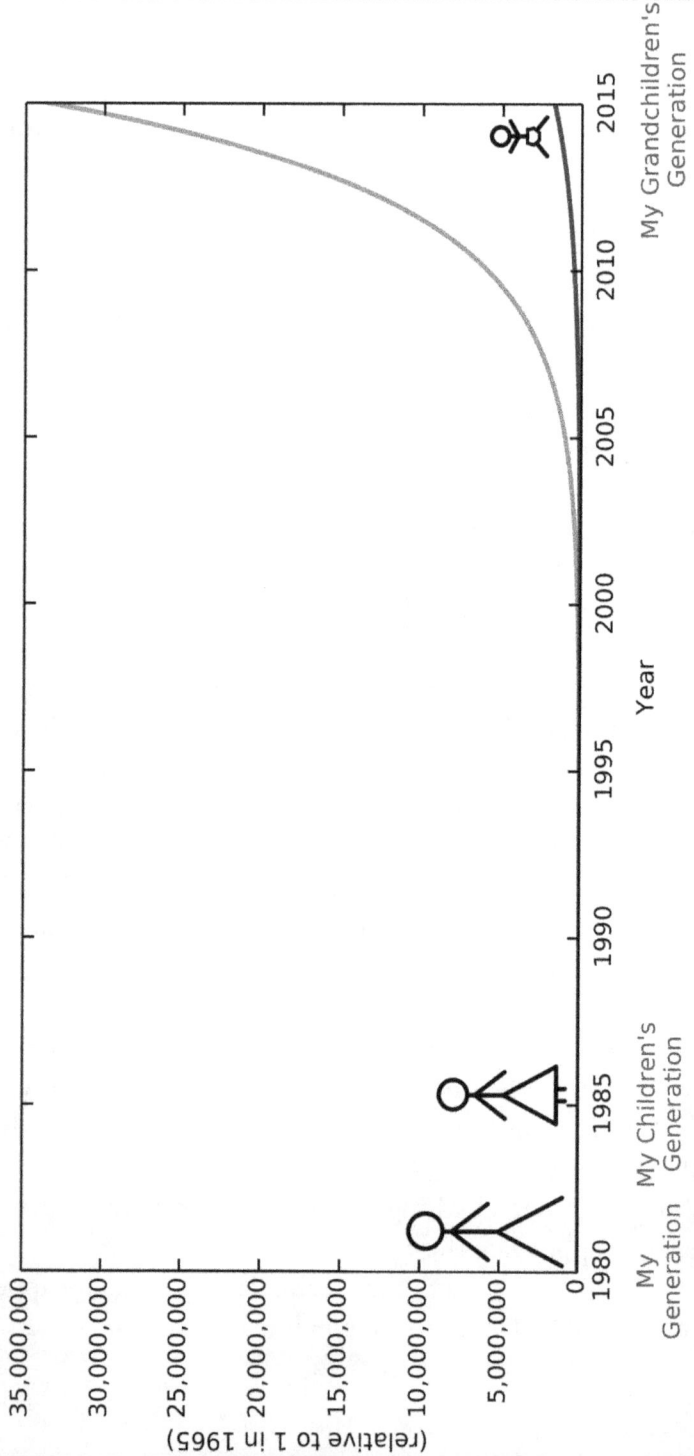

**Exponential Growth: Three Generations of Experience**

Exponential Growth of Computer Power (red)
versus
Applied Transformative Technologies (green)

changing, but not radically. Their computers, smartphones, as well as their Facebook, Twitter, eBay and PayPal accounts, and even Siri, work just fine for them. My grandchildren, who will grow up fondling children's computers in their cradles, are ready for the future; they just do not know it yet. They started ascending the knee of exponential change from birth. It is all they will ever know. Some day, after they learn to talk, they will say, "it is no big deal."

Hopefully, these anecdotes and charts will help raise your consciousness of the pace of change in our current lives and provide you with a warning of how these forces will radically alter the direction of the future. Today, we are relatively comfortable that our future will be *essentially* an extension of our past experience. On the flat stage of exponential change, this assumption works rather well. As we enter the knee of this curve, the signs of a paradigm shift in our experience become much more apparent. As we climb the knee of exponential change, a lack of appreciation of the force of Radical Change on our lives and on the lives of our children may be a tragic mistake.

Before examining how the nature of new technologies is being transformed by Radical Change, it will be useful to examine the process of how exponentially increasing computer capacity will, and must, drive transformational technologies that will alter our lives and our assumptions and approaches to our place in the universe. The following chapters in the remainder of Part One will address some of the dimensions of this process.

# Chapter Five

## POSITIVE FORCES FOR CHANGE:
### It Takes a Village

To understand how Radical Change will affect the advancement of technologies in our future, I need to examine the driving force for this development -- the accumulation and application of knowledge. History can teach us a great deal about how knowledge is developed, what forces and processes can help to accelerate the accumulation of knowledge, and also what forces have historically impeded or prohibited either the development of knowledge or its application to change the way our society lives and functions. Despite the impact of Radical Change on the nature of progress in our civilization, the essential nature of how knowledge develops and how it is either applied or suppressed will not be significantly altered.[40]

I will begin by examining how knowledge is created and what can expedite this process. In its simplest form, new, beneficial knowledge is best developed if existing knowledge can be accumulated, reviewed, analyzed and reformulated effectively and quickly. Bringing more participants into this process will also help, as will providing effective and larger incentives to motivate people to participate in a highly focused

---

40 There is one very important exception. The growing intelligence of computers may create an "Explosion of Knowledge" never before experienced. This possibility is the subject of Chapter Six.

and energized manner. In this chapter I will examine how the power of Radical Change, driven by the exponential force of advancing computational power, will dramatically affect each and every one of these factors.

Knowledge has always been derived from the meticulous review and consideration of massive amounts of raw data, as Charles Darwin commented in 1887: "My mind seems to have become a kind of machine for grinding general laws out of large collections of facts."[41] Computers today have the capacity to organize, store and process massive amounts of information and raw data at a scale that was unimaginable to Darwin. Supercomputers, operating at computational speeds in the billionths of a second, far exceed the capacity of any brain to crunch raw collections of facts. This capability is providing extremely important advances in many fields. Recently this capability has been used to predict the spread of infectious diseases and to prognosticate economic, political, social and cultural trends by analyzing overwhelming masses of raw data. Some of this data might otherwise have been dismissed as relatively trivial information on Facebook, Twitter and countless other sites for social interactions. As computer programs continue to be developed that can examine in milliseconds the staggering amount of data now available, this will inevitably lead to increasing discoveries of new knowledge.

The mere capability of accumulating and processing massive amounts of data is, however, just the beginning of the impact that exponentially advancing computer power will have on the formulation of new knowledge. Knowledge will also grow more rapidly if it can be cheaply shared and utilized by very large numbers of people. With the ubiquitous expansion of access to the Internet, well over three billion people have a staggering amount of information and knowledge available, virtually for free. Better yet, it comes very well organized and easy to use. Through the use of very sophisticated search engines, browsers and other applications on websites, knowledge is not only easier to access,

---

41 Charles Darwin, *The Autobiography of Charles Darwin*, Chapter II.

but it is also much easier to compile and understand. This capability was never before available to any great thinker, inventor or layperson.

Let's take an example. Suppose you wish to research a subject that you do not know very well, such as cognitive behavior.[42] During the Industrial Revolution, you would (if you lived in Boston) go to the Boston Public Library and ask the librarian to guide you to the right section. However, you were already ahead of 99.9 percent of the world that couldn't go to a library as useful as the Boston Public Library. Once there, you would slowly work your way through the pivotal works in the field and retrieve each one to read. Some cross-referenced works would require a trip to the Harvard Library, if you could get in, and some would not be available at all. Very slowly you would get part of the job done. Today on Wikipedia or thousands of similar sites, you type in the subject matter and immediately get a well-researched paper. As you read the paper, every footnote can instantaneously lead you to another source that is almost always there, never checked out and almost always free. In a few moments you have gathered what would have taken months of collecting research reports, newspaper articles, and papers at symposiums and conferences. Every area of specialized knowledge now has its own dedicated search engine(s) and website(s) that provide this function. In the age of the Internet, the challenge of locating and sorting relevant information has been dramatically reduced, and yet we take it for granted.

Making this information available to the world is wonderful, but obviously not everyone with access to this information will benefit from it or use it wisely, nor will most create a transformative technology. History is, however, full of examples that demonstrate that you do not need to be a recognized expert or genius in any field to make a great discovery. Albert Einstein, perhaps the most brilliant mind since Thomas Jefferson, began his career as a third-class patent clerk in the Swiss Patent Office in Bern, Switzerland. In a single year (1905, now

---

42 Try doing a little research in this area of knowledge if you wish to see how dense and impenetrable experts can make a subject.

dubbed the "miracle year"), Einstein, at the age of twenty-six, delivered four papers that transformed our fundamental understanding of how the universe was created and how it works. Those papers included his theory of the photoelectric effect for which he was subsequently awarded a Nobel Prize, Brownian motion, the theory of special relativity and the equivalence of mass and energy, which led to the most famous equation of all time: $E = mc^2$. It was a period of great achievement for Einstein, but it also had its disappointments. In 1903 the Swiss government denied his request for advancement to be a second-class patent clerk, and a year later he attempted to change careers; however, his application to teach third grade in Bern, Switzerland, was rejected by the local school committee.

Everywhere we look today, many great achievements are coming, surprisingly, from unlikely sources. We all know that Apple was created in a garage by Steve Jobs, but one of the most unlikely success stories of this era may be the remarkable Mr. Craig Venter, born in Salt Lake City in 1946. After an undistinguished early education (he was an indifferent student more interested in surfing, and he nearly flunked eighth grade), he went on to suffer a traumatic experience in the Vietnam War. This experience inspired him to begin a college education at the community college in San Mateo, California. Despite an early, undiagnosed case of ADHD (attention deficit hyperactivity disorder), Venter graduated with a PhD in physiology and pharmacology from the University of California, San Diego. Notwithstanding this unpromising start, Venter went on to become one of the first to sequence the human genome, and he may be the first scientist to create a form of synthetic life.[43] He was listed by Time Magazine in both 2007 and 2008 as one of the one hundred most influential people in the world. In July 2009, Synthetic Genomes, a firm he founded, entered into a joint venture with ExxonMobil to develop a synthetic biofuel, based on his past work in the field of genetics. This collaboration may lead to a new generation of biofuel that could not

---

43 There is a significant scientific dispute on this point.

only help resolve the world's energy crisis, but it might also play a vital role in battling climate change.

There may not be a great many undiscovered "Einsteins" out there (I disagree, if you lower that bar just a little), but there are plenty of people who, when focused, incentivized, and teamed with people from other disciplines, can achieve great things. Today, collaborative cutting-edge research and development efforts can be undertaken by multidisciplinary teams separated by thousands of miles, national boundaries, even barriers of language.[44] As knowledge-sharing technologies continue to improve, they will exponentially increase this aspect of the creation of new breakthrough technologies.

In all of this technological splendor, we should not lose track of the role of the greatest motivator of all -- the hope or promise of achieving great economic wealth and popular recognition and acclaim. As knowledge expands, creative minds will use this knowledge to invent technologies that transform our lives. For a technology to accomplish this goal, it needs to be cheap, be simple and work well enough to be implemented throughout society (applied transformative technologies, ATT). With the power of Radical Change, this process and the immense financial rewards that can come with it are occurring remarkably quickly all around us. Nearly every day, we hear stories of immense wealth being generated by young startups. The media and the Internet tend to sensationalize this news by focusing almost entirely on the almost unimaginable financial wealth of a few, such as Mark Zuckerberg, founder of Facebook, or Travis Kalanick, CEO of Uber. But for each of these rock stars, there are hundreds or thousands of supporting participants who become "only" millionaires – think of the early employees at Apple, Google, etc. who have benefited financially, all because they were there at the birth of a new idea. In the age of the Internet, an idea can be immediately presented and marketed worldwide and at virtually no cost. This has never before been possible, and it contributes to the paradigm

---

44 Computer programs capable of simultaneous translations are improving dramatically.

shift of opportunity that now inspires, empowers and energizes millions of people around the globe to give it a shot. It may be like playing the lottery, if you consider the odds of success, but the vision of reward of this magnitude has lifted many out of disillusionment.

There are numerous other manifestations of the way in which new technologies are creating opportunities for people around the world to achieve substantial economic achievement and recognition. When adjusted for inflation and the graduated federal income tax, whether these opportunities exceed the creation of the great wealth of the Rockefellers, Mellons and Carnegies of the Industrial Revolution may be debated, but it is beyond question that these opportunities are now available to a far greater number of individuals if they are willing to expend the effort and incur the risks of seeking out these opportunities. Today there is increasing concern with the economic inequality that results from the creation of astronomical wealth by the one-percenters, and the even more mind-boggling concentration of wealth by the 1 percent of the one-percenters. This issue will be addressed at some length in later chapters of this book, but what is important to note here is that an increasing percentage of this magnificently fortunate group of one-percenters derived their wealth from their own efforts.[45] There should be a serious discussion of the effects of such a concentration of income and wealth in the hands of so few people, but as a message of hope and inspiration to those who may create the transformative technologies of the future it is a powerful part of the process fueling Radical Change.

Efforts to concentrate the best minds with sufficient resources to create wonderful new technologies have been going on for hundreds of years. One example of a current revival of an old approach is exemplified by the increasing use of the concept of the incentive prize. One of the first incentive prizes was established in 1714 by an act of the British Parliament. It offered a reward of ten thousand pounds[46] for the first

---

45  Thomas Piketty, *Capital in the Twenty-First Century* (Belknap Press, Harvard University Press, 2014).

46  In constant dollars, in 1714 this was a staggering amount of money.

person to invent a simple and accurate method to determine a sailing ship's location. The prize led to the discovery (by a watchmaker) of the first instrument to measure longitude with some precision. Since then, an incentive prize has been offered for the first nonstop flight over the Atlantic, won by Charles Lindberg in 1927. More recently, incentive prizes have been popularized by the Ansari X Prize foundation (for the first privately funded orbit into space) and the US Defense Advanced Research Projects Agency (DARPA) (for the first driverless vehicle to navigate a one hundred fifty mile course in the desert). The incentive prize is a very effective way to leverage efforts at discovery for very focused results. It is also a form of democracy since the competitions are generally open to all and, surprisingly, some of the winners of these competitions are individuals without formal education or proven experience in the field of science subject to the prize.

The forces for change and the technologies accelerating these forces, as described above, provide an unprecedented capability to share knowledge and to be rewarded for these efforts beyond anyone's previous wildest dreams. Despite these amazing impacts, the most transformative force to accelerate the growth of knowledge in the twenty-first century may arise from the growing acceptance of the revolutionary principles upon which the Internet was founded. These principles are based upon the premise that information, knowledge, inventions and ideas should never be proprietary; namely, everyone has a right to universal and essentially free access to everything that is known and/or knowable. These concepts are blasphemous to, at least, two centuries of individual and corporate secrecy and protectionism. Over this period, there have been cosmic efforts by legislators, lawyers and business people (i.e., the Brakemen, described in Chapter Seven) to protect these intellectual property rights through the use of the most elaborate and thorough forms of national, regional and international patent, copyright, trademark, licensing, tax treaties and regulatory constraints that brilliant and very well-paid minds can concoct. The very existence of the

Internet and the principles on which it is based and has been defiantly operated have called all of this protectionism into question.[47]

Given that this philosophy represents a massive challenge to those who wish to protect their intellectual property, this shift in attitude has been met with stiff resistance. Despite this reaction, throughout the world there is a rising new generation of inventors and entrepreneurs that include many of our most brilliant, creative and energetic young people. These individuals have forsaken traditional career paths in major institutions, corporations, and/or universities to pursue their dreams. They gather together in garages, warehouses, artists' lofts, Starbucks, basements in their parents' homes, etc.

Superficially, you could dismiss and denigrate what is new about this generation. Yes, there is a quality of rebellion and counter-culture. They are the children of the Internet, imbued with its values of hating secrecy and private property. This is a generation that has chosen to not only believe in the principles of the Internet, but to also try to embody these principles into a new sense of entrepreneurism. This is a generation that believes that people have a *right* not only to share but also to have access to the energy, creativity, knowledge and ideas of others. For the corporate America of my generation, these are frightening, anti-capitalistic statements, almost un-American. Or are they? They may be, in fact, much closer to the basic values of the founders of this country than the corporate secrecy, protectionism and avarice of IBM and many other companies and institutions of the 1980s.

The emergence of this new generation is just beginning to be felt. It is a sad fact that one of the great forces that has led to its creation is the shrinking opportunities that exist in more traditional career paths. Working as an underground generation and in an underground economy, its members often do not appear as employed in the United States Bureau of Labor Statistics. Their current contributions, no matter how

---

47 One of the most remarkable impacts of open-source technology may be the development of the sequencing of the human genome by the Broad Institute. This discovery is not patented, which has resulted in an exponential explosion of efforts to utilize this knowledge in the fields of health care and pharmaceuticals.

hard they work, are rarely reflected in our gross national product, productivity or employment statistics, nor in the number of new patents being filed (thank God!). Many in this generation subsist on welfare, unemployment benefits, food stamps, and part-time jobs as bicycle messengers, cooks and counter help at Wendy's and McDonalds. Some live on their mothers' and fathers' decreasing goodwill and patience. We don't even have a good name for this generation of entrepreneurs, and yet they embody the American Dream. They may provide the single greatest hope for the economic future of our country.

I have a personal interest in this development because my oldest daughter, Kristen, is part of this new generation. She left not one, but three, jobs in established investment banking firms to pursue a career in journalism at Stanford University. There she was bitten by the bug of Silicon Valley and has spent the last four years without, until just recently, a salary, creating a startup software company in the educational industry.

As this generation has matured, it has struggled with the inherent conflict between the founding principles of the Internet and the reality that without capital, nothing happens, and without property rights of some form, there is no capital. Unless you are very young and very idealistic, you must have an economic incentive. This concession is not to betray the lofty goals of the Internet, it is to try to honor and nurture them, and still make a decent living. How these competing interests can be reconciled will be one of the many challenges that this generation must face.

One last observation about the geek generation. Despite its ideology, it is getting organized. All over America, innovation centers are beginning to appear. They take many shapes and sizes and some are more formal and structured than others. What they have in common is cheap space and open environments -- both physically and intellectually. People on a shoestring come to share their energy, ideas, insanity, creativity, and sometimes even their lunch. At no time in American history have more young people been attracted together to dream big dreams and share their aspirations, with the possible exception being the many immigrants who passed through Ellis Island.

One of the first and most successful of such centers is the Innovation Center, 100 Broadway, Cambridge, Massachusetts. I knew of this center years ago, long before ever imagining I would write this book, because I represented the landlord, MIT, in a number of tenant/landlord disputes with its energetic, iconoclastic founder, Tim Rowe. The importance of innovation centers to direct the forces of Radical Change in positive directions will be discussed in later chapters. For now, it is important only to note that the development of such centers and the intellectual culture upon which they are based will play a very important part in the development of wonderful new transformative technologies in our future. The creation of many more innovation centers has now become a major focus of efforts to redevelop and rejuvenate many neighborhoods in American cities. Using the example of the Cambridge Innovation Center, Boston has renamed the Fort Point Channel, historically an undeveloped area on Boston's waterfront, The Innovation District. They even hired Tim as a consultant. Recently, he opened a second innovation center in this district. Similar efforts are being undertaken in many cities across America and the world.

These centers are not being formed to help people create traditional goods and services. They are being formed to create new ideas and inventions. The marketplace they will enrich is not a market of hard goods and services but a marketplace of knowledge and innovation. Hopefully, while some of these technologies will be sold to the highest bidder, many will be open-sourced -- available to all, and virtually free.

Despite the naysayers, who will be discussed at the conclusion of the following chapter, based on all of the factors described above, the outlook for the development of new knowledge that will become the driving force for new ideas, inventions and ATT in the future has never been brighter.

# Chapter Six

## WHEN TECHNOLOGY REACHES THE TIPPING POINT:
### The Explosion of Knowledge

The development of massive amounts of computational power in recent history is a fact no one challenges. Whether the exponential growth of this astounding capability will inevitably, quickly and radically change the world is subject to great debate. In Chapter Five, I discussed how the astounding capabilities of computers have increasingly accelerated the forces that have historically contributed to the growth of knowledge and the creation of applied transformative technologies. A growing number of experts believe that as computer intelligence advances, it will inevitably reach a "tipping point" causing an evolution of knowledge not measured in millennia, as was the case with the evolution of Homo sapiens, but in milliseconds. This scenario was first predicted by Irving Good in 1965 (the birth date of Moore's law) in "Speculations Concerning the First Ultraintelligent Machine"[48]:

> An ultraintelligent machine could design even better machines.
> There would, unquestionably, be an "intelligence explosion,"

---

[48] I. J. Good, "Speculations Concerning the First Ultraintelligent Machine (HTML)," *Advances in Computers*, Vol. 6, 1965. Among his many accomplishments, Good was a colleague of Alan Turing and an important part of the effort of the British code-breakers at Betchley Park to decipher the German code, Enigma.

and the intelligence of man would be left far behind. Thus, the first ultraintelligent machine is the last invention that man need ever make.

That sounds ominous, but could computers ever achieve this level of ultraintelligence?

We know that the mere existence of computer capacity will not transform the world. In fact, except for a few geeks in offices at Google, Intel, Apple, Stanford University, MIT, etc., no one really even appreciates the height, and certainly not the view of the horizon from the top of the Himalayan-size pile of computer power that now exists. But you do not need to be an expert to recognize that the potential applications of this powerful capacity have only begun to be explored. And remember, in the next two years this capacity will more than double. The objective evidence of the growth of AI in the past few decades (witness the progression from IBM Deep Blue in chess to IBM Watson in "Jeopardy") would seem to a layperson to support the conclusion that the creation of artificial ultraintelligence is only a matter of time. In fact, almost all of the experts agree that increasing computer capacity will *inevitably* lead to the creation of nonhuman ultraintelligence. The only real issue of disagreement is whether this will occur within twenty years (Kurzweil) or one hundred years (Michio Kaku, in *Physics of the Future*).[49] Given that this book is written for our children and our grandchildren, this range of forecasts is not comforting. Nor is the reason for this consensus: The creation of ultraintelligence is right in the sweet spot of computer capability, alongside of the ability to play chess and "Jeopardy" better than any human.

To understand why the phenomenal growth of computer capacity may drive an Explosion of Knowledge, we need to examine the process of how transformative technologies are developed. A tremendous body

---

49 Michio Kaku, *Physics of the Future* (Random House, 2012); *The Future of the Mind* (Random House, 2014).

of incredibly important, erudite work has been crushed into these simplistic propositions:

1. The capacity to collect, transmit, process, formulate, reformulate, and share information and data will lead to the development of greater and greater amounts of useful information and knowledge.
2. As the body of useful knowledge increases, the number of inventions and ideas based on this increased knowledge will also increase.
3. Many of the applications of technologies based on these inventions and ideas will also increase. Some of these new technologies will transform our lives as ATT.
4. ATT will rapidly improve because of steps one to three above, and as they do, technologies will become much better and much cheaper.
5. These technologies will be developed at an ever-increasing rate, reducing the time of transition from steps one to four above, and reducing the costs of applying newly developed ATT.

One could easily characterize this summary of progress in the formation of knowledge and its transformation into ATT as an oversimplistic, naive view of issues that are fundamentally extremely complex, subtle, and very difficult to quantify or comprehend. Certainly experts can discuss these points in far more sophisticated terms, but this progression is based essentially on common sense. Bear in mind, also, that this is a laypersons guide, so I will take certain liberties to keep this material understandable.

When you break down the process of developing knowledge and ATT into its subparts, as described above, it becomes much more evident that massive computational power today and the tsunami wave of new capacity heading our way could very easily accelerate this process beyond any human capability. Supercomputers can obviously store and process vast amounts of information and knowledge. We have a new generation of computers such as IBM Watson that are able to "learn" new knowledge, and they are improving exponentially. Also, in the research and development stage, computer intelligence is being developed with the ability to process information and develop new useful information and knowledge based on absorbing vast amounts of information in much the same manner as humans learn. Experts in this new field of computer development term this ability *deep learning.* There are also numerous technologies, such as voice recognition and language translation, in which computers are able to reprogram themselves in reiterative steps that improve their performance. These capabilities are in a preliminary stage of development, but we should expect to see significant progress in this area. If we do, the incredible speed of computer calculation will clearly create a new generation of computers that will be able to process existing knowledge in a reiterative process of self-improvement, culminating in highly advanced computers that will reach the tipping point and become ultraintelligent.

For many years, Ray Kurzweil has been a strong advocate of this form of explosion in knowledge. In *How to Create a Mind,*[50] he restated his Law of Accelerating Returns (LOAR), first enunciated in his seminal work *The Age of Intelligent Machines.*[51] The underlying premise of this theory is that as knowledge expands exponentially (due to the power of advancing computer intelligence), it will drive the further exponential growth of new knowledge. This accumulation and improvement of knowledge is occurring at the virtually incomprehensible speed of computer computation. Kurzweil argues, in defining his theory of LOAR, that as AI develops (i.e., emerges from the knee of exponential change), an Explosion of Knowledge will become a self-fulfilling prophesy. Each new generation of AI will be more powerful and therefore more capable of creating the next more powerful generation of AI. With the amazing

---

50 Ray Kurzweil, *How to Create a Mind: The Secret of Human Thought Revealed* (Viking Press, 2012).

51 Ray Kurzweil, *The Age of Intelligent Machines* (MIT Press, 1990).

advances in the speed and capacity of computers, these reiterations will become separated by seconds, and then even milliseconds.

Obviously, the arguments by the proponents of an Explosion of Knowledge are essentially theoretical since we have no prior experience with anything remotely similar to our current computer capabilities. The future may not witness an Explosion of Knowledge, or LOAR, on the scale envisioned by Irving Good or Kurzweil, but on our journey to the Near Horizon, the process of creating new knowledge and ATT will accelerate dramatically -- maybe not exponentially, but "fast, really fast." The acceleration in the evolution of knowledge will be discussed at greater length in Chapter Nine, "Accelerating Evolution: Darwin on Steroids."

Despite the logic and the growing number of experts who believe an Explosion of Knowledge is imminent (within twenty-five to forty years), there is a vocal group of very authoritative critics who disagree.[52] One such expert is Robert Gordon. Gordon concludes in his widely read work, "Is U.S. Economic Growth Over?", 2012, that the United States ran out of "good inventions" by 1970 and has been tinkering with old ideas ever since.[53] He is in very good company. Tyler Cowen, another well-known economist, concludes in *The Great Stagnation*, 2011, that we are running out of "low-hanging fruit." This is Cowen's image of great ideas. We are, according to Cowen, at a "technological plateau, and the trees are more bare than we would like to think."[54]

It is difficult to understand where all these people have been for the past few decades. It is as if Lord Kelvin[55] had returned to earth. In 1900,

---

52 One of the most renowned and respected is Paul G. Allen, cofounder of Microsoft. Paul G. Allen and Mark Greaves, "Paul Allen, The Singularity Isn't Near," *Technology Review*, October 12, 2011.

53 Robert J. Gordon, "Is U.S. Economic Growth Over? Faltering Innovation Confronts the Six Headwinds," the National Bureau of Economic Research Working Paper No. 18315, Issued in August 2012.

54 Tyler Cowen, *The Great Stagnation: How America Ate All the Low-Hanging Fruit of Modern History, Got Sick, and Will (Eventually) Feel Better* (Dutton, 2011).

55 Lord William Thomas Kelvin (1824-1907), noted British physicist who, among many achievements, formulated the first and second laws of thermodynamics.

Lord Kelvin regretfully told a peer group of scientists at the British Association for the Advancement of Science: "There is nothing new to be discovered in physics now. All that remains is more and more precise measurement." Lord Kelvin was a colorful figure, nicknamed "Senior Wrangler" by his fellow students at Cambridge for his overconfidence and distain for anyone who disagreed with him. While there, after taking the final exam in mathematics, he asked his servant to "run down to the Senate House" to see who came in "second." His servant returned and pronounced, "You, sir!" Kelvin also regrettably proclaimed in 1896 that "heavier than air flying machines are impossible." At the time, the Wright brothers had already descended on Kitty Hawk and took flight in December 1903.

Given the force of rapidly advancing technologies on the process of creating knowledge and the clear possibility of an Explosion of Knowledge, it appears that the naysayers may be remembered as closer to modern-day Luddites. This misconception is not, however, simply a harmless disagreement; it may seriously delay our recognition of the effects of Radical Change. So before moving on, I should examine some common misconceptions held by those espousing conservative views of the growth of knowledge and ATT, such as Lord Kelvin and his modern-day counterparts.

First, the failure of the rapid development of a single technology is often used as an indictment of the growth of all technologies. In "Is U.S. Economic Growth Over?" Robert Gordon argues that the failure over the last thirty years of automobiles and commercial aviation to transport us dramatically faster demonstrates technology has very finite limits of accomplishment.[56] If you carefully pick the technologies, you can support this conclusion, but as an observation of the effects of overall technological growth, it is severely myopic and provides a very dangerous false sense of comfort that things are just about the same. In 1985

---

56 Robert J. Gordon, "Is U.S. Economic Growth Over? Faltering Innovation Confronts the Six Headwinds," National Bureau of Economic Research, Working Paper No. 18315, August 2012.

what were our expectations of the growth of the Internet? Are we disappointed at the slow development of the applications of the human genome sequencing? Has the growth of AI been disappointing compared to our expectations? Many technologies as they are developed do run into serious problems with fundamental laws of the physical world, but often technology provides an answer, such as the advancement from vacuum tubes to silicon wafers or horse-drawn carriages to automobiles.

To compound the misconception that technologies develop slowly, we often form childish expectations of how quickly a technology will magically transform our lives. The science fiction of Asimov and others in the 1950s convinced many that we would soon have robotic servants to take care of us, driverless cars, hovercraft and space ships to move us around and time machines to go visit the future and/or the past. It didn't happen, but this is not an indictment of technology; it was bad science from the beginning. Time travel and teleportation are science fiction technologies that caught our fancy but *may* violate the fundamental laws of science. When reality sets in and we realize these unrealistic expectations are not going to be fulfilled by technology, we sometimes wrongly blame technology.

Finally, as will be discussed later, many technologies are introduced to the public long before they work very well, such as the very early introduction of mobile phones, personal computers or automated 411 "assistance." Our frustration with the many shortcomings of these technologies often convinces us that *all* technologies will be mired in a similar primitive, dysfunctional condition forever.

While all of these factors affect our judgment about new technologies, many are but temporary hiccups. If we look back at history, we can learn an important lesson in this regard. No prior technology that, in retrospect, was considered by historians to have transformed a civilization did so rapidly after its invention. The Guttenberg printing press, assumed to have been invented by Johannes Guttenberg in 1450, is considered such a transformative technology. However, the technology of moveable type was first developed in China around 1040, and movable metal type was first developed around 1250 in Korea. Even if 1450 is a legitimate jumping off point, it was several centuries before this invention revolutionized the manner in which knowledge was disseminated in the world.

Thomas Newcomb is credited with the first commercial application of the steam engine in 1712. Newcomb invented a primitive steam engine that could pump water out of the coal mines of England. It was not, however, until 1776 that James Watt introduced the first commercially viable steam engine. Even Watt tinkered with his invention for several decades before it was ready to empower the Industrial Revolution. In fact, the full impact of the steam engine on the course of the Industrial Revolution was not clear until well into the nineteenth century. Even as late as 1870, John Henry allegedly challenged the steam hammer to a competition.

Thomas Edison invented and patented the incandescent light bulb in 1878. This invention is widely recognized as the beginning of the transformation of society by inventions powered by electricity. However, the technology had been demonstrated by Humphry Davy as early as 1802[57] and perfected by many subsequent inventors in the ensuing seventy-five years. Even following Edison's invention of the light bulb, it took decades to electrify the developed world and replace the steam engine with the electric motor.

In many respects, the growth in the applications of computers, the Internet and AI has already transformed our world (ask any teenager), but the true magnitude of the impact of these technologies has not yet occurred. We have, however, become a very impatient society, and our expectations for how quickly these new technologies should transform our lives have become unrealistic. In an age stressed with the initial pressure of Radical Change, these unrealistic expectations are understandable, but they should be discounted when we consider how quickly these technologies will realistically transform our lives in the future.

---

57 Actually, you could go back to Ben Franklin and his kite in 1774.

By studying the historic progression of prior major transformative technologies, it is clear that it takes time for any new technology to impact civilization in a significant manner and even longer for society to actually appreciate the degree to which the technology has done so. When you examine the progression of such prior transformative technologies, one other lesson is also clear: The period required for each technology following its initial discovery to the time it transforms society has become increasingly shorter, not exponentially shorter but significantly shorter. We should expect this trend, enforced by Radical Change, to continue despite the negativity of the naysayers.

There are, however, very powerful forces that impede the growth of knowledge and the application of ATT. We will explore some of these factors in more detail in the next chapter, "Things That Do Not Like Change."

# Chapter Seven

## THINGS THAT DO NOT LIKE CHANGE:
### The Brakemen and the Heavy Load

As much as I would like to dwell only on the positive forces that will accelerate the formation of knowledge and the creation of ATT, there are many forces that wish to see this progress fail. Some of these forces are apparent and are deeply rooted in political, religious and/or personal beliefs, but some are not. Some are forces that we create and regulate by the "Brakemen"[58] and presumably can modify to accommodate Radical Change, and others arise out of the limitations inherent in the very physical laws of the universe that govern the nature and potential development of certain technologies (the "Heavy Load").

To forecast how technology will dramatically affect our future, it is important to recognize how powerful and profound these obstacles can be in, at least, hindering, if not prohibiting certain technologies from moving forward. A technology that does not suffer from attracting a great many Brakemen (such as computers) can progress very rapidly. However, a technology such as genetically altered agricultural crops or stem cell research will progress far less rapidly due to the influence of the Brakemen. Other technologies challenge basic physical laws of science, such as cold fusion

---

58 Brakemen is a sexist choice for this dubious distinction, but I cannot bring myself to use the term Brake people. Rest assured, women are well, but not exactly equally, represented among the Brakemen.

and space and/or time travel, or are otherwise extremely technically difficult to implement, such as battery storage, solar power and electric cars. The fact that these technologies are not progressing very rapidly is not a failure of the power of technology -- it is a reflection of the limitations imposed by the fundamental laws of nature that govern the development of any technology (the Heavy Load). As a result, to be able to forecast which technologies will rapidly develop in the future, we need to anticipate the role of the Brakemen and the Heavy Load in that process. When a technology meets stiff resistance by one or both of these forces, it will rarely develop quickly no matter how much effort is expended or how much benefit it may promise.

I will begin this discussion by examining the forces that do not wish to have a new technology succeed. Many of these forces have been established to protect "economic privilege" or "moral, ethical, political or religious values" or, potentially the most pernicious of all values, "the common or public good." Some of these values are important but are negotiable with those who hold them, but many are held by "True Believers,"[59] who do not negotiate with anyone. These forces will be broken down and defined as belief systems for lack of a better term. Some of these belief systems are as follows:

**Governmental Restraints:** These are local, state and national laws, rules, regulations, and procedures that regulate just about everything we do. While they are generally well intentioned, in practice these restrictions can be used as tools by special-interest individuals and/or groups to thwart many creative ideas. Prime implementers of these restraints are the US Patent and Trademark Office, the Food and Drug Administration, Federal Trade Commission, Securities and Exchange

---

59 *The True Believer* by Eric Hoffer offers a brilliant insight as to how intractable the mind of a True Believer can become -- think of the National Rifle Association (NRA), the Environmental Defense Fund (EDF), the American Civil Liberties Union (ACLU), the Tea Party, etc. Eric Hoffer, *The True Believer: Thoughts on the Nature of Mass Movements* (Harper & Brothers, 1951).

Commission and other governmental regulatory and licensing agencies too numerous to list.

**Politics:** It is very important to distinguish politics from governmental restraints, especially in today's political environment. Politicians have agendas that, for the politically innocent, are baffling and seemingly inconsistent, but they have clear and well-organized systems of reward and punishment that must be understood and sometimes honored and/ or rewarded. They are rarely found in company with good intentions, but even when they are, keep an eye on them.

**Economic Self-Interest:** Any new technology creates Winners and Losers. Radical Change creates radical Winners and Losers. Whenever a new technology begins to attain the status of ATT, it forces the creation of organized groups to protect the self-interest of those who hold an economic advantage or benefit that is threatened by the existence of it. From Ned Ludd and the Luddites fighting the cotton gin to the United Auto Workers (UAW) fighting the robotic assembly line to the recent efforts of the taxicab drivers of the world fighting Uber, these forces play an extremely important and sometimes underrated role in *how* and, sometimes, *when* or even *if* a new technology rolls (or does not roll) out. Each has its own turf to defend, but taken together, these interest groups cover a lot of territory. Construction unions and unions representing public employees have rarely seen a restrictive work rule they didn't love. Patent lawyers and big corporations continue to feel that our current licensing, trademark, copyright and patent laws are too weak to protect their economic interests. NIMBYs are almost always supportive of progress and development; it is just a question of geography -- as in "not in my backyard."

Finally, there are many oddly eclectic groups that are galvanized solely due to a new technology such as wind power. To understand how new technologies can sometimes create some interesting and odd, yet powerful, bedfellows, wind power provides a great example. For over twenty years, an epic battle has been raging over the development of a proposed wind farm off the coast of Hyannis Port, Massachusetts. The developer, Cape Wind, plans to construct the wind farm approximately ten miles off shore on some rather shallow shoals, but sadly for the economic backers of Cape Wind, the site, on a very clear day, is just barely within view of the residents of Hyannis Port, including the residents of the Kennedy Compound. Allegedly, this area is a prime place for sailing (why the shoals are not considered a problem is not clear). To make matters even more apparently appalling, according to the wind farm's opponents, these shoals contain an irreplaceable and fabulously diverse ecosystem. Curiously, this environmental treasure was previously unknown -- that is, until the announcement by Cape Wind of its intentions to construct the wind farm there. This intrusion into the playground of the wealthy and the proposed desecration of the pristine beauty of the ocean so valued by the environmental True Believers has created an eclectic alliance of opponents, The Alliance to Protect Nantucket Sound. This group includes the poor and the rich, sailors and bird watchers, beachcombers and beachfront property owners, the left and the right, and even some Native Americans protecting their heritage, a truly rainbow coalition. This unlikely coalition has found enough common ground to fight a monumental battle with Cape Wind, and has successfully delayed the project for years, costing the company millions. Due to this delay, Cape Wind recently lost its power contracts with the region's major utilities. This may prove to be a death knell for this project. This precedent has sent a powerful message within, at least, the United States, and perhaps other parts of the world, that seriously discourages future investment and development efforts in this very promising and environmentally friendly technology.

**Personal Religious, Ethical and/or Moral Beliefs:** These groups fiercely defend their own personal belief systems. Since Copernicus postulated that the earth was not at the center of the universe, many organized religions have kept a wary eye on technology. Stem-cell research turned out okay, but only because science invented a way to do the research without the need to rely on fetal matter. Today we have fierce debates on issues as divergent as abortion, birth control, mandatory inoculations, DNA research, the reengineering of the human brain, organ transplants and the creation of new forms of life. When the belief systems are held by True Believers such as those protecting the sanctity of life from new technologies in areas such as birth control or stem-cell research, or the unsuspecting world from the dangers of genetically altered food products, the intransigence of the Brakemen cannot be overestimated.

**The Common or Public Good:** Brakemen empowered by calls for the common or public good are especially difficult to constrain. These calls to protect us from ourselves have been particularly effective in slowing the advance of just about everything, including, for example, many common-sense applications of technologies such as the fluoridation of drinking water or mandatory inoculations for measles.

Most people would agree that nearly all of these belief systems serve legitimate purposes, especially if it happens to be your belief system that is in question. If this was not the case, the belief system would not attract many or certainly not very effective Brakemen. Radical Change will, however, aggressively challenge the status quo (often confused by some as the common good), in ways never previously imagined. This will in turn result in an outpouring of outrage that the common good is being endangered.

In addition to the restraints imposed by the Brakemen, the development and implementation of some technologies face much greater technical obstacles than others. Generally, technologies that are knowledge-based (such as DNA sequencing, brain scanning, voice recognition, applications on the Internet, AI, etc.) do not encounter this problem and are developing rapidly. The development of other technologies, however, sometimes challenges basic physical laws of science. Cold fusion, battery storage capacity, solar energy and robotics are just a few of these technologies. We have also fantasized about other technologies, such as time and space travel, mental telepathy and teleportation ("Beam me up, Scotty"), that created unrealistic expectations but were easy for writers of science fiction to glorify.

Another difficulty in developing new technologies arises from the fact that some technologies require massive infrastructure to be widely adopted. The commercial application of electric cars is one example of a technology that struggles with this limitation. Obviously, the difficulty of developing sufficient battery-storage capacity (the Heavy Load) is one major technical stumbling block. But even as this technical hurdle is overcome, the existing infrastructure in the United States will require a major overhaul to create electric refueling stations before this technology can replace fossil fuels on a meaningful scale.

There are numerous other technologies that face problems of this nature, but occasionally technology also provides an answer. The enormous growth of applications on the Internet has transformed the world. This technology is, however, entirely dependent on the capacity of the fiber-optic network, satellite receivers and routers around the world to handle this exploding traffic. The capacity to serve these functions exists only because of a series of breakthrough technologies that have dramatically increased the capacity of every element of this network. Other technologies have fared less well.

Technology is relentlessly challenging both the Brakemen and the stubborn Heavy Load technologies. To accurately predict the progress of new technologies, we must appreciate the true nature of the challenges that each technology must overcome. The failure to fulfill the dreams of Asimov or Captain Kirk of the Starship *Enterprise* does not portend that our future will not be full of other technological breakthroughs that will profoundly change our lives.

The previous chapters have tried to set the stage for how technology will evolve in our future and what the forces will be that encourage or inhibit this process. Since this is a laypersons guide, I will conclude Part

One by proposing a simple analogy that may capture the sense of what we might experience on our journey. It is a simple image that most readers have experienced, riding on a train -- actually, riding in the Caboose of a freight train (the Cannonball Express) pulled by a very, very special engine.

# Chapter Eight

## THE LITTLE ENGINE THAT COULD:
### Are You on Board?

The analogy that follows attempts to capture the look and feel of the effects of Radical Change on the transition from computer capacity to knowledge to ideas and inventions to ATT with the image of an imaginary Freight Train. The Engine of our Freight Train is a magnificent Steam Engine pulling a train of Freight Cars and a trailing Caboose. Yes, the complexity of this analogy gives you a frightening look into the depths of my grasp of this subject, but I ask you to suspend the possible proclivity to find fault with things and try to sense the imagery and dynamics. The Engine of the Cannonball Express left the station in the village of TIR (The Industrial Revolution) over sixty years ago. The Freight Train consists of an amazing Steam Engine (representing computer capacity/AI) and three types of Freight Cars. The first type of Freight Car is full of knowledge (the K Car), the second type of Freight Car contains new inventions and ideas (the I-I Car), and the third type of Freight Car contains Applied Transformative Technologies (the ATT Car). Trailing all the Freight Cars is the Caboose. It is filled with society -- all of us staring out the windows and wondering what the hell is going on, where we are going, and how soon we will arrive. In the Caboose there are a number of very wise Conductors to act as our guides on this fantastic journey and, if we become restive, afraid or unruly, they will restore a sense of calm and order. There it is! The development of the future of our civilization captured in an image from our past. But, of course, it is more complicated than that.

This Steam Engine is no ordinary steam engine. It is full of engineers. They are brilliant graduates of MIT and Stanford with PhDs in mathematics, physics and computer science. The engineers are constantly at work improving this Engine and they are amazingly good at what they do!

Each type of Freight Car comes in different weights, which roughly correspond to the relative ease with which their contents can be pulled along by the Engine. To control the speed of the Freight Train, there are Brakemen riding in each Freight Car. The Freight Cars are arranged on the Freight Train in accordance with the relative weight of each Freight Car's contents, namely, the combination of the Heavy Load of the particular technology and the number of Brakemen along for the ride. In the first car (a K Car), there are forms of knowledge that tend to progress much more easily by the pull of our Steam Engine. Research projects heavily dependent on computer capacity, such as telecommunications, the Internet, DNA and RNA sequencing and brain scanning, are examples of this easier-to-develop light knowledge. Subsequent K Cars are filled with research in areas where there has been less rapid success due to either the Brakemen or the Heavy Load or both. These technologies include robotics, solar power and the cognitive learning capabilities of computers. Due to the fact that they have drawn many powerful Brakemen, other technologies, such as genetically altered agricultural products and stem cell research, are found in subsequent heavier K Cars. The last K Car is filled with technological research into areas that seem to be much more difficult to develop such as cold fusion, manned interplanetary space flight, immortality, cloning of individuals, etc.

Similarly, each of the I-I Cars is filled on the same principle of lightest cars first. The first I-I Car is filled with inventions that can be developed most quickly and most easily from knowledge, such as applications of the Internet, stock market algorithms, computer chess games, GPS systems, etc. This Freight Car attracts only a few Brakemen. The second I-I Freight Car contains more technically difficult inventions, such as language translation and voice and facial recognition systems. This Freight Car also attracts more Brakemen because these inventions are beginning to be perceived as competition to vested economic or political interests and/or they otherwise threaten personal belief systems. The third I-I Car contains ideas and inventions that are even more difficult to develop and/or that attract many more Brakemen. Alternative fuels, nanotechnology, battery storage devices, 3-D printers and wind power fall into this category.

The ATT Freight Cars are loaded with a similar priority for the weight of each Freight Car (the Heavy Load and the number of Brakemen). Transformative technologies such as digitized music and films, smartphones, the Internet, personal laptops, and social media such as e-Bay and Facebook are all in the first ATT Freight Car. Subsequent ATT Freight Cars contain ATT that either attracts more Brakemen (nuclear power generation) or suffers from a Heavy Load (robots, driverless cars, etc.).

Finally, imagine that the Engine, the Freight Cars and the Caboose are all attached to one another by amazingly strong, but incredibly flexible and stretchable bungee cords, yes, bungee cords! When our remarkable Engine left the Station of TIR, it was an old Steam Engine. But the brilliant engineers aboard the Freight Train have been constantly fidgeting, pulling, pushing, and inventing new ways to make it go faster and faster. They have been very good at this -- better than anyone had ever predicted. Not long after departure, their efforts had improved the Steam Engine so remarkably that it morphed into a Diesel Engine. With the benefits of all these improvements, the Cannonball Express was able to achieve an exponential increase in its rate of speed since it left the station sixty years ago. It is now being fitted out with Saturn rocket boosters so that it looks as if it will continue to accelerate exponentially for the foreseeable future.

Well, what happens? We sort of know, because we've been riding in the Caboose for quite a while now. As the Engine of the Cannonball Express begins to accelerate, it pulls on Freight Car number one (the light K Car). This Freight Car begins to move forward, but the bungee cord that connects the two begins to strain and lengthen slightly because, although the K Car is light, it does have inertia so it tends to fall back slightly from the Engine. As the first K Car pulls forward, it begins to pull on the bungee cord that attaches it to the first light I-I Car. As this Freight Car begins to move forward, it likewise begins to pull on the bungee cord that attaches it to the next semi-light K Car. Slowly, all the bungee cords begin to tighten, and all of the Freight Cars begin to move forward and accelerate.

Our Engine has been accelerating for a long time, and by now it is moving "really fast," and its remarkable engineers are still busily making it faster and faster. The Freight Cars behind the Engine are also moving faster and faster, but each Freight Car is moving just slightly slower than the one before it. The bungee cords are beginning to stretch almost unimaginably long, especially the ones up front, as each strains to pull the remainder of the Freight Train and its valuable Caboose forward.

Now let's ascend to ten thousand feet and look down at our remarkable Cannonball Express. The Caboose is beginning to pick up speed, but by now it is miles behind the Engine of the Cannonball Express. The Engine has been doubling its rate of speed, at least every two years since 1955. If, at the very beginning, it was moving at the rate of one meter an hour, it would now be traveling at the speed of 3,400,000 kilometers an hour! And remember, those engineers are still at work trying to find a new breakthrough technology that will continue this Engine's remarkable accelerating progress. There is a growing chorus of doubters saying that this cannot keep happening, but these guys from MIT and Stanford love to piss the doubters off!

Meanwhile, each of the Freight Cars is also accelerating, each a little bit slower than the one ahead due to its own inertia and the lengthening of the bungee cords. Even the Caboose is really moving now, and we are beginning to feel a new sensation -- things outside are passing by faster and faster, but we are still moving rather slowly -- we are on the flat stage of the exponential curve of acceleration. As Winston Churchill famously stated with regard to the Battle of Britain, "We are not at the beginning of the end, but we are at the end of the beginning." The Engine, now adapted with Saturn booster rockets, is climbing out of the knee of exponential change, and it is moving like a son of a bitch! From ten thousand feet above, we can see that the bungee cords are straining enormously, especially the ones up front. They contain a tremendous amount of kinetic energy that has been created by our miraculous little Engine. In fact, if this Engine were to slow down now, or even stop, the force of the straining bungee cords would still pull the Freight Cars and the Caboose forward with a frightening rate of acceleration. The leading Freight Cars are now entering into the knee of exponential acceleration. But our little Engine has not stopped. The engineers are still feverishly working to improve it. They are now working on something called "warp speed."

Over time, the Caboose will also accelerate rapidly. Exponentially? Perhaps not. Certainly never at the rate of our Engine, but faster than any caboose has ever gone before. The Conductors, consisting of a small group of scientific experts, writers and even a few enlightened politicians, are working the aisle of the Caboose to alleviate our growing fears of how fast we are moving and where the hell we are heading. We have not had that "holy shit" moment yet, but the forces that will inevitably make this happen have all been put into operation. Our journey is now guaranteed; there will be no stops, no halfway station or platform on which to exit, no turning back and no way to slow down. The Cannonball Express is already "locked and loaded" -- those bungee cords have been stretching for over sixty years (they are tighter than the bands on a sling shot), and, to make matters even more exciting, our Engine is still accelerating. We are in for one hell of a ride!

Now I am not so naive as to believe that my model train is not a simplistic analogy of where we are and how we will enter the future. This analogy does, however, capture not only what has been happening for over sixty years, but also how dynamic the current situation has become. We are sitting in a Caboose that is being inexorably pulled by miles of very tightly stretched bungee cords. Even if our Engine begins to slow, we will be thrust forward into the future of Radical Change, whether we are ready for that future or not.

# Part Two

The Evolution of the Nature of Technology

# Chapter Nine

## ACCELERATING EVOLUTION:
### Darwin on Steroids
### Dimension One

Part One examined the exponential growth of computer power and provided a harbinger for what is coming our way on that horizon. Part Two, The Evolution of the Nature of Technology, explores the changing nature of new technologies *and* the subtle and the dramatic ways in which these technologies will radically alter our lives in the future. As advanced technologies, particularly knowledge-based technologies,[60] continue to develop, they will not only become more powerful due to the operation of Moore's law, but they will also evolve in the very nature and *form* in which they manifest themselves in our society. Because these changes are evolutionary (even at the pace of Radical Change), we have been slow to appreciate how profoundly this transformation has already changed the world in which we live. Without this appreciation, we will not be able to forecast which new technologies will develop, how quickly

---

60 The term *knowledge-based technologies* refers to those technologies that are primarily driven by pure knowledge and are, therefore, more directly impacted by vastly increased computer capabilities. An example of a knowledge-based technology would be DNA research, as compared to solar technology, which relies more heavily on physical structures. Obviously, all technologies rely on, at least, some component of knowledge. As a result, this distinction is sometimes blurred. In considering which technologies will develop most rapidly in the coming years of Radical Change driven by the remarkable growth of computer power, this distinction may, however, be useful and will be used throughout the remaining chapters of this book.

these technologies will lead to new inventions, or the manner in which these technologies will cause a quantum change in our lives and, more dramatically, the lives of our children and our grandchildren.

Chapters Nine through Thirteen identify five dimensions of the transformation in the role and nature of new technologies and discuss how this transformation will redefine the relationship between humanity and technology in the twenty-first century. In summary, these five dimensions are as follows:

1. The pace of technological evolution is accelerating (due to the force of Radical Change) so that we now experience new, reiterative generations of technological development within our own lifetimes; examples include the evolution of the laptop computer, mobile phone, the Internet and DNA sequencing.

2. As technologies get smarter, they are increasingly able to perform tasks that historically were considered to be strictly the province of human intelligence. One important aspect of this new capability is the fact that these technologies can increasingly make decisions on their own volition (self-actuating); examples include stock algorithms, drones, Big Blue (chess), IBM Watson ("Jeopardy") and musical composition.

3. Technologies are now so deeply integrated into every fabric of our lives that we are struggling with our natural reluctance to accept, embrace and trust the full capability of nonhuman intelligence; examples include our nascent relationship with Siri and Echo, reliance on investment, medical and legal advice and driverless cars.

4. As certain technologies have become more powerful, they have transformed many physical goods and services into pure knowledge; examples include goods such as digital music and film, the smartphone (which also functions as a camera, calculator, calendar, alarm clock, etc.), and 3-D printers; and services such

as the many applications on Internet websites that provide travel, educational, entertainment and retail services.

5. Many of the benefits, challenges and economic impacts that are created by new technologies cannot be properly quantified, described or appreciated using the metrics, standards of measurement and/or terminology that defined the twentieth century; examples include the forces for interactive social change due to the interconnectivity of the Internet (Facebook and Twitter, etc.), the educational opportunities and entertainment value of the Internet and its power for political change (the Arab Spring Revolution).[61] These technologies have had enormous impacts on our world but are difficult, if not impossible, to quantify with traditional metrics.

All five of these dimensions reinforce one another. Combined, they have empowered technology to thrust us into a new age that represents a paradigm shift from the era of machines from which we have now just emerged. In this chapter we will analyze the first dimension described above, namely, the rapid acceleration in the rate of development of new technologies.

For many years, progress in technology has been described, with good reason, as analogous to the evolution of Homo sapiens. Most technologies pass through a series of evolutionary stages of development before they become powerful enough to profoundly change the quality of our lives. Since the primary focus of this book is on the economic consequences of present and future technologies, I will begin with a simplified look at the evolution of technologies that affect employment opportunities. As with all evolutionary processes, at the beginning of the development of a new technology it emerges in a very primitive

---

61 The seeming failure of this movement should not be equated with a failure of the technologies that, for a brief moment in time, galvanized the people in a number of nations striving for democracy. Technology has provided a revolutionary way to communicate the power of political information and ideas, but it cannot guarantee how these ideas will be accepted or acted upon.

form. At this stage, the technology may reflect a brilliant idea, but it simply does not work very well. These technologies are often thought of as status symbols or toys, but they have little effect on society as a whole. Examples of such technologies would be mobile phones of the 1970s or personal computers of the early 1980s. These early inventions are referred to in this book as Stage I Technologies.

As a technology evolves to Stage II, it becomes more sophisticated and useful. For one thing, it has the benefit of all the negative feedback it generated as a Stage I Technology. Depending primarily upon the scope of the economic incentives to reintroduce the technology into the marketplace (with, at least, a straight face), the turnaround time from Stage I to Stage II may now take only months or several years.[62] This was the case for online bill paying services that went from a disaster to a great success in just a few years. For technologies that are driven by computer intelligence, we are not talking about decades. If the marketplace is calling, technologies are often reintroduced still long before they work very well. This sometimes happens because people always want new toys or the newest high-tech gadget even if it remains relatively dysfunctional. Often, however, we are forced to use Stage II Technologies whether we like them or not. Why is this possible? Because business is driven to improve its profit margins, and a great way to do that is to reduce labor costs by "employing" a Stage II Technology as soon as it can be defended as a replacement for human service. Think of the 411 automated "service" from your local phone company or the quality of the information provided by automated switchboards or the automated customer "services" provided by virtually every corporation and government agency today. We encounter this experience daily when we attempt to get information about our accounts or make a complaint or seek information about how to assemble a new product or make it work, such as with the new wireless printer you just bought. The use of Stage II Technologies

---

62 Of course, the roles of the Brakemen and the Heavy Load may play an important part in the timing of the development and reintroduction of any technology into the marketplace.

is prevalent because, in effect, using them transfers the burden and the cost of the service from the provider to the user. If the Stage II service is really crappy (like 411), people will even stop using it. This is a particularly useful result for businesses that can't make a profit by responding to legitimate consumer requests, such as obtaining a telephone number from a telephone company or attempting to get a business to answer your complaints or questions regarding why their new product doesn't work.

The combination of these strategies by business creates a consumer backlash of anger and frustration and fantasies of revenge because of all the time, money and effort we waste trying to get more out of these technologies than the technologies are worth. I refer to this phenomenon as the *premature introduction of technology* or, affectionately, "PIT." I am not trying to be funny here. PIT has long-term consequences on our perception of how fast technology can develop and leads to very low expectations that certain technologies, such as voice recognition,[63] will ever get better. By experiencing so much PIT, we tend to believe that all technologies are bad and/or hopelessly slow to improve. These perceptions are very wrong and short-sighted and lead people to dramatically underestimate what technology will be capable of performing very shortly, especially with the power of Radical Change.

The good news for our collective dispositions and blood pressures is that Stage II Technologies often quickly evolve into Stage III -- think of smartphones and automated bill paying. In this stage, the technology works very well and is reasonably inexpensive. It gains consumer confidence fairly rapidly, despite former PIT. As technologies evolve to Stage III, they become not only much better but also much cheaper, as Moore's law predicts. At Stage III, a technology becomes a wrecking ball for the jobs it can replace. The evolution in the development of all new technologies (not just the ones that replace jobs) from Stage I through Stage III has been chronicled by countless observers for many years. What is different in the twenty-first century is the increasing *rapidity* of

---

63 My experience with Siri is an example.

this progression. As we approach the Near Horizon, this compression in the time between new generations of technological advancement will continue to accelerate.

To appreciate how this progression will affect jobs in the future, let us take the example of the plight of the bridge or highway toll collector. This is not a job that many would have predicted could be eliminated by technology. For years, being a toll collector was a peach of a job to have. You worked for the government in a business that was a monopoly. By way of "belt and suspenders," your job was also protected by an impenetrable maze of civil service laws, rules and regulations, the power of unions, and political sponsors. With the benefit of all of this support, these jobs led to higher and higher levels of compensation and presumably lifetime job security. In fact, the position of toll collector had more Brakemen protecting it per square foot in its Freight Car than any other job, with the possible exception of US postal workers.

Finally, a Stage II-III Technology (the transponder) was introduced to challenge this bastion of protected employment. The job function was easily mechanized and the savings were dramatic. Slowly, transponders began to invade this job market. The early transponders worked pretty well, were rather cost effective, and drivers (voters) liked them because they could get through the tollbooths faster.[64] But in the early days, the transponder remained basically a Stage II Technology. The signals from the tollbooth and the transponders themselves did not work very well, and the computer programs governing billing, complaints and appeals for improper tickets often led to bureaucratic nightmares. Also, for some unfathomable reason, there were (and remain) an irritating number of drivers who, despite the cost savings and the shorter, faster lines at the tollbooths, do not subscribe and use a transponder. To make matters worse, these people also have the infuriating habit of incorrectly driving up to the Fast Lane booth. When they try to back out, it creates a traffic jam and lots of road rage. Because this technology does not

---

64 The fact that voters were enthusiastic about this technology is important because many of the Brakemen for this technology are politicians.

work very well, sometimes you have to stop (well, you should stop) to get human assistance. This also creates a nasty backup and more road rage in the Fast Lane. This is not good news, except for the remaining toll collectors. Consequently this technology only made an inroad into the job market, admittedly a big one, but there was still room for the very politically well-connected tollbooth "operator" to keep his or her job.

But very quickly came a Stage III Technology -- tollbooth cameras to take a picture of your license plate and automatic billing sent to your home. With a transponder you could still save money, but since you do not need one with this new technology, there is no longer a need for a cash lane. Everyone can drive through the tollbooths, going like hell. At this stage, soon almost all the toll-collector jobs will be gone. The service that is provided is also cheap, and everyone is happy except the toll collector and his or her family. If this was the toll collector's only previous employment experience, it will not be easy to find work (forget comparable pay and the same level of job security) in any replacement job. Hopefully, this simplified description of the evolution of technologies that affect employment may resonate with your everyday experience. To appreciate the accelerating evolution of technology, we will, however, examine a few current knowledge-based technologies where there exists objective evidence of exponential development.[65]

One example is the development of the Human Genome Project. This was a highly focused, billion-dollar effort to achieve what many had considered to be the impossible -- the sequencing of the human genome. After almost eight years of intensive work, the project was able to sequence only 1 percent of the human genome. With the enormous assistance of the exponential growth of computer capacity, the project was, however, completed approximately six years later, almost two years ahead of schedule. When plotted on a chart, the progress in sequencing the human genome is shown to actually have exceeded the exponential

---

65 Technologies that are the most dependent upon the growth of computer power and capability (knowledge-based technologies) are, obviously, the first to experience an exponential acceleration in the evolution of their development.

rate of change predicted by Moore's law. The exponential decrease in cost and time in producing genome sequencing has now allowed for a myriad of applications in the treatment of disease and the creation of many new genetically engineered drugs that are dramatically altering many aspects of the future of health care and prevention of disease. Today, genome sequencing has become so inexpensive and rapid that it is (or at least until a recent Federal Food and Drug Administration [FDA] decision) readily available to the general public over the Internet or on sites such as "23andMe" and for about one hundred dollars.[66]

In *How to Create a Mind*, Ray Kurzweil persuasively argues that the effort to re-engineer the mind is also proceeding on an exponential curve.[67] The development of MRI technologies with exceedingly high resolution as well as other related technologies that rely on massive computing power has played a large part in allowing for this progress.

These are only a few of the technologies that have been made possible by the vastly increased computational power available in the last few years. In summary, the rate of growth, measured in objective and quantifiable terms, in the capacity of many new particularly knowledge-based technologies such as telecommunications, DNA sequencing, brain scanning and genetic engineering, often exceeds the exponential rate of growth predicted by Moore's law.

While less dramatic, the force of exponential growth of computer capacity is now transforming the rate at which many other technologies are developing. This is apparent in the fields of robotics, voice and object recognition by AI, deep and cognitive learning by computers,

---

66 In November 2013, the FDA issued a letter warning companies such as 23andMe that there was insufficient documented evidence linking illness to the factors identified by genome sequencing to warrant the commercial dissemination of this information. Based on this ruling, you can still get the results of your genetic test but no explanation of what they may mean for you -- at least not from 23andMe. In early 2015, the FDA signaled that it was about to reverse itself on this issue.

67 Kurzweil has many detractors, since he challenges the status quo with a brazen self-confidence and sometimes apparent disregard for his opponents' arguments (some might add their intelligence as well). For his detractors, he has also had the annoying habit of often being proven with the passage of time to be correct.

and language translation. Even many technologies that have historically struggled with the Heavy Load of very difficult challenges with the laws of science are beginning to experience a similar but less dramatic form of acceleration. Recent developments in battery storage, water purification and solar power attest to the fact that even technologies that seemed mired in quagmires of technological challenges are now moving forward at unprecedented rates of progress.

The ultimate result of the accelerating pace of technological development was described in Chapter Six, "When Technology Reaches the Tipping Point." While the date that AI becomes ultraintelligent (triggering an Explosion of Knowledge) may not occur before we reach the Near Horizon, almost all experts in the field agree that it is only a question of time. In *Superintelligence*, Nick Bostrom,[68] director of the University of Oxford's Future of Humanity Institute, presents the results of a compilation of surveys of over two hundred experts on the question of whether they expect human-level machine intelligence (HLMI) to be developed, and if so, when. HLMI was defined by Bostrom as the intelligence required to "carry out most human professions at least as well as a typical human."[69] Over 90 percent of the experts polled believed that HLMI would be achieved by 2075, and 50 percent believed it would be developed by 2040. Given that this book is written in large part for the benefit of our children and grandchildren, if you are concerned with the dark side of an Explosion of Knowledge, even the conservative prognostications of 2075 are not comforting.

Regardless of whether technology reaches the tipping point leading to an alien ultraintelligence, the acceleration in the evolution of technology is rapidly altering our society. But, this does not mean that all technologies are advancing. There will always be examples of technologies that have reached the practical end point of meaningful advancement (i.e., they are beginning to confront the fundamental physical laws

---

68 Nick Bostrom, *Superintelligence: Paths, Dangers, Strategies* (Oxford Press, 2014).

69 This is not ultraintelligence, as that term is used in Chapter Six, but with the reiterative power of ultra-fast computing, Bostrom asserts and most experts would agree that HLMI would morph into such a level of intelligence very quickly.

that govern the universe). In the nineteenth century, it was widely recognized that after centuries of tinkering, the stage coach as a means of
transportation had reached its limits -- but other modes of transportation were invented that did not suffer the inherent limitations of this
technology. Another example of this transition was cited earlier – the
demise of vacuum tubes that empowered early computers due to the
development of integrated circuits using silicon chips. The progress of
particularly knowledge-based technologies over the past two decades
indicates that it may be only our inherent fear of change that restrains us
from admitting that this acceleration of technology will create a future
for our children and grandchildren that will not be just an extension of
the progress of our past -- it will be a quantum transformation in their
lives.

# Chapter Ten

## TECHNOLOGY COMES OF AGE:
### From John Henry to the Wolf of Wall Street
### Dimension Two

Early technologies such as the lever and the screw augmented the physical power and capabilities of men and women. In the ensuing centuries, technology grew more sophisticated, but it still continued to provide a blunt-force approach to progress. It did not take a great deal of thought to drive a steel spike into a railroad track or to weave cotton. The impact of advancing technologies today, however, involves AI performing tasks that require a great deal more intelligence than applying sheer brute force. Public awareness of this new dimension of computer intelligence has recently increased significantly. The exploits of IBM Watson defeating the two greatest champions of "Jeopardy" at their own game received a great deal of public fanfare. While Watson represents far more than an IBM "publicity stunt," as Noam Chomsky once termed it, for most laypeople computer intelligence is still viewed as either romantic science fiction or an amusingly primitive technology that does not possess even a modicum of true human intelligence. The truth is closer to science fiction than most people would believe.[70] In this chapter I will explore the recent progression of computer intelligence (AI) as it is affecting employment, but advances in AI are readily transferable to many other aspects of our lives.

---

70 In fact, the truth is much closer to science fiction than many experts concerned about the future of ASI feel is in our best interests.

Where will we see rapidly increasing computer intelligence creating significant job destruction and the formation of new jobs in the future? We could extrapolate from the data of the past to project out into the future, but we would come up way short on the side of the number of jobs that will be lost and we would miss the mark of where, when and which types of new jobs will be created in the future. To understand why this process of job loss and job creation is occurring, we need to look back *not* on which *jobs* have been subjected to technological elimination but which *types of functions* have been replaced. This may seem to be a distinction without a difference, but here it is not, and it makes all the difference in foreseeing where there will be a significant progression in the capabilities of computers and AI to replace jobs in the future.

Historically, technology has generally eliminated unskilled, repetitive, labor-intensive jobs. The reason for this is that in the nineteenth and most of the twentieth centuries these were the only functions technology could perform. It simply wasn't good enough to save other forms of labor.[71] This perception has survived, but relying upon it will result in a great deal of error in forecasting the role of technology in job creation and destruction in the twenty-first century.

We all know that robots can perform simple repetitive manual labor. We should have finished the sentence. Robots have historically performed the functions of unskilled labor *for robots*, but this is very different from what is unskilled labor for humans. This distinction is subtle, but it is crucial to be able to accurately forecast which types of jobs will be eliminated by new technologies in the near future. Also, due to Radical Change, the definition of what constitutes unskilled functions for robots is changing rapidly, and to the detriment of the employment opportunities of the average worker.

Many experts have argued that AI can perform the hard problems of intelligence easily but finds it very difficult to perform activities that require

---

71 As described in Chapter Two, this assumption has never been entirely true, since in the early days of the Industrial Revolution some of the early job victims were the skilled workers in the guilds who had previously produced, by hand, a variety of very skilled work products such as leather shoes, boots, plowshares, rifles, candlesticks and silver bowls.

low-level sensory-motor skills. This dichotomy was described in the 1980s as Moravec's Paradox.[72] Hans Moravec believed that it was relatively easy for computers to achieve a high level of performance on intelligence tests but it was difficult or impossible to create AI with the skills of a two-year-old when it came to perception and mobility. Moravec supported this conclusion, in part, by an analysis of the history of human evolution. Basic motor skills and spatial, facial and object recognition were required by the most primitive life forms at the earliest stages of evolutionary development. Therefore, these skills have been evolving for over a billion years. More advanced skills that we tend to associate with human intelligence arise from the exercise of abstract thought, which is a trait that was developed approximately one hundred thousand years ago. Whether this theory is correct or only an historic circumstance, part of the Moravec Paradox is incontrovertible. The tasks that a two-year-old can effortlessly undertake, like running and recognizing and relating to his or her surroundings, have been reduced in our evolutionary development to simple functions for humans (they can be performed almost without thought), but they are extremely hard to duplicate with robotic AI. Despite these difficulties, technology is assaulting these barriers with unprecedented force.

Robots and AI have tremendous strengths and horrible weaknesses. If the skill is chess or "Jeopardy," or trading stocks and bonds on the New York Stock Exchange, we are already out of our league. These are all very skilled functions; however, if a function requires spatial or object recognition, a two-year-old toddler can crawl circles around Watson. As smart as Watson may seem in the context of the game of "Jeopardy," it cannot distinguish a cat from a dog. And as intelligent as robots have become, they are a very far way from possessing even basic common sense. Nor does Watson have any understanding of the concept of right and wrong. Therefore, although a busboy in a fine restaurant or a chambermaid hold relatively unskilled positions, it will be a long time before robots and AI replace these jobs.

---

72 Hans Moravec (Robotics Institute, Carnegie Mellon University) was an early pioneer in the study of the growth of AI. In *Mind Children: The Future of Robot and Human Intelligence* (Harvard University Press, 1988), and subsequent follow-up articles, Moravec predicted that AI would reach a level of intelligence approaching ASI by 2040.

To forecast the economic consequences of technology in the future, we need to redefine what is meant by *unskilled* labor for robots. Actually the concept of *unskilled* for robots has very little to do with what we consider to be unskilled manual labor. When we discuss which jobs robots and AI can and increasingly will perform, we need, therefore, a new definition of this concept. Workers who should particularly fear elimination or substantial displacement by AI (whether in the form of robots or not) before the Near Horizon will have jobs with the following, admittedly rough, characteristics:

- jobs performed in an environment that can be relatively well defined and that is stable and predictable;
- jobs that can be broken down into repetitive and physically simple and routine motions and/or functions, and/or jobs that do not require physical movement, such as investment and travel advice, call-in centers, etc.;
- jobs that do not require great sensitivity or ability to relate to, understand or provide comfort to humans; and
- job functions that do not require intuitive or creative abilities or the application and restraint of common sense or right and wrong.

Robotic AI already possesses the skills to memorize, calculate, make complicated decisions, coordinate multiple tasks and communicate (voice recognition and speech are much closer than you think). Computers can obviously also process and analyze massive amounts of sophisticated information and draw conclusions from pattern recognition and probability analyses of information and statistics. These undeniably intelligent functions are well within the sweet spot for AI. Recently, computers have been developed that are capable of learning new information and knowledge[73] and engaging in primitive forms of cognitive thinking. These new capabili-

---

73 IBM Watson possesses this ability and has assimilated (learned) a great deal of information and knowledge all by itself. The next generation of computer programs will learn through experience in much the same manner as we do as humans. This general form of computer ability was referred to earlier in this book as deep learning and will be discussed in Chapter Eighteen, "The Transformation of the Service Sector."

ties require enormous computer capacity, but Moore's law assures us that if that is the limiting factor, then help, lots of it, is on the way.

In practice, applying the limitations described above, AI works very well on an assembly line operating a drill press or putting parts together, but it doesn't work very well sorting loose objects on a conveyor belt. Also, technology works better on an assembly line than in clearing tables in a busy restaurant. The tables are covered with clutter, the aisles are full of moving objects, and sometimes these objects can be a little "tipsy." Recognizing a bowl of soup, as opposed to the centerpiece, is a tremendous challenge for robots and, even if a robot could recognize it as a bowl, is the bowl empty or half full? These are important facts to know before the robot attempts to move the bowl.

For robots, now and certainly in the future, if a function can be performed within the limitations described in the four parameters listed above, it will soon be performed by robots/AI, if it isn't already. This is true no matter how complicated or intellectually demanding the job function might otherwise be if it was performed by a human. Chess, an extremely complicated and sophisticated game, fits nicely within these limitations, and AI rules the chess world. Investment advice, reports on stock market fluctuations, tax returns, news reports on sporting events or financial trends, legal analysis and litigation support and other functions that require processing massive amounts of information and/or that utilize word association, pattern recognition, etc. are now routinely performed by computers. Busing tables does not fit into these limitations, so there is job security there. These are, of course, generalizations, and not every job function either fits or can be defined by these characteristics. But in predicting the course of job destruction and job creation in the future, these four guidelines will be far more useful and much less subject to leading to false conclusions than the terms *skilled* and *unskilled* labor.

More troubling for the current job opportunities in the market is the fact that technology is hard at work breaking free of even these limitations. As technology improves, all of these barriers will be tested and many will be breached. In fact, many of these barriers have already fallen, at least in part.[74] Take Siri, for example; you know how I feel about her. Despite her faults, version six is a major improvement over version five (separated by a little over one year). Even my version five could give me the date on which Easter falls next year or tell me when the Red Sox are playing in Boston, give me directions to just about anywhere or the names of Italian restaurants in Brookline (well, almost). Yes, she has a bad attitude -- but she is intelligent enough to *have* an attitude. Also, I need to accept my part in this. Although Siri still remains rather "dumb," a big part of the problem in getting her to work with me is that the user (me) is also "dumb" (i.e., I do not interface with technology very well).[75] This dimension of our unfolding relationship with computers will be analyzed further in the next chapter, "Comfort with Computers."

Despite my shortcomings, Siri clearly needs to be improved, but she *is* being improved, even while I am annoying her. My iPhone is less than two years old, but I have been informed by my Apple Genius Bar advisor, Keith, that I desperately need a version six for many obvious reasons (at least to him). One reason -- version six has a much-improved version of Siri. Keith tells me that all the Siris of the world are tied into one great supercomputer located somewhere (it really doesn't matter where, Keith informed me), and every time we use Siri, the supercomputer learns from its experience with us, no matter how bad or infuriating our behavior. Keith tells me that I will find the version six Siri to be much more user friendly and that even I will have a better attitude. I am dubious.

---

74 Recent developments in the field of deep learning may provide the seminal breakthrough that will lead to a new generation of computers that can learn by themselves, self-program future operating capabilities and engage in behavior that we would objectively refer to as cognitive learning if a human were to do it. This could be the first historic step to the reiterative process of an ultraintelligent machine predicted by Irving Good in 1965. See Irving John Good, *The Scientist Speculates: An Anthology of Partly-Baked Ideas* (Capricorn Books, 1965).

75 I am working on this problem and hope to develop a new version of me (version two) within a few months. This version will realize, for example, that in speaking with a computer, you do not need to comply with social courtesies -- such as beginning each question with a formal salutation -- "*Siri, ...*" This just confuses a computer.

While not a scientific law, there is a quality about technological development that hates technical barriers and inherently wants to break them down. It may be as simple as the creativity, optimism and brilliance of all the engineers that program AI. These geeks want to prove to us that all the walls we have created to box in technology, especially AI, are of our own making and not set by the boundaries of technology itself.

History can teach us something timeless here. The spirit of this battle with barriers -- both the intrinsic limitations of science (the Heavy Load) and those maintained by the Brakemen -- is beautifully captured in Robert Frost's moving poem, "Mending Wall," a portion of which follows:

Something there is that doesn't love a wall,
That sends the frozen ground-swell under it,
And spills the upper boulders in the sun,
And makes gaps even two can pass abreast. ...

I let my neighbor know beyond the hill;
And on a day we meet to walk the line. ...
There where it is we do not need the wall. ...

Before I built a wall I'd ask to know
What I was walling in or walling out,
And to whom I was like to give offense. ...

I see him there
Bringing a stone grasped firmly by the top
In each hand, like a stone-aged savage armed.
He moves in darkness as it seems to me. ...

And he likes having thought of it so well
He says again, "Good fences make good neighbors."

This is an old poem and a favorite of mine, written during the Industrial Revolution (1914), but it is fresh and immortal in its message of our love/hate affair with barriers and Brakemen.

Once a technology can perform an intellectually sophisticated function, watch out, because it is capable of almost unimaginable improvement. Earlier, I referred to the widespread use of stock market algorithms because they could trade stocks and bonds on the world's stock exchanges much faster than humans. This doesn't seem like much of an advantage, since how much more can you make with a millisecond head start? Actually if you do it a billion times (sort of nanotechnology on Wall Street), you can make a lot. Trading is now *so* fast with modern technology that the brokers using this technology are moving physically closer to the trading centers because the time of sending the trades across fiberoptic networks (measured in milliseconds) is reducing the advantage of the fastest robotic traders. This is hard for me to comprehend, but it is the subject of an excellent book, *Flash Boys*, by Michael Lewis.[76] In his book, Lewis insightfully explores the development of computer-driven stock trading. It could provide a very valuable lesson in assessing what happens when computers reach Stage III capabilities and beyond.[77] Our experience

---

76 Michael Lewis, *Flash Boys: A Wall Street Revolt* (W.W. Norton & Company, 2014).

77 Today the advantage in the speed of responding to market information that algorithmic trading provides is so advanced that some have argued it is the equivalent of allowing some traders on the stock market to profit from "insider" information -- i.e., the information on which the trades are based is not available to the general public. Ultimately, this issue will be settled by the Securities and Exchange Commission and the courts because the economic stakes involved are enormous. In 2014, there were only a handful of supercomputers in the world capable of algorithmic trading at the highest level of technology. This technology empowers 2 percent of the brokers on the New York Stock Exchange to engage in over 60 percent of the entire volume of sales on the Exchange. Is utilizing this technology by a very privileged and incredibly wealthy few inherently unfair? Is it "insider information"? I am not certain, but it feels unfair to me. It may be the modern-day equivalent of the early days of the stock market: namely, the difference between an investor owning a chair on the stock market or a ticker-tape teletype stock printer competing against an investor in Atlanta making trades on the stock market by use of the US Post Office.

with algorithmic stock trading demonstrates beyond any doubt that humans cannot compete against the incredible speed of computers in making decisions. This may account for the recent acknowledgment by the US Department of Defense that the newest generation of military drones will be programmed to make decisions to employ deadly force without prior direct human authorization. The reason is that a drone operating with the time constraint of how long it would take for a human to react would be useless in combat with a hostile drone operating without such a limitation.

As technologies continue to evolve, the division of the roles of humans and technology performing skilled and unskilled functions, as we have historically understood that distinction, may be significantly reversed. Certainly, until the advent of ASI, there will be a role for the truly gifted, creative people in the world, but for the rest of us, many of the functions left to perform to make a living will increasingly be the unskilled jobs that robots simply cannot perform, or cannot perform economically. As AI becomes increasingly intelligent, it will, of course, also create many meaningful jobs for humans, some in fields of employment that are now either in their infancy or do not even exist. Later chapters of this book (Chapters Seventeen through Twenty-One) will address this struggle of job creation versus job destruction and the increasingly difficult challenge of technological unemployment identified by John Maynard Keynes almost one hundred years ago.

# Chapter Eleven

## COMFORT WITH COMPUTERS:
How Do You Act on Your First Date with Samantha?
Dimension Three

Unlike prior technologies, computers and, more specifically, the development of AI pose unique and previously incomprehensible challenges to our deeply held belief that humans hold a special place in the universe. The sense of unease arising from this challenge manifests itself in a number of related ways, all of which create impediments to our ability to integrate the full benefits of computers and AI into our lives. We first encountered this problem in the process of learning how to properly operate a computer and access the Internet and its myriad applications. My generation referred to this challenge as learning how to "think like a computer." As AI has developed, particularly in its ability to think like a human, our relationship with this technology is facing a new set of issues.

Notwithstanding our innocent fascination with the benign robots portrayed in the science fiction of Isaac Asimov, most of us are not comfortable with embracing a cold, alien intelligence, and we are certainly not comfortable with allowing that intelligence to become an integral, essential part of our lives. This reluctance inevitably contributes to our inherent lack of trust that such an intelligence will provide us with valuable advice and guidance in many of the most important aspects of our lives.

There are many ways that these prejudices are expressed. As advancing AI develops the ability to perform services that previously could only be performed by humans, the greatest impediment to AI's rapid implementation in these areas may not be the issue of how well the technology can perform the function -- but how willing we are to accept technology doing so. This is a new dimension in our ongoing love-hate affair with developing technologies. In fact, it may be the final frontier that will define our relationship with AI as it transcends into a higher form of alien intelligence.

How well do you relate to your computer? Would you consider having an affair with your laptop as Theodore did with Samantha in the movie *Her*? Or is your laptop a frustrating challenge that at times seems obtuse and cantankerous and even seems to have a mind of its own? These are not gossip-column questions. Our comfort level with computers, while well recognized as a source of humor, is generally not appreciated for the subtle but enormous effect it has on how we react to AI as it plays an increasing role in our lives. Our relationship with AI has really just begun. Personal computers were first available in the late 1970s and remained within the province of the geeks for, at least, the next few decades. So our love-hate relationship with the computer is a relatively short-lived affair. As a result, like any nascent relationship, we have deep-seated issues of trust and comfort with what works and what doesn't. Just like a first date. Some of the dimensions of this budding relationship are readily apparent to all of us, and some are not. For most of us over the age of thirty-five, our first experience with computers was PIT, discussed in Chapter Nine. The computer was complicated and counterintuitive, crashed at exactly the wrong moment, "spoke" in its own language or, in fact, in numerous languages (most of them unintelligible), and it had a will of its own. To benefit from all the advantages computers could provide, you needed to spend an enormous amount of time and effort learning how to operate one. This often resulted in frustration, sometimes rising to the level of rage. And just when you thought you knew how to use your computer, it became obsolete. In the past thirty years, there have been many dramatic improvements in personal computers, laptops, iPads, smartphones, etc., making them increasingly easy to use (Stage II to III Technology), but this technology will continue to change and there are many computer skills we still must master. You need to have very good typing skills and an extensive knowledge of how to navigate the architecture of the computer and effectively use the astounding number of applications available on the Internet. There is a major generational issue here. By the time computers were at Stage III, most of my generation were too old to naively and innocently embrace this new technology. We have paid a heavy price for this understandable misjudgment.

There are many consequences that arise from our inherent lack of trust, understanding and acceptance of computers and computer intelligence (or AI). These factors create subtle but very clear barriers in how we can best utilize and benefit from AI. This will become more of a factor in leading a happy life and competing in tomorrow's workforce as Radical Change brings AI increasingly into the everyday fabric of our lives. To appreciate our discomfort with AI, we need to appreciate how ingrained and deep these prejudices are. Our society recognizes the generational gulf between how America's grandparents and grandchildren think and feel about and use their computers. This often becomes apparent in observing older people refusing to even use a computer or a smartphone or, more likely, the many applications they empower, but some level of distrust and discomfort lies within all of us, even those toddlers playing with children's smartphones in their cribs. Radical Change will make this very clear, as it challenges the limits of how many daily activities will *require* us to interact with and rely on computers.

Noam Chomsky is one of the greatest intellects and moral forces of the twentieth and twenty-first centuries. He is professor emeritus of linguistics at MIT, and among his many brilliant achievements, he is a noted observer and commentator on computer development and AI. In an interview in 2014 on TED Talks, Chomsky expressed some of his views on this subject. According to Chomsky, IBM Watson was a "publicity stunt" and "good advertising." He also stated that computers would never be able to translate a foreign language, at least not very authentically, and expressed a number of other somewhat unflattering thoughts about the limits of future computer accomplishment. I will never be a Noam Chomsky; I have no pretense of having his intellect, wisdom or even his moral values, but I detect that he is not, and never will be, comfortable in his relationship with computers.

Our current generational struggle with computers was brilliantly captured by the Visio TV advertisement: "So simple even an adult can use it." To date, this dilemma is more the butt of jokes than a subject of serious thought. It shouldn't be. I will lay off further references to Noam Chomsky -- he has done way too much good for us. My own shortcomings with computers provide the example I am looking for. Computers will never feel warm and cuddly to me. I will always prefer the *New York Times* scattered around my sunroom on a Sunday afternoon than that same news on my smartphone. Yes, I have always had a bad attitude regarding computers, but it is way too late for me to unlearn my prejudices. I, for one, still struggle with the question of literally where the letters of my laptop message go when I push the keyboard to send my email to a foreign country, with no more than an email address for guidance. This computer illiteracy severely interferes with my comprehension and ability to benefit from all the blessings of my Apple computer. I will never be a ballerina either, and that is okay. But in the era of Radical Change, these attitudes about computer literacy are not okay.

These attitudes are changing, but not fast enough. My children do not possess my innocence or incompetence in comprehending how to best benefit from the amazing capacity of laptops and smartphones.[78] Their comfort levels are much higher than mine, and they seem intuitively to understand how to think like a computer in a manner that no matter how many trips I take to the Genius Bar at Apple (and I've taken many), I will never be able to duplicate. This is not to say that they

---

78 Remember that my children were born at the point in time (late 1980s) when computer capacity was just beginning to enter the knee of exponential change.

understand how computers work -- they really do not. They don't even seem to *care* how computers work; they just use them. The process of our acclimation to computer technology and AI will continue to improve as our now streaking Cannonball Express continues to pull us toward the Near Horizon. Today it is commonplace for two- or three-year-olds to find that their greatest form of entertainment is a children's iPhone. When these toddlers are in their teens, they will relate to robots and AI with, at best, as great a gulf between their parents as I have with my children.

Last year, my wife and I were staying at our farm in Woodstock, Vermont. We decided to have dinner at Richardson's Tavern, a cozy restaurant with a fireplace and warm surroundings at the Woodstock Inn. We took a table next to a young couple, tourists up for a weekend of skiing. Their son, three years old or so, was seated with them, intently watching something on a child's laptop with headphones implanted in his ears. He seemed totally absorbed. My wife remarked that it was a pity that such a beautiful moment for the family to be together was ruined by Junior being engrossed and on another planet. From the perspective of family values and an opportunity for a young and active family to bond, it was a shame. But Junior did the unexpected! At one point during his parents' conversation, he came to life, sat up and pulled an earplug out of one ear and babbled something inaudible to his parents before cramming the earplug back in his head. His parents seemed to find what Junior had to say both apropos and amusing. Somehow Junior had emerged from his own virtual reality and made a fleeting connection with his family; he had learned to multitask. Despite this momentary diversion, Junior was far more absorbed and comfortable in his own electronic world, even though this could have been a special moment for his family. If I were to take a wild guess -- Junior will be one of the Winners (at the age of twenty-three), as we arrive at the Near Horizon.

Junior's generation will not only have wonderful computer skills, but it will instinctively accept and enthusiastically embrace AI in performing many human service functions including many professional jobs that today seem unimaginable being performed by computers. The children of this generation will not suffer from the nostalgia of quiet winter Sunday afternoons in the warm sunlight of a sunroom reading the *New York Times*, nor will they experience the anger and frustration of being forced on an everyday basis to attempt to utilize PIT. They will not sense as I do that their relationship to computers must be cold and impersonal. The AI that this generation will come to know will show emotion, and it will detect and be able to respond to emotions *appropriately*. This AI will be smarter in many ways than they will ever be. It will certainly possess much greater knowledge and information than they will ever be able to master. This AI will be friendly, happy, never tired or grumpy and much better behaved and tolerant than even you or I. It will be so central to their daily lives that their relationships with it will become virtually indistinguishable from their relationships with humans.

When we attempt to predict how far computers and AI will progress in the next twenty years, we must also predict how far humans will come in their ability to embrace this technology. It takes two to tango. Even in my own lifetime, I have experienced subtle but clear improvements in my ability to understand and feel a level of comfort with new technologies. When I began the practice of law, it was an unquestioned principle of the profession that any important transaction, meeting or serious negotiation had to be done in person. The unchallenged nature of this assumption caused business and professions to expend millions, if not billions, of dollars in wasted time traveling to meetings, closings and conferences that could have been undertaken by telephone, speaker phone and/or video conference call. The cost of cab rides, airplane fares, hotels, meals and (perhaps the greatest cost of all) the legal time that was spent just traveling, was astonishing. Yes, the legal downtime of traveling was billed to clients.[79] All of this expense was justified by the unchallenged assumption that you couldn't accomplish serious business until everybody was seated around a conference table. There, you would

---

[79] This is one of the few areas in this book where I speak from personal knowledge and experience.

be able to appreciate the nuances of body language and facial expression, including, for example, a twitching eye when someone was lying or the tone of someone's voice when he or she was nervous. This attitude persisted even when relatively high-quality conference calls and office speaker phones were developed (Stage II Technologies).

The ingrained attitude that prolonged the time of this transition was assisted by the unpleasant first experiences of using many technologies, principally video conferencing. This may have been the ultimate PIT. The problems with this Stage I Technology began with the fact that neither I nor virtually any of my partners could even turn the damn things on. We often, in front of our clients, had to call the mailroom, or later the IT department, just to set up the picture and sound. The cameras rarely pointed in the right direction, so you often would see the artwork in the conference room in New York and the potted plants in Washington instead of the clients. Sometimes the video conferencing didn't work at all, and other times just one of the systems in one of the participating offices didn't work, but the "conference" was still a total failure. It was a miracle if anything, forget serious, was accomplished. However, as these technologies improved, the pressure of the wasted time and the costs of travel made this technology more and more acceptable. In fact, clients demanded it. Video conferencing equipment also quickly evolved to a Stage III Technology, and such attitudes about the importance of face-to-face meetings began to become antiquated.

Another dimension to the lack of trust in computers and AI is less recognized. As stated earlier, because we are not fully comfortable with computers and AI performing functions normally reserved for humans, we do not trust technology when it performs these functions. This sense of the inadequacy, unreliability, and/or immaturity of AI is a great opening for the Brakemen to "protect" any field of human employment that could otherwise be replaced in whole or in part by AI. By preying on our inherent lack of trust and confidence in the advancing capabilities of AI, the Brakemen can demand rigorous regulation and thereby stifle the application of these new technologies. With the accelerating growth of AI, this understandable exercise in the preservation of the status quo will become an increasingly contentious source of economic conflict and a major impediment to the expeditious and ubiquitous application of these technologies in society.

One example of this conflict that is just beginning to emerge is the use of Dr. (IBM) Watson. IBM sent Watson back to medical school after the "Jeopardy" triumph. At the time of the writing of this book (2015), Watson had graduated, but its usefulness to the health-care community remains confined to acting as an assistant to physicians in making diagnoses on patient conditions. In this capacity, Watson is, in fact, a magnificent data base and a great "second chair," but it remains just a resource -- admittedly an amazing resource -- for the attending physician following the traditional practices of medicine. If Watson can beat the two greatest champions in "Jeopardy," would any fully licensed clinician wish to challenge Watson to a medical version of that game? Wouldn't it make sense to put Watson's capability to a more direct and impactful use, such as making diagnoses directly?

Millions of the world's poor, particularly in the Third World, die or become gravely ill due to lack of an early diagnosis of life-threatening illness, but Watson will be restrained from directly addressing this crisis -- not by the limits of technology but by the Brakemen protecting the practice of medicine. Certainly these standards have great merit and (when the technology is ready) we should expect these standards to be modified accordingly and applied with good intentions. But licensing any new technology that involves human health and/or safety, even when faced with an obvious immediate need, creates a difficult and sensitive balancing of legitimate but conflicting interests. The debates over genetically engineered agricultural products such as Golden Rice and the licensing of potential miracle drugs promising relief from tragic, fatal illnesses pose similar dilemmas. What will distinguish the discussion over the licensing of Dr. Watson will be the fact that the doctor to be certified will not be human. This will force us to confront our innate conviction that something as fundamental and basic as medical care should be administered *solely* by humans. To overcome this prejudice in any regulatory setting will require an overwhelming body of evidence that Watson can perform this function *far* better than a human doctor. Even if Watson (or more likely some partnership of humans and Watson) could pass the licensing hurdles to practice medicine, the patients (at least those with a choice) would also need to have confidence in their doctor. These hurdles will be difficult, but not impossible, to overcome, because our comfort level and trust in applications of AI are growing rapidly.

IBM Watson as an aid to medicine is but one example of this difficult balancing act. Rapidly advancing computer technology will create similar challenges in many other professions, such as consulting, investment banking, law and psychotherapy. Soon this battle will take to the streets as the transportation workers of the world face the emerging threat of driverless cars, buses and trucks. Not only will this technology face the challenge of lots of Brakemen, but it will need to engender consumer acceptance before it can become a commercial reality. As of the end of 2014 Google's driverless cars had logged well over one million miles with only two accidents -- both caused when a human reassumed control of an otherwise driverless car. As driverless cars continue to advance, they will pose enormous and very complicated issues of driver, passenger and pedestrian safety, as well as property loss. These issues are inherently part of driving a car, truck or bus, but they will be of special concern when the driver is AI. The Brakemen and their lobbyists and lawyers will express a remarkable level of concern for the safety of the *public*, as their economic interests are threatened by a change of technology of this magnitude. These forces will combine to create a myriad of regulatory constraints prohibiting or at a minimum impeding the widespread use of these vehicles, long after the technology has proven the obvious safety advantages of allowing AI to drive America.

No matter how good driverless cars become and no matter how outstanding their record of safe performance in the eyes of the regulatory bodies, the last barrier that these vehicles will have to surmount is the fundamental consumer distrust that these vehicles are safe.[80]

Playing into this distrust will be all of the special-interest groups threatened by the widespread introduction of driverless vehicles. This debate will be extremely difficult because there is a fundamental risk to human life at stake here. The fact that humans driving vehicles have a very long and not very enviable safety record is obvious. But this is the risk we know; in fact, tragically, this risk has been graphically quantified. Even faced with this reality, our inherent prejudice and distrust of robotics will be extremely difficult to overcome before these cars will be licensed to drive on our highways. Acceptance of the technological capability of driverless cars will occur long after there is an overwhelming body of evidence of the benefits of getting human operators off the road.[81]

The examples contained above are dramatic, but the issue of consumer acceptance of computers interacting with people on a personal level will become increasingly commonplace as technologies such as voice recognition, interactive intelligence, emotional sensitivity and interactive speech capabilities become more and more integrated into every facet of our daily lives. Areas such as retail sales, legal, medical, investment and tax advice, elder care and daycare, governmental services, real estate and insurance brokerage and teaching are already within the capabilities of advanced computers.[82] The issue is not whether AI will be ready for these challenges, but whether we will be. There are

---

80 This will be the second time that the automobile has faced this problem. The first experience came when Model T Fords were introduced. At that time, there was a major public outcry, from almost everyone who could not afford a Model T, that these vehicles were "too dangerous," "untested," and even "against God's will."

81 In fact, in some ways other technologies have already breached this barrier of confidence. When weather conditions become extremely severe, it is not our friendly pilot who lands a commercial aircraft; it is a sophisticated system of aviation powered by AI. Recently, the Federal Highway Administration has mandated that certain early-warning sensors empowered by AI be installed in all new automobiles beginning in 2017 to safeguard against driver carelessness.

82 Travel agents were the "canaries in the coal mine" for this trend.

no easy answers to these conundrums. Radical Change will, however, ensure that these dilemmas will intensify in the near future.

Objective, solid evidence of the efficacy of a new technology will always be the absolute foundation of licensing, regulating, or otherwise allowing a new technology to be accepted and to proliferate. However, our basic instinct that humans will always be better, smarter and more able to perform a task than AI will need to be fundamentally and constantly reviewed as Radical Change creates technologies that far surpass not only the PIT that helped form these instincts but also our own human abilities and limitations.

# Chapter Twelve

## APPLIED KNOWLEDGE:
### The Transformation of Physical Goods and Services
### Dimension Four

Beginning in the late twentieth century technology began to take on an entirely new dimension: It began to replace hard goods and services with knowledge-based technologies that better served the same purpose. For the sake of simplicity, this transformation will be referred to as a replacement of such goods and services with knowledge.[83] In the early stages of this transformation this new attribute of knowledge did not seem very significant, but as with so many other developments in technology, once this capability was created, it developed exponentially.

A good starting place to examine the growing capability of technology to transform physical products and services into knowledge is the music industry. In 1979, Warner Brothers introduced the first popular digitized music album, the immortal "Bop till You Drop" by guitarist Ry Cooder. When records and albums were digitized, the resulting product was no longer physical. It didn't just replace the vinyl record with a substitute, the replacement possessed fundamentally different properties than the product it replaced. Records no longer needed to be produced,

---

83 Obviously almost every form of new technology consists of both knowledge and a physical component, but for the rapidly developing new knowledge-based technologies, that physical element is secondary and does not drive the capability of the technology.

distributed, sold or stored in the traditional sense of those words.[84] The death of the record player soon followed. Once music was transformed into a digital format, it was no longer physical, and, therefore, there were virtually no limits on how it could be copied, transferred, shared or combined with other knowledge-based technologies. In the early stage of the development of this technology, this transformation did not seem very remarkable. But digitization revolutionized how the music industry produced, protected, and made a buck off music. It also dramatically changed the way we all listened to music and bought music or, let's be honest, didn't buy music.

These developments did not go unnoticed by the Brakemen. Immediate legal challenges of copyright, royalties, patents and licensing infringements were raised by the best lawyers that the entertainment industry could find, and a young generation of frightened and bewildered teenage music "pirates" was put on trial. Government regulatory agencies were also understandably concerned that some of their jurisdiction might be slipping away and reacted accordingly. New technologies are almost always challenged by the traditional Brakemen, and they came armed with their tools (laws and regulations), which had been meticulously crafted in the previous era to protect their vested interests. Sometimes, however, these tools do not fit very well because the new technologies that they attempt to stifle do not look, feel or operate like the products and services they replace. This troubles the Brakemen, among others, whether they are tax collectors (think of the early days of attempts to impose state sales tax on Amazon and eBay) or the music industry in its attempts to stop teenagers from making illegal copies of their most popular songs.

As a first-year law associate, I was asked to write a memo to substantiate a TV station's claim of property rights to the musical productions it produced and televised. There was, however, a problem. The culprit

---

84 Who knows why the term Gold Label signifies the success of a song? The CD replaced the album and both were obviously physical, but the music captured by the digital process was now electronic.

was copying them on electronic discs that did not look, feel or behave like the TV broadcast signals or the reels of film that the station had produced and that were legally protected. My research unveiled a similar conundrum that had come up many years prior in the battle of sheet-music publishers to squeeze royalties out of the makers of the cylinders that made the player pianos play. In the pivotal case in this battle, the sheet-music publishers demonstrated that the cylinders were just like sheet music by producing an expert who, by running his finger over a player piano cylinder, could determine by the shape and location of the holes on the cylinder which song the cylinder could play, thereby proving that the cylinder was just like sheet music. (Try running your fingers over a CD.) This was a stretch, but at the time of the lawsuit music was protected by laws and regulations that assumed the music had to be printed on a sheet of paper -- hence, the term "sheet music." Technology had evolved into another form entirely. The sheet-music industry won this case, as did my client, but technology won the war. This example from history exemplifies a quality of new technologies that is critical to understanding the challenges that these technologies create as they evolve from their traditional physical nature to pure knowledge.[85]

Music may have been the first commodity that was digitized into something that was essentially different in all of its characteristics, but it was far from the last. The technology quickly spread to include films, but these applications still did not truly portend where technology was heading. All of these forms of media had already come over

---

85 A more recent example of this type of challenge to the Brakemen and their tools has come from Uber. The taxicab industry is one of the most highly regulated monopolies in every major city in the world. It seemed so safe from competition that the sale of taxicab medallions is a multibillion-dollar business. Unfortunately for the industry and the holders of all those medallions, the laws and regulations protecting them from competition were drafted in a far simpler era, an era that never contemplated the power of new technologies such as cell phones, GPS positioning and mapping and/or the ubiquitous use of credit cards. Even with all this technology, it took some creativity to avoid regulation, but the founders of Uber seem to have done it and, in the process, they created a fifty billion dollar business and left a great deal of economic chaos in their wake.

the air, so they did not seem completely defined as "hard" or "physical." Immediately, however, photos were transformed to knowledge, as were books and newspapers, greeting cards, calendars, notepaper and schedulers.

The development of the uses of the smartphone is the best current example of the evolution of physical goods and services into knowledge. The cell phone was originally just a mobile phone. With exponentially expanding computer capacity, the cell phone quickly gained so much knowledge that it had to be renamed a *smart*phone. With this knowledge, it became capable of replacing an amazing array of physical products and services, a partial list of which is contained in Chart 12.1, "The U-Haul Trailer." In effect, all of the products in the U-Haul and the functions they perform have been transformed, in essence, into knowledge. These once physical goods need not have any independent physical presence. They exist as AI in your smartphone that fits in your pocket. Yes, you still need a physical smartphone, and periodically you need to purchase a new version, but everything it replaced is gone. At some point, as you review all the "stuff" in the U-Haul trailer, you cannot keep saying to yourself, "It is in my smartphone." Knowledge is in your smartphone. The goods are in your attic or rental pod -- that is, if you ever bought them in the first place. For my children, this is a no-brainer. They, and nearly anyone else under forty, will never buy a calculator, calendar, alarm clock, or, for that matter, have a land-based telephone ever again.

| Chart 12.1 | |
|---|---|
| **The U-Haul Trailer: What the Smartphone Had for Breakfast** | |
| 1. camera / telephoto lens | 26. Dictaphone |
| 2. film | 27. digital recorder |
| 3. photos / prints | 28. newspapers (worldwide access) |
| 4. photo albums | 29. magazines (worldwide access) |
| 5. movie camera | 30. encyclopedias |
| 6. movie projector | 31. dictionaries (in virtually every language) |
| 7. movie screen | 32. flashlights / penlights |
| 8. compass | 33. calculators |
| 9. notebook (endless supply) | 34. checkerboard (with built-in opponent) |
| 10. calendar (always current) | 35. chess board (with built-in opponent) of samples or your own design) |
| 11. greeting cards (from a nearly limitless set | 36. restaurant guides |
| 12. envelopes (same as for greeting cards) | 37. maps |
| 13. writing paper (see #12 above) | 38. GPS |
| 14. pens | 39. barometer |
| 15. pencils | 40. thermometer (so far, only outdoors) |
| 16. ink | 41. personal organizer / scheduler |
| 17. stamps | 42. books (only a few less than are in the Library of Congress) |
| 18. sticky pads / note pads | 43. iPod |
| 19. want ads | 44. telephone (landline) / telephone books |
| 20. file cabinet / files / folders | 45. video games |
| 21. CDs / CD player | 46. deck of cards |
| 22. DVDs / DVD player | 47. clock / alarm clock |
| 23. radio /stereo | 48. wristwatch |
| 24. TV | 49. graph paper |
| 25. address book | 50. laptop access to the Internet with over one million applications |

A similar, if not even more dramatic, transformation has occurred in the area of human services. Once again, the early stages of this transition did not appear very remarkable. The technological replacement of telephone operators and billing and accounting personnel appeared to be the normal progression of increased productivity resulting from the introduction of new labor-saving technologies. However, as technology became smarter it began to replace other functions that were far more complex and sophisticated. This second generation of job loss of service functions included travel planning (Travelocity, Kayak, etc.), tax preparation (TurboTax, etc.), legal work (LegalZoom) and toll collecting (E-Z Pass). As we become more comfortable and trusting in our relationship with technology, we will embrace another generation of job loss in the service sector, including insurance agents, financial consultants, real estate agents, legal associates, elder and day care workers, etc. I could have prepared another chart for these services similar to Chart 12.1, which lists products, but I would still be working on it given the rapidity of new service applications being developed on the Internet.

You could attempt to quantify the value of all these products and services, but even if you did, you would miss an important point. The smartphone not only replaces the physical object or service, but it also performs the function much better. The smartphone is a calendar and a scheduler, but, unlike its physical counterparts, it can be linked to groups or other applications, it is never out of date and you can make as many copies of it as you wish -- all for free. Photos taken by your smartphone have similar advantages -- you can stream them in the Cloud, share them with anyone for free or even alter or touch them up in ways that would be impossible with physical photos or negatives. How about travel services? Was there ever a travel agency that could offer you the array of bargains that you can effortlessly obtain on Kayak or Travelocity, and without a fee?

This is not a singular phenomenon of these particular technologies. This is a fundamental property of many advancing technologies. The conversion from physical goods and services to knowledge can be seen in every aspect of our lives. The US Bureau of Labor Statistics does not keep measurements that quantify the degree to which this transformation has changed the way the world satisfies many of its most basic needs and/or desires.[86] But this is far from saying that this trend does not have an enormous economic impact. For example, with the increasing use of smartphones, the goods and services listed in Chart 12.1 are, in large part, not being produced. This significantly and adversely affects our gross national product and has caused the loss of many jobs. If you need proof, ask former employees of Kodak or Polaroid, or residents of Maine still reeling from the decline in their forestry and pulp industries due to the decline of newspapers, or the sales staff that used to work at neighborhood record stores. In the next twenty years new technologies will be invented that will push the barrier of what functions, products and services can be transformed into knowledge.

We are entering an era where teaching is being augmented by the tremendous proliferation of free classes and lectures on the Internet. Virtually every institution of higher learning is putting almost all of its classes on the Internet. You can get more than just a good education on the Internet. MIT will issue you a certificate of completion if you complete a prescribed curriculum of its Internet courses. In effect, we have transformed the physical presence of a teacher, school, college or university into a knowledge-based technology as nearly as we have transformed the camera. We will, of course, always need teachers, but long before the Near Horizon, the best high school math teacher will hold a class for one hundred thousand students who will participate in classrooms or at home with 3-D imaging, surround sound and *interactive* capability, not with *that* teacher, but with a highly sophisticated form of AI. How would that experience stack up against today's sometimes chaotic schoolroom with a teacher who is having a bad day or who lacks sufficient training? In Chapter Eighteen, "The Transformation of the Service Sector," I will explore what the classroom of the future may look

---

86 Not only are there no statistics, but we do not have standards of measurement that even address this transformation.

like, but one characteristic should be noted now: The classroom and the teacher of the future will not need to be physical, and the educational services will largely be provided by AI. As technologies continue to improve, we will increasingly look for knowledge-based solutions to address our problems rather than costly, inflexible equipment and/or unpredictable human services.

Supplanting physical goods and services with knowledge-based technologies will, of course, take time.[87] And we will always need physical objects and people with whom to socialize. I will never relax by sitting on my smartphone, so there will always be a need for lawn chairs, and our educational system will always require the guidance of well-educated teachers.[88] The scope of physical goods and services that can be transformed into knowledge will, however, be limited much more by our imagination and our personal willingness to embrace the technology than by the capability of the new technology.

A glimpse at the promise of 3-D printers may give us an insight into what the future has in store for us as this transition progresses. Today the 3-D printer is largely a toy.[89] It is a Stage II Technology, but even at this early stage it can transform many objects that have been considered hard or durable into knowledge. The dishes on your table in 2025 will still be made of something very solid, but that plate will be knowledge for most of its life. It will be created as knowledge (stored and transported as an algorithm), and it will be produced by an algorithm running a 3-D printer. When you order a product over the Internet, it will

---

87 The role of and potential for mischief by the Brakemen in this process will certainly lengthen the period of this transition.

88 Although with technology, as Eric Brynjolfsson and Andrew McAfee point out in their book *The Second Machine Age: Work, Progress, and Prosperity in a Time of Brilliant Technologies* (W.W. Norton & Company, Inc., 2014), "Never say never."

89 In fact, 3-D printers are already becoming much more than toys. In the field of medicine, 3-D printers provide a very important role in fabricating high-quality, precise custom-fitted stents and other replacement parts used in micro-surgery and dentistry. These miniature parts are making revolutionary medical procedures possible. Recently, 3-D printers have begun to produce custom-built artificial limbs, especially for children who outgrow prosthetics fairly quickly. The promise of 3-D printers will be explored in more depth in Chapter Seventeen, "The Death of Manufacturing Jobs."

arrive at the 3-D printer in your local outlet as an algorithm, and only then will it become a physical object. Until then, it will be subject to the limitations of knowledge, not the limitations of physical objects.

That brings us to consider the uncertain but potentially brilliant future of nanotechnology, which will be discussed in Chapter Nineteen, "Employment in the Twenty-First Century." Nanotechnology, if it reaches practical scales of application for manufactured goods, will be another and virtually final step in demolishing the historically clear distinction between our hard, physical world and knowledge. Even if its full potential is never achieved, it will still have a major impact on how we view physical goods.

To understand the full impact and nature of the transformation created by these technologies, we need to appreciate that the new knowledge-based technologies do not just replace a hard product or service with a cheaper, better model. This is not a substitution of product A for product B. The knowledge-based replacement for a traditional product or service is no longer constrained by the rules and limitations of the physical world. It must, in fact, follow the limitations and be subject to the characteristics of knowledge. These limitations are very different and a great deal looser than the laws governing physical matter.

To understand how profound this transformation is, we should review some of the basic characteristics of physical matter versus knowledge. Some of the rules governing physical goods and services are as follows:

- Physical goods and services are scarce.

No matter how many golf putters a man or woman may have in the garage, that number is finite. If you want another one, you have to go out and purchase one. If your friend wants one of your putters, you can give it to her or him, but then you do not have it. If you are writing notes to friends on your note pad, you are fine until you run out of ink and/ or paper. If you are reading today's newspaper or looking at a calendar, you are fine, but tomorrow or next year you will need a new one. If your golf clubs become obsolete, you need to buy a set of new, state-of-the-art clubs; even Titleist will not send you a free upgrade. If your kitchen plumbing is broken, you need to call a plumber (they are very scarce), and if your new television does not work, God help you!

- Physical goods and services are costly.

No matter where you go to obtain something physical, whether it is to Walmart or a consignment store for "experienced" clothing, there is a cost. Sometimes the cost is low and sometimes it is high, but there is never a free lunch. If you want three of the same thing, it costs you about three times more. If you want your lawn mowed or your sidewalk shoveled, the kid next door needs to get off the couch and he must be paid to do so. If it snows again, he may be pissed that you keep interfering with his playing video games, but if you plead with him, he may agree to get off the couch. If he does, he will definitely need to be paid a second time.

- Physical goods and services must conform to the other laws and limitations of physical objects and/or human frailties.

Physical goods require and deplete finite resources and need to be stored and transported to where they are needed. These items can be damaged or broken and they often need repairs and services. People who perform services get cranky, temperamental, resentful, sick, disabled, old and disinterested, and they may develop bad attitudes.

Finally, in the twenty-first century, the most important difference between physical goods or services and knowledge will become increasingly clear: Physical goods and services cannot increase exponentially.[90]

These properties of physical goods and services are so much a part of our experience that we do not view them as limitations. However,

---

90 The term "exponentially" in this context refers to a rate of growth similar to the doubling every two years predicted by Moore's law.

knowledge as it exists on the Internet or otherwise, is pretty much a free spirit.

The rules governing knowledge are very different:

- Knowledge is not scarce.

When you share knowledge it increases, and when you give it away you can keep it at the same time. You also can distribute knowledge to a staggering number of people at virtually no cost and in real time and make as many copies of it as you want (other than for some "lawyer rules" and the Brakemen). It also does not run out; if you want to make a "To Do" list or write to a friend or send a greeting card, you never run out of paper, envelopes, ink or stamps. If you need tomorrow's newspaper or magazine or you need a calendar or road map for directions, there will always be a current one on your smartphone. If they improve the applications on your smartphone, you generally are sent a free update. However, if your new television does not work, you still are out of luck.

- Knowledge is not costly.

There is a caveat here. Creating new knowledge can be very expensive. Unlocking the secret of the human genome cost well over one billion dollars. Efforts to obtain the knowledge of what is causing climate change and how to reverse it will cost billions. The expense of creating other forms of new knowledge has, however, been radically reduced, and the creation of some types of new knowledge is no longer costly and, in fact, a great deal is free (think of Wikipedia or TED Talks). Crunching enormous amounts of information to find trends and correlations is not very expensive. If you wish to utilize massive amounts of computer capacity, you can rent time at a very low cost on some of the world's supercomputers through a Cloud application from Amazon, IBM or Google. The increasing use of crowd sourcing to solve difficult problems of information gathering, as well as open-source technologies, has also reduced the cost of creating new knowledge. The spread of Asian flu can now be tracked by monitoring social networks for key words indicating the presence of a new flu season. Processing large amounts of data is a prime driver in creating new knowledge, and increasing computer capacity can achieve this goal at levels millions of times faster than the human brain and very inexpensively. Other technologies such as DNA sequencing and brain scans are now exponentially better and cheaper. And remember, once knowledge is created, transmitting, sharing and utilizing it is virtually free and accessible worldwide.

- Knowledge is not subject to the other laws and limitations of physical objects or human frailties.

Knowledge can be transmitted almost instantaneously everywhere on the Internet, it is always available and travels and stores well in very small spaces, it isn't very fragile and it can be programmed to be eternally friendly, upbeat and courteous.

Finally and most importantly, any product or service that can be transformed into knowledge may, therefore, be subject to rapid exponential growth.

This list may sound simplistic, but there is a very profound lesson here. When a product or service is transformed into knowledge, it can in most instances become virtually free and ubiquitous, except for the efforts of some of the ever "helpful" Brakemen. These qualities are not a change in degree for a product or a service or a mere extension of its usefulness, they represent a fundamental transformation of the very nature of the "thing." By replacing goods and services with pure knowledge, technology has taken on a new dimension that was never encountered during the Industrial Revolution. Driven by Radical Change, this evolution is just beginning. Digitizing music may not have seemed very astounding. But at the time, did anyone predict that within ten or twenty years technology could transform a camera, calculator, road map, CD player, television, travel agent or a teacher, etc. into knowledge that would fit in your pocket? Remember, the smartphone is only one exam-ple of a knowledge-based technology satisfying many functions that pre-viously required a physical piece of equipment or a human.

Three-D printers and applications of the science of nanotechnology will be the new wave of technologies to radically complete this paradigm shift for physical goods. The advancing technologies of AI including voice recognition and speech, deep learning, cognitive thinking and emotional sensitivity will create the same transformation for many ser-vices historically performed by humans.

# Chapter Thirteen

## How Do You Measure Progress:
### Quantifying the Unquantifiable
### Dimension Five

Each dimension of advancing technologies contributes to the impact of Radical Change on our lives. Collectively these forces are creating a paradigm shift in the world our children and grandchildren will inherit. Our ability to comprehend and appreciate the extent of this transformation will, however, be limited by our prior experience and the terms we use to define this experience. These constraints will become ever more obvious as Radical Change causes a fundamental shift in our lives, not only quantitatively, as evidenced by more abundance and better objective standards of living, but qualitatively, in a quantum change in the basic nature of our lives. This shift has already begun, but we tend to mischaracterize it and denigrate the degree to which there have been alterations in our lives and our relationships with others and, on a macro scale, the way in which the people and the nations of the world relate to one another.

On a simple level, the art of letter writing as a way of communicating is considered nostalgic, at best. The art or even reliance on conversation versus texting one another is following the same trend. Terms such as "24/7" or "the now generation," "virtual reality," and "real time" seem to have emerged from a quaint but antiquated age. We have moved beyond those clichés, and the pace of this change is quickening.

In many ways, when historians look back on the twenty-first century, the societal changes caused by Radical Change may, in fact, seem even more remarkable and revolutionary than the technological improvements that will dramatically change the objective standards of living all around the world.

Today we have choices to have a social night out going to the theater, the movies or a concert, or in lieu of a night out we can stay at home and enjoy virtually the same experience on a big-screen TV with surround sound. If we have decided to stay in, we can also amuse ourselves with tweets to friends and engage in gossip or voyeurism on Facebook or innumerable other social networks, all basically for free. If we are feeling serious, we can take in a lecture on TED Talks or any one of a thousand other educational websites. If we are really serious, we can go online with any one of thousands of university open-source course curriculums. As staggering as these choices seem, they are growing exponentially! Long before the Near Horizon, we will have the choice to take a physical trip to Rome to visit the Sistine Chapel and see the works of Michelangelo or to have a relaxing evening at home curled up on our favorite living room chair while taking that same tour in virtual reality without the travel, crowds, distractions and expense. In fact, we will be able to choose to take that tour with a personalized tour guide preprogrammed with our own personal interests. If we want the thrill of a hike in the Alps, skiing at Alta or white-water rafting on the Rio Grande in Colorado without having to unduly exert ourselves physically or financially, we will don a headset that provides us an immediate, virtual experience. Led by the makers of video games, the newest generation of technologies in these fields provides early-stage forms of these choices today. Virtual reality has progressed very dramatically from the early days of Nintendo. Today, state-of-the-art virtual-reality equipment is bulky and awkward to utilize (Stage II Technology), but the experience it creates feels almost real. In fact, in a series of tests of cutting-edge equipment showcased at the Electronic Entertainment Expo in Los Angeles in 2014,[91] the participants in follow-

---

91 The Electronics Entertainment Expo (E3) is the largest trade fair for computer and video games in an industry that exceeded $25 billion in worldwide sales in 2014.

up interviews reported difficulty in remembering which prior experiences were real and which were memories induced by virtual-reality technology.

There is no way accurately to measure the economic effects of the transformation in the quality of our lives caused by these new dimensions of technology, such as the way we choose to spend our leisure time, but they are immense. For leisure-time activities, our traditional metrics would show a negative economic impact on the entertainment and leisure industries offset by the economic benefit due to the creation of new products such as video games, but these numbers would not reflect the actual impact of this transformation on our enjoyment or the quality of our lives.

The lack of appreciation for how fundamentally different new technologies have made our lives is somewhat difficult to explain. But this quantum change in how we now *choose* to live must be understood to appreciate how different our future will be from the experience of previous generations. Part of the answer to this riddle may rest upon the fact that we have always struggled, without success, to quantify and distill the *degree* of change in the human experience and/or to find ways to objectively rank the merits of otherwise unrelated human achievements. And yet we are obsessed with the need to quantify and measure everything. This primordial drive may be based on the simple proposition that anything we can measure we can control. Or in a somewhat more charitable sense, if something can be quantified, it can be harnessed and used to improve our lives. Historically we have been very good at measuring just about everything. Lord William Thomson Kelvin enabled us to understand temperature by establishing the correct value for absolute zero (–273.15 Celsius). Lord Ernest Rutherford did the same for radioactivity by discovering the concept of the radioactive half life of matter, which provided a basis for many forms of measurement, including radiocarbon dating. In the years that followed, scientists explored our universe with such precision that new measurements were needed to record their achievements. Research on the atomic level of molecules and the subatomic level of quarks required us to create the terms nanometer (one-billionth of a meter), *picometer* (one-thousandth of a nanometer or one-trillionth [$10^{-12}$] of a meter), and *femtometer* (one-quadrillionth [$10^{-15}$] of a meter). To examine matter this small, science also needed to create new measurements of time such as the *attosecond* (one-billionth of a billionth of a second, or one *quintillioth* [$10^{-18}$] of a second). These measurements are all beyond a layperson's comprehension and do not represent measurements of anything we can observe or experience. This does not, however, mean they are not potentially very useful. Today we have atomic-force microscopes that can resolve features one nanometer wide (about one or two atoms). For a brilliant insight into why technologies at this scale may revolutionize everything in our world, read *Engines of Creation* (1986) and *Radical Abundance* (2013), both by K. Eric Drexler, the founder of nanotechnology.[92] For a less erudite explanation, see Chapter Nineteen, "Employment in the Twenty-First Century," which briefly discusses the nature and possible applications and risks of nanotechnology.

Our efforts to precisely measure things have not, however, been limited to scientific matters nor other subjects that allow objective standards to be established. We rely on the decibel to measure the intensity of sound, but not the beauty of a song. The decibel is a useful measure if you are complaining about the noise from motorcycles, airplanes or boomboxes in your neighborhood, but it is not useful as a way to appreciate a concert. To a layperson such as myself, these well-intentioned efforts seem to be misguided and even counterproductive. In the diversity of life, there are many qualities and characteristics that should not be reduced to simple, objective metrics. In fact, in science, there is a well-known principle that in measuring something, especially at the atomic and subatomic levels, you will alter or destroy it. We could learn a great deal from this principle when we attempt to dissect and measure the breadth and richness of the human experience beyond the bounds

---

92 Eric K. Drexler, *Engines of Creation: The Coming Era of Nanotechnology* (Doubleday, 1986), and Eric K. Drexler, *Radical Abundance: How a Revolution in Nanotechnology Will Change Civilization* (Public Affairs, 2013).

of scientific exploration or measurement. There is no purpose in inventing or imposing scales to measure or compare two hours at the Boston Pops to a quiet evening at home listening to iTunes on a laptop headphone. What is the value of Mona Lisa's smile? It cannot be quantified, and that is good.

Despite the appeal of common sense and a great deal of good advice from the skeptics, historically many individuals have tried to establish rating systems, subjective standards or other forms of metrics to place relative values on just about every facet of our lives and the world in which we live. Some writers, generally historians, have attempted to track this progress by creating elaborate systems to identify and place values on great ideas or inventions throughout history. Some economists, business leaders and politicians have tried to track trends in economic well being by utilizing standards such as the gross national product and/or productivity or income per worker. Reading these studies, one cannot help but be left with the impression that each writer wishes to define the world in terms of his or her own image and/or discipline. Economists, based on their faith and understanding of economics, would have us understand the history of the world by way of unemotional economic charts, statistics and trends. Historians would rely on major historical events, ideas or figures in history. This bias in defining the world may or may not be misguided, but it certainly can produce some baffling results that sometimes defy common sense. These efforts have not been limited to measuring human progress in technology or economics. There have been some notable attempts to establish relative values for music, philosophies and even happiness. No less a genius than Michael Porter, Harvard professor of business, was engaged in 2014 in a project in Bhutan to quantify happiness. Other than a great excuse to spend some time in what I have been told is a very exotic place, what is the point? Attempting to reduce our finest artistic achievements and deepest-felt emotions into values and metrics that can be charted, compared and, otherwise, crunched with our computers is not a valuable use of time, except that in its failure we are reminded that these achievements are timeless and awe-inspiring, and that is why we cherish them.

Why this digression? It isn't one. Knowledge-based technologies will continue to supplant and/or transform previously hard (measurable) physical goods and services, and these technologies will radically alter the ways in which we communicate, work, relax, seek a sense of connection and express our artistic and creative forces. The effects of this transformation on the quality of our lives cannot be properly appreciated or quantified by our traditional standards of measurements, metrics, approaches, assumptions, or economic valuations. This is another manifestation of the paradigm shift we are experiencing. As a result, using the historic hard measures of progress developed during the Industrial Revolution and later twentieth century will not help us in understanding how quickly our world is changing. In fact, these forms of measurement may reinforce our own misconception that not much is new. Some economists are beginning to appreciate this problem, as traditional indices of our economy such as unemployment, productivity and gross national product all seem to increasingly belie the true state of well-being in our nation.

In the new age we have entered, we need to reassess the way in which we measure change. For example, for years we have relied upon the calculation of gross national product to provide a reliable indication of how well America is doing economically. But with the impact of the transformation of hard goods and services into knowledge, gross national product as measured by traditional approaches and assumptions is no longer as accurate a measurement of how our economy is performing or, more importantly, how we as individuals are doing. Look in your pocket and consider your pint-sized friend, the smartphone. It has largely replaced every product listed in Chart 12.1, "The U-Haul Trailer," and that list is growing fast. As discussed earlier, it would be difficult, if not impossible, to quantify the aggregate loss of economic value that has occurred by the transformation caused by the smartphone alone. But this is just one of the more obvious knowledge-based technologies that are transforming our lives. TurboTax has alleviated some of the pain, suffering and expense of tax season, but it adds very little to our gross national product. It has, however, replaced the need for thousands of accountants. Automated bill paying has simplified our lives and mitigated the monthly drudgery of writing all those checks, but it has resulted in the loss of thousands of jobs in billing and collection departments across America. Applications such as Kayak and Travelocity have sealed the fate of an already endangered species, the travel agent, resulting in the loss of thousands of jobs and small businesses. Despite the loss of these businesses and lots of good middle-class jobs, the travel industry itself may have benefited by offering lower-cost travel packages that encourage more and different types of individuals to travel. The same observations can be made about the music and camera industries. The benefits to society have been *increased* by the improvement and greater accessibility to us of all these goods and services, yet we assign no value to this. What does get recorded is the loss of economic benefits and the jobs that used to service our needs and produce, sell, support and service the physical products that these technologies have replaced. Using the metrics of the past would lead us to believe that our economy has been diminished, but yet our lives have been enriched.

To better appreciate this phenomenon, consider the impact of some simple applications of the Internet on the fabric of our lives. What is the value of a tweet, a message left on Facebook or a call on Face Time? If it is a teasing remark about that good-looking boy you were staring at while you were falling over the curb, probably not much. But what if that message was a video from a friend consoling you after the loss of a parent, or a video conference with your mom while she was fighting in Afghanistan? Recently the reality of *how* profoundly new technologies can impact our personal lives was brought home to me with the birth of my first grandson, Max. For weeks after his birth, my daughter Anna called us nightly on Face Time. We were able to watch Max roll over in his crib for the first time and eat his first bite of solid food. Despite the separation of Boston from Santa Fe we got to experience first-hand the joy, frustration and sometimes exasperation of Anna's struggle to keep up with her firstborn child. You cannot place a value on this experience for her mom and me.[93]

These new technologies enrich and change our lives in both subtle and dramatic fashions. We intuitively sense this, but we tend to denigrate these feelings by referring to most of these developments as merely amusement or harmless (or not so harmless) diversions. Those who embrace these technologies are often dismissed as geeks having a personal absorption with the Internet or computer games. Yes, many are fixated by violent games, smut and other questionable benefits of our World Wide Web. Yet we also learn, enjoy music or lectures, or research topics of interest, and we save lots of time finding good restaurants, a job, even a new soul mate, all on the Internet. We connect and share our personal lives with our friends and acquaintances as never before through Facebook, Twitter, Instagram, etc. The effects of the Internet on our society are far more radical than the impact of radio and TV on their respective eras, and yet we have no objective standards to measure the influence or the contribution of the Internet to the quality of our lives.

What is the value of Facebook? In 2014 it had a market cap of approximately $200 billion, employed only about five thousand workers, and yet it connected over 1.2 billion people around the world. These individuals spent countless hours communicating, staying in touch, learning and just plain amusing themselves, virtually for free. This ability to easily and freely connect with one another is transforming interpersonal relationships in our society in a very profound manner. We tend to dismiss this attention to social media as an overabsorption with the Internet or as merely a new form of twenty-first century entertainment, but it is redefining our relationships with one another in ways that were unimaginable just twenty years ago. The power of the Internet has also transformed the course of nations and has placed fear into many

---

93 Only God knows what Max was thinking, seeing our faces and hearing our voices on a smartphone that he certainly could not comprehend.

totalitarian governments around the world, something our billion-dollar diplomatic corps hasn't been able to do. But what have we added to the gross national product to reflect how profoundly our lives and the world have changed? The Internet now provides free and open access to virtually every educational course given in most of the great universities in America. We know how much a degree at MIT costs, but what is a certificate from MIT open-source courses worth? In 2006 Salman Khan created what may be one of the largest institutions of higher learning in the world, the Khan Academy, online and virtually for free. Notwithstanding the impact of the Khan Academy on society, the costs of the buildings and campuses with classrooms and laboratories to replicate what can be learned on the Internet from the Khan Academy are not in our gross national product. The Khan Academy does not employ large numbers of professors or assistants, not even janitorial help, yet it delivers an educational product that in many ways is as valuable as that of any university. It is a virtual institution, it is essentially knowledge, and it is free. For those not ready for a rigorous educational experience from MIT or the Khan Academy, there are the endless educational opportunities on TED Talks, Wikipedia or thousands of similar educational sites, and for a few dollars a month we can subscribe to incredible new websites on every subject in creation. What do we add to the gross national product due to the existence of all of these educational opportunities? Virtually nothing.

How about the value of movies, books, music and newspapers that can be obtained either for free (I am not condoning piracy) or for much, much less on the Internet than on the street? What is the economic value of the million or more applications on the Internet? What is the economic value of Siri making reservations for you, calling friends, answering questions or acting almost like a personal assistant? And she will get better, a lot better!

Of course, we have always had great ideas and thinkers -- Socrates, Plato, Mother Teresa, Mahatma Gandhi, Golda Meir and Yogi Berra, for example -- but we have never been able to objectively quantify the value of their contributions to our lives. We have communicated great feelings to each other in many modes for generations without being able to place objective value on them. With our new technologies in telecommunications, however, there is a new immediacy and accessibility to this knowledge. If we are to appreciate the true effects of Radical Change on our journey to the Near Horizon, we must understand the growing limitations of relying on our old metrics to measure and quantify these values and benefits. In the future, our traditional measures will become not only less useful, but they may also badly mislead us. As technology transforms more and more goods and services to knowledge, this paradox will only intensify.

Despite these inadequacies, statistics such as those historically compiled by the US Bureau of Labor Statistics (i.e., measures of gross national product, productivity, unemployment, etc.) should not be disregarded. These objective standards are all we have (at least for now), and they can help us plot the course to the future so long as we fully understand how dynamic our society has become and how this tension should affect our reliance on these standards. As we journey to our future, we occasionally need to glance in the rear-view mirror of history and at our traditional measures of progress, but for the most part, we should keep our eyes on the road ahead because the future will be coming up fast, really fast!

The knowledge-based society of 2035 will have an abundance for many and a lifestyle for virtually all that is almost unimaginable today, but the true magnitude of this new abundance will not be fully reflected by our historical standards and metrics of economic measurement. For us fully to appreciate and be grateful for some of our new abundance, we must keep this dimension in mind.

# Chapter Fourteen

## THE KNOWLEDGE REVOLUTION:
### Artificial Intelligence Is Not a Machine

We have left the age of the Industrial Revolution behind us. But where are we? Are we in a Machine Age, as Ray Kurzweil describes in *The Age of Spiritual Machines*,[94] or as Brynjolfsson and McAfee more recently describe in *The Second Machine Age*?[95] Other commentators have referred to this new era as the Digital Age, the Age of the Internet or the Knowledge Revolution.[96] Each of these terms captures from a different perspective the very powerful technological advances that are revolutionizing the twenty-first century. But beneath all these bedazzling advances lies one common denominator -- the astounding growth of computer capacity and AI and their applications to every aspect of our lives. This is the force that has been expanding exponentially and has transformed the machines of the twentieth century to something far different today.

There is tremendous historical precedent to refer to computers as *machines*. In fact, the earliest computers were nothing more than an extension of machines. The code breakers used to decipher German

---

94 Ray Kurzweil, *The Age of Spiritual Machines: When Computers Exceed Human Intelligence* (Penguin Books, 2000).

95 Erik Brynjolfsson and Andrew McAfee, *The Second Machine Age: Work, Progress, and Prosperity in a Time of Brilliant Technologies* (W.W. Norton & Company, Inc., 2014).

96 K. Eric Drexler, *Radical Abundance, How a Revolution in Nanotechnology Will Change Civilization* (Perseus Books Group, Public Affairs, 2013).

messages that helped to win the Second World War consisted of very complicated contraptions that depended principally on moving physical components in extremely complex patterns.[97] These code breakers looked, felt and operated like machines, but they produced something fundamentally different -- not physical products, but knowledge. It isn't surprising that as computers developed from vacuum tubes to integrated circuits and silicon chips, the terminology of *machines* followed. In 1988, *Time Magazine* proclaimed the computer to be the greatest *machine* in the world. At that time the forces of exponential change had not yet transformed the computer into something else. Computers were an extension, but only an extension, of the physical contraptions used by the code breakers in the early 1940s.

From 1988 to 2015, computers' way of thinking (AI) evolved dramatically. The information computers could learn by themselves, the cognitive manner in which they could process this information with deep learning into knowledge and the virtually incomprehensible speeds at which they could compute were not an extension of what went before.[98] As described in the earlier chapters of Part Two, the very nature, function and product of computers and AI have become fundamentally very different. As part of this transition, computers and the technologies empowered by AI stopped looking and acting like machines, but more importantly, they stopped being limited by the physical laws that have historically defined machines. Even the product of these *machines* (knowledge) changed not just in quantity but in the very nature of what knowledge could accomplish, including many functions that previously could not be done with physical machines at all. The smartphone replaced hundreds of machines that formerly we manufactured, bought, sold, repaired and used every day, but the functions of these products are

---

97 The role of computers in this process was recently dramatized by the poignant, if not historically accurate, movie, *The Imitation Game*, 2014, directed by Morten Tyldum. Christopher, the name of the computer in this movie, looked like a machine.

98 From 1945 (the approximate time of the code breakers) to 2015, computer capacity has actually doubled approximately forty-five times -- computers today are, therefore, about thirty-five *trillion* times more powerful than Christopher, the code breaker.

now served much better by a technology that is essentially knowledge. The Internet and its one million-plus applications also replace functions that were performed by goods and services with, essentially, knowledge. Technology has begun to develop into functions and forms incapable of being defined, quantified or even measured by the terminology and/or metrics of the machines of the Industrial Revolution. Although we are engaged in a debate over whether computers will ever be able to think in the same way as humans do, everyone would agree that computers (applications of AI) can now make decisions on their own volition, learn and create new information and knowledge. No machine in the Industrial Revolution possessed any of these characteristics.

Radical Change is quickly creating new means to enrich our lives, to learn, love and/or annoy one another, and to express our beliefs and emotions (unfortunately, at least with regard to chat boxes and other social media, without any apparent decorum or restraint) by means that are not machine-like. These benefits to our way of living are difficult to quantify, but, as described in Chapter Thirteen, "How Do You Measure Progress?", they are very real, they are expanding exponentially and they are dramatically impacting how we live.

The full implications of how Radical Change will fundamentally impact our lives in the future are extremely difficult to grasp because such dramatic change has never occurred before. To appreciate its effects, to quantify this change and to try to understand these forces will require a reevaluation of the basic terminology of how we described "progress," "productivity," and "value" during the Industrial Revolution. *The Age of Spiritual Machines, The Second Machine Age* and many other books that are imbued with the language of machines are seminal works. But these visionaries, who delivered their message as an evolution of machines, have attempted to describe the future in the terminology of the past.

With all due respect to their collective work, today the astounding growth of knowledge-based technologies is not the second phase of anything we have ever experienced before. It is not a continuum of the age of machines that ushered in the Industrial Revolution. The Internet is no more a machine than the steam engine was a horse or a sledgehammer. During the Industrial Revolution, agriculture still remained an essential part of our economy, but we did not define the new technologies of the nineteenth and twentieth centuries primarily with terms historically identified with the Age of Agriculture. Similarly, the technology of the twenty-first century cannot be defined or properly understood using the terminology and metrics of the Industrial Revolution. Of course there will always be machines, such as amazing new driverless cars. The physical parts of these machines will be more or less the same as they were in the twentieth century, but what will be new is that they will be "driven" by artificial intelligence. Our children will not recall this era as defined by machines; it will be defined by knowledge. We have entered the age of the Knowledge Revolution.

This is not a debate about naming rights. As a lawyer, I know that the definition of terms determines the outcome of the debate. If you allow me to define the terms we use in any discussion, it will come out the way I desire. As a result, to understand the magnitude and appreciate the comprehensive nature of the paradigm shift we are entering, we must choose our words carefully and examine our fundamental metrics for measuring our progress with the same care.

The importance of placing a new, profoundly more powerful technology in the correct context was captured by President Harry S. Truman in a message to Congress on October 3, 1945, following the use of atomic weapons on Japan:

> The release of atomic energy constitutes a new force too revolutionary to consider in the framework of old ideas.

We are entering into another revolutionary age, but in this revolution we will be armed with knowledge!

In the age of the Knowledge Revolution, we will still utilize machines, just as in the Industrial Revolution there remained an important role

for agriculture and hunting and gathering. But what will characterize this new age will be the fact that the engine driving our economy,
indeed our civilization, will be knowledge, not machines. Do not, however, take false comfort that by replacing the sometimes harsh terminology that defined the machinery of the Industrial Revolution with the
terminology of knowledge, we will avoid in this transition the historical consequences of the growing pains that accompany all revolutions.
In the Knowledge Revolution, along with great abundance will come
hardship, violence and the threat of economic and potentially existential Armageddon. In fact, the knowledge of the twenty-first century will
be far more dangerous than the physical machines and weapons that
defined our prior revolutions, and the stakes will, therefore, be much
greater. In this coming age, our greatest challenge may not be a battle
with machines; it may be a battle with our greatest invention yet, the
unruly child of computer intelligence developing into advanced applications that escape our control or, worse, evolve into an alien artificial
super intelligence.

The chapters that follow will explore what can be safely forecast
about how Radical Change will shape the growth and development of
advancing technologies. We will examine how the technologies of the
twenty-first century will evolve, how they will create abundance for some
beyond previous comprehension, and yet how they will also save labor
so successfully that we will face unprecedented challenges in unemployment, wage stagnation and inequality. Because this is no longer a
struggle with machines, we will need to readdress our basic assumptions
and approaches to our relationship with these rapidly evolving new technologies. The challenge we face will be far greater than the one posed
by the advent of the Industrial Revolution because we will enter this new
era with the force of Radical Change.

Since the days of the ancient Greek soothsayers, forecasting the
future has always been a very uncertain business. Predicting a future
evolving at the rate of Radical Change is a much more difficult task. As
a result, in Part Three we will focus primarily on the period of the next

twenty years (the Near Horizon) and the economic legacy we will leave to the next generation.

While it is not the purpose of this book to forecast the development of an ASI (benign or malevolent), Part Four will briefly describe what Stephen Hawking, one of the most brilliant minds of our time, has described as our "possible worst challenge," the inevitable day when we and/or our offspring face the threat of an emerging alien super intelligence that, as it matures, may no longer need our nurturing support nor even wish to have our tacit consent for its existence.

Part Five will briefly address a few basic principles that may help us set a new direction to our path to the future.

# Part Three

---

## The Near Horizon

# Chapter Fifteen

## BRAVE NEW WORLD:
### Can You Stand the Truth?

As Radical Change creates a paradigm shift in our views and attitudes about life, we will feel a growing sense of discomfort. As humans, we inherently fear change. This human reaction has for centuries been the subject of great novels, plays and musicals. In 1933, Aldous Huxley wrote *Brave New World*. It is a story about a very strange new world. At the time when it was written, it both frightened and excited its readers. It drew its energy and enduring message from our deep-seated fear of the uncertainty of the future. To put the message of this famous book in a correct historical perspective, *Brave New World* is based on the vision of William Shakespeare's *The Tempest* (V, 1), published in 1610. *The Tempest* tells the story of Miranda, a young, innocent maiden who was raised on a very remote and primitive island. On her travels, she discovers the mainland of modern England. As she is coming ashore to her new civilization, she sees a group of drunken sailors staggering onto the same land off the wreckage of their ship. In her bewilderment, she exclaims:

O Wonder!
How many Godly creatures are there here.
How beauteous mankind is!
O Brave New World,
That has such people in it.

Miranda clearly suffered from an innocent view of the beauty of her new world. A group of drunken sailors staggering ashore is not an image of "how beauteous mankind is"!

If the vision of *Brave New World* is a correct vision of our future, then Yogi Berra had it right: "The future just ain't what it used to be." This dark view of the future, while understandable, is unwarranted by any fair evaluation of technological progress to date. Advancing technologies in the twenty-first century will benefit humanity in a much more profound sense than in any previous era of human experience, but with this abundance will come new and difficult challenges because some of the new technological advances will harbor a dark side. One thing on our journey will be certain -- as our rate of progress rapidly accelerates, we will face greater misgivings as to where we are heading and how safe our passage will be. As in the past, we will latch on to what is familiar and known to us until it becomes painfully obvious that it is no longer working. In an age of Radical Change, this may be a reaction that will not serve us well.

As *The Tempest* teaches us, the sense of a world in seemingly endless and rapidly accelerating change has been around for awhile, and we have endured. As we progress, we need to take a deep breath and accept the things we cannot change, particularly because there will be a lot more of those challenges coming up. We all crave certainty, but it rarely occurs until we are confronted with it. As Golda Meir once remarked while walking on a beach with friends to celebrate her seventieth birthday, "Of this one thing I am now certain..." (her friends gathered closely to better share this pearl of wisdom), "I shall live to be an old woman." This may not be overly encouraging, but simple truths bear witness that there will be some certainty on our journey.

In facing uncertainty, we need to be guided by the same common sense and sense of humor that has served us well for generations. This advice is, of course, easier said than done, especially if you have just watched *The Terminator* or any one of its genre or if your identity has been stolen by some crook using the seemingly trackless Heartbleed "virus,"[99] So in lieu of offering moral, spiritual or other types of fortitude, I will offer a few simple guides that technological progress has already taught us for a saner passage to the future. Even in the paradigm shift ahead, these basic attributes of technology should not materially change. These six rules of technology and frequent looks into the rearview mirror of history may be all we have for guidance on our journey to the Near Horizon. They do not provide a great deal of help in forecasting our journey drawn by Radical Change, but they are a start.

**Rule One:** New technologies create greater abundance, but sometimes this abundance comes with painful consequences.

With the acceleration of the development of new technologies caused by Radical Change, we will experience an order-of-magnitude increase in both the "highs" (the Winners) and the "lows" (the Losers) that this rule anticipates.

**Rule Two:** Technology is amoral.

As technologies develop, there is little evidence that they (including AI) will be utilized for or inspire a higher level of moral, ethical or spiritual enlightenment. Technology, at least until it reaches the level of ASI, is solely a tool, and, like a lever, it will amplify the finest and worst instincts of the human beings who employ it.

**Rule Three:** No matter how heinous the potential consequences of the use of a new technology, someone or some entity will be willing, often in the name of their Higher Power, to inflict that loss or harm on humanity.

---

99 The Heartbleed "virus" uses a technology that can attack a computer without leaving a trace, making it virtually impossible to identify the perpetrator. Technically, it is not a classic "virus," but the result to the victim feels the same.

Through the concerted efforts of the Manhattan Project, the United States developed the atomic bomb. Despite the fact that we consider ourselves one of the most enlightened and civilized nations in the world, we used this technology in war in 1944.[100] Since that date, the world has been fundamentally changed because for the first time in history, we live with a technology so powerful that it could annihilate our civilization.

**Rule Four:** Never assess the risk of a new technology on the assumption that humanity can effectively control that technology from manipulation or misuse for any sustainable period of time.

We have benefited beyond description from the Internet, yet we are now extremely vulnerable to devastating cyber attacks on the fundamental infrastructures that make life possible and we are now exposed to massive invasions of our privacy and personal freedoms. We continue to struggle with the issues raised by nuclear weaponry and chemical and biological warfare. Advancing forms of AI and the new and powerful technologies that it will create may finally test this rule to its limits.

**Rule Five:** Never assume that a technology created for humanitarian or beneficial purposes will not be converted by someone else's creativity and ingenuity into a terrible threat to life and human liberties.[101]

Laser technology benefits many aspects of our lives, from health care to telecommunications, but recent breakthroughs in this technology may pave the way to create satellite wars in space and/or compact, relatively

---

100 Prior to the testing of the first atomic bomb, a very respected group of experts warned that an explosion of this nature would result in a cataclysmic atomic chain reaction annihilating life on the planet. Obviously we did it anyhow. If there was any doubt that if the stakes are high enough, otherwise reasonable and sane people will employ any dangerous technology, no matter what the potential consequences, this historical precedent should settle the matter.

101 Early technological progress in a field often occurs long before the lethal implications of the misuse of that technology become apparent. This was certainly the case in the fields of atomic research, laser development, AI and genetic research.

cheap nuclear weapons. Advances in genetic engineering have provided wonderful benefits in health care and nutrition but have opened up what some consider to be a very real threat of human cloning, the creation of new life forms, genetically engineered offspring and possible adverse and severe long-term effects of improperly genetically altered agricultural crops.

**Rule Six:** New technologies challenge our basic understanding of the fundamental premises of how the world operates and our own place in the world.

As technologies develop, they often redefine many of our basic conceptions of the complexity of life, the universe and our place in creation. In the early part of the sixteenth century, Copernicus developed the theory that the earth was not the center of the universe. To put it mildly, the world, and in particular the Roman Catholic Church, was not prepared for this revelation. As a result, this discovery caused a great deal of religious, ethical and political unrest and unhappiness. Humanity's entire relationship to the physical universe was forever altered. The acceptance of the theory of evolution and, more recently, the unlocking of the secrets of the subatomic world, the discovery of potentially billions of Goldilocks planets within the Milky Way,[102] advances in genetic engineering of DNA and the possible creation of synthetic life have profoundly altered our understanding of the universe and the sanctity of human life. The promise of future breakthrough technological developments in the field of ASI that far surpass human intelligence (Singularity) may cause many to question the basic nature of humanity's relationship to God and the universe.

---

102 Goldilocks planets are planets of far distant stars that possess similar characteristics to those of earth (i.e., size, atmosphere, liquid water and other characteristics compatible with the origin of life). The discovery of the existence of such planets was only recently possible due to major advances in telemetry, such as the Kepler space observatory.

These Rules do not provide a great deal of help in forecasting our journey to the Near Horizon, driven by Radical Change, but they are a start.

Before we begin an exploration of our future, we need to be reminded of how fast we will be traveling on our journey. Think for a moment about even the terminology we are forced to use. When in history did a society believe that forecasting twenty years into the future (the Near Horizon) will be truly uncertain and that the next forty years (to the Far Horizon), will be truly unpredictable? This latter period is about the length of the relatively staid and stable legal career I expected when I began to practice law in 1970.

Well, it took us a long time to get here. If I knew a shortcut, we would have gone down it, but predicting where our journey into the future will lead requires an understanding of where we started, a bit about how technology got us here and what the guides will be for our journey: So buckle your seatbelts; the Engine of the Cannonball Express has passed the speed of sound and is approaching the speed of light! Our Caboose is trailing far behind the Engine, but in the eyes of history and certainly in the scale of time in the cosmos, we are not very far behind at all!

# Chapter Sixteen

## A GLIMPSE INTO THE FUTURE:
### Be Careful What You Wish For

The scope of the change we will certainly experience on our way to the Far Horizon (2055) may rival the impact on society during the entire period of the Industrial Revolution. It will accentuate the highs and lows, provide new challenges to our basic individual rights and freedoms, and it will test our resolve, patience and tolerance to the limits. Radical Change will bring for many, but not all, an abundance, a new way of life and a standard of living that will constitute a quantum change in the way we work, live, love, communicate, amuse ourselves, trade, annoy and hurt one another, and just plain get along. The noneconomic challenges described in this chapter may not seem to some, especially the unemployed and struggling, to be as serious or as threatening as unemployment and inequality, which are the subject of the last chapters in Part Three. These noneconomic challenges will, however, shape and define our lives and enrich and/or degrade the quality of our society in ways that now seem almost unimaginable. For the most part, we will be able to adapt and learn to live with the compromises these challenges will force. But these choices will be extremely difficult and often painful. The dilemmas created will often offend those with deeply held ethical, moral or religious beliefs. There will be horrible errors in judgment (there already have been -- think of the National Security Agency (NSA) surveillance debacle of January 2014). The decisions we ultimately will be forced to make may seem to some to be horrible compromises, but as a society we will move on.

The following are some, but certainly not all, of these challenges. They do not appear in any particular order because the possibility of each one occurring and the magnitude of its consequences are uncertain. Also, the importance that each individual places on these values is a very personal judgment.

## CREDIT CARD AND FINANCIAL FRAUD

It is interesting that we refer to this phenomenon as identity theft, which implies that somehow our identity equates to our credit status, personal net worth, and whatever else is in our wallet. But this fraud is truly *just* very inconvenient. Most of our financial institutions have already realized that it is cheaper for them to chase the perpetrators of these crimes than to harass the victims of this form of fraud. Since it is occurring to all of their competitors, it is now a necessary cost of business and is placed as an embedded cost in their services. In reality, this cost is reflected in higher costs of credit and comes right back to us. There is a lesson here when technology promises you something for nothing, such as credit card security. As the recent outbreak of the virulent Heartbleed virus reminded us, as technologies improve, the consequences of this problem will only get worse.

## VULNERABILITY OF INTEGRATED, HIGH-TECHNOLOGICAL SYSTEMS

The growing vulnerability of every electronic system controlled by computer intelligence is much more troubling and increasingly recognized as a serious threat. Even now, that's almost every system that is the basis for our survival. Our banking and financial systems, the infrastructures that deliver communications, energy, and drinking water and those that control the operation of our systems of mass transit, flight and nuclear power generation, even the systems controlled by the US Department of Defense including ICBMs and drones, are entirely dependent on our ability to maintain the security and integrity of these systems and keep them safe from cyber attack. We have already seen examples of how these systems can fail, be manipulated or be misused.[103] In assessing the risk of these technologies, we need seriously to consider the implications of Rules Two, Four and Five mentioned previously.

Just in time for the 2014 holidays, North Korea, acting through the clever pseudonym The Guardians of Peace, launched an amateurish cyber attack on the equally unsophisticated cyber security protecting Sony Entertainment's deepest secrets. The outcome of the dirty laundry of the Hollywood stars being dumped into the insatiable appetite of the Internet was a public-relations feeding frenzy. Many felt little sympathy for the anguish that this caused the box-office superstars, but when the Guardians threatened violence at movie theaters that wished to show *The Interview*, the scope of the problem began to show its truly ugly, sinister side. Sony collapsed and pulled the movie, so the precedent of cyber blackmail has now been established.[104] On a more substantive level, the United States and Israel recently codeveloped an extremely sophisticated computer virus, Stuxnet, to infiltrate the Iranian nuclear weapons development program. The virus has the ability to hack its way past the security barriers protecting the Iranian high-speed centrifuges that produce enriched uranium necessary to build nuclear weapons. Once Stuxnet was successfully installed, it directed the centrifuges to spin faster than their maximum performance standards, thereby self-destructing. Stuxnet performed flawlessly and the Iranian nuclear program was set back for, at least, two years. Unfortunately, Stuxnet was not programmed to self-destruct. In fact, to assure its success against

---

103 Recently Chrysler recalled over 1.4 million cars when two reporters demonstrated the ability to electronically take over some of the computer-driven operating systems in these cars.

104 In fairness to Sony, they did reverse this decision and scheduled a very limited release of the movie.

computer security defenses, it was programmed to duplicate itself. As a result, numerous (the actual number is unknown) versions of Stuxnet have now escaped to computer files around the world. For Stuxnet to go viral again, someone with extremely advanced computer skills would need to detect its presence and potential power, but there are many computer geeks out there with those qualifications.[105]

Unfortunately, the technology for much more terrifying applications of cyber attack already exists; we are just waiting for the other shoe to drop. On November 17, 2014, Admiral Michael S. Rogers, Director of NSA and head of the US Cyber Command, appeared before the House Intelligence Committee. In response to a question sparked by alleged Chinese cyber attacks on the US power grid, Admiral Rogers responded that China and "one or two" other countries are capable of mounting cyber attacks that would shut down a significant portion of the US electric grid and "other critical systems" in the United States. In Roger's words, "It is only a matter of when, not if, we are going to see something dramatic."[106] When asked if this meant we were now as a nation in a position equivalent to nuclear deterrence (which defined the Cold War), Admiral Rogers responded that it was worse because nuclear attacks could be detected and attributed to a specific source in time to retaliate. In his words:

> By contrast, the source of a cyber attack can easily be disguised and the capability ... is possessed not only by nation states but by criminal groups and individuals.

These integrated systems are not safe from attack, compromise or failure. And they are not safe because they violate many of the rules of technology described in Chapter Fifteen. Security barriers to contain the power of these technologies have historically not served us well. I am

---

105 Please consider Rules Three and Four.

106 As this book was going to print, the world learned that the Chinese had orchestrated an ongoing attack on US government agencies, compromising confidential information of twenty million (and climbing) US citizens.

certain that if you give me a few dozen very bright teenagers, the most sophisticated computer technology that money can buy, a big basement, two hundred pizzas, fifty cases of Diet Coke and two long weekends, there is virtually no computer code in the world that is safe from our attack.

In the future, the efficiencies, increasing capabilities and further integration of all of our electronic infrastructure and support systems will prove to be so appealing that we will devise and implement new technologies on a grand scale to improve the performance of these systems far beyond current levels. But the integrated nature of these systems will also render them even more vulnerable to cyber attack, and it will dramatically increase the consequences of a cyber attack were one to occur. Why expose ourselves to so much more vulnerability, especially when we are already faced with so many internal and external threats of terrorism and sabotage? Because these systems will work better, they will be more productive, they will make a few people a lot of money, and they will save some money and work much better for all of us. We will not just tolerate these changes; we will demand them.

## PERSONAL PRIVACY, FREEDOM OF SPEECH AND PERSONAL LIBERTY

In late 2013 the world learned that the well-intentioned, highly motivated National Security Agency had engaged in an unprecedented invasion of personal privacy and liberty. The NSA wasn't being a voyeur; it had a higher purpose in mind, the protection of our freedoms and our way of life from foreign and domestic terrorists! But as they say, "The path to hell is paved with good intentions." With the help of some truly amazing technology, the NSA really went to work, and our worst fears of the consequences of Rules Two, Four and Five of the rules of technology were confirmed by our own government's good intentions. If this misuse of technology is what we should expect from those whose mission it is to protect us, what could be in store for us from those who may wish to control or hurt us? The technologies that the NSA used were extremely powerful. But with the rate of computer development and the virtually complete integration of all our computerized networks, how much further could the NSA or a rogue nation or a terrorist group go by the year 2035?[107] Consider the potential threat if one giant super-computer tied together all the security cameras in every mom-and-pop convenience store, every parking lot and street corner, every commercial building, school or movie theater -- you name it and cameras will be there. This security equipment will continue to be upgraded, and soon we will have voice and facial recognition systems that will work extremely well. Add to this the information from all of the GPS positioning systems in our smartphones and cars; all the information available on Facebook, Twitter and Google; every email, text, credit card entry, and barcode transaction; and the sum of all the information that could be derived from "the Internet of Things." The chilling fact is that computer capacity and technology can do most of the integration and processing of this data today. What will change in the near future will be the ease, cost, scope and ability of computers to access and process this information. In 2014 Google announced that it had developed a new computer capacity that was able to examine all of its existing mobile truck camera films and indentify and catalog all of the street address numbers visible in that film for the entire country of France. It took the computer just over two hours! Now I have no idea why Google felt it needed to know the address of virtually every citizen in France, but the use of this technology in the wrong hands could go very badly, especially if it was programmed to identify objects and information that are more threatening than a street address. What if an extension of that technology could be combined with enhanced satellite photos used on Google maps? Our government already possesses satellite technologies far better than the ones we now get on Google. And compare the quality of the Google maps five years ago to today's; if you have not seen those maps

---

107 Taken in this context, the recent popularity of technologies such as the "Internet of Things" takes on an ominous but unintended consequence.

lately, Google one up. It will blow your mind! Take the Google "street address" technology -- expand it exponentially, add to it an unbelievably expanding information base from satellite surveillance, put all of this information into a supercomputer, and you have the technology to produce the "Big Brother" society described by George Orwell in *Nineteen Eighty-Four.*[108]

The power of these advances in security will, taken together, severely threaten personal privacy and freedom. These technologies will, of course, be met with governmental regulation. But remember Rule Four of the rules of technology -- governmental restraints will not be infallible. Consider what would be left of your privacy and how this information could be used to limit your freedom of speech and personal liberties. This will, of course, also cause a great battle by organizations such as the American Civil Liberties Union to save us from ourselves, and they will be very busy. But because so much of this technology will also create great abundance and security for so many, there will be great resistance to being "protected." The rise of terrorist violence across the world will be an ongoing powerful force leading us to choose more security versus less privacy, which is good, unless you are concerned with your own loss of personal privacy.

One final example of how good intentions in the future *may* get us into trouble is in the area of health care. In only the last few years, America and the developed nations of the world have converted most of the health care records of hospitals, health care insurers and even government agencies to digital files. It is easy to see the possible abuse of widespread or even discrete, but unwanted, access to this information. America has passed far-reaching privacy laws such as the Health Insurance Portability and Accountability Act (HIPAA), but remember the limitations of the rules of technology and what good intentions

---

108 George Orwell, *Nineteen Eighty-Four* (Signet Classics, 1949). This book tells the story of the repressive, totalitarian government of Oceania, which through an omnipresent government surveillance is able to persecute all individualism and independent thinking as "thought crimes." This tyranny is epitomized by Big Brother, the quasi-divine leader of the state.

can get us. Consider the advances in health care diagnostics and treatments that could occur if, rather than relying only on clinical trials, all of the health care histories of all Americans, indeed of all patients in the health care communities of the developed nations of the world, could be pooled and processed by one great supercomputer that could determine patterns, correlations and relationships between environmental factors, genetic predispositions, drugs and drug interactions, quality and specific methods of treatment. The advances in health care that would be identified by this process would be magnificent but at what cost to personal freedom, privacy and liberty? What if your life or health-care insurer, your employer or one of your competitors had access to this information?

## GENETIC ENGINEERING

Bioengineering on a molecular level has been around for a long time, if you count creating hybrids by crosspollination. But today, with super powerful molecular engineering, we are beginning to unlock the secrets of life. The human genome was first sequenced in 2000. This was a dramatic task that had for a long time been considered impossible. It was completed by a concerted effort that brought together some of the greatest intellects, concentrations of capital and focus of technological capability since the Manhattan Project. With the DNA code finally understood and open sourced (not patented), it opened the flood gates to a worldwide effort to apply this technology to many fields of health care and the prevention of genetically transmitted diseases and disabilities.

These applications are wonderful and filled with the promise of a much better, longer and healthier life, not only for us, but also for our children and grandchildren. But this knowledge can also be a double-edged sword. Do you really want to know your propensity to contract cancer? Angelina Jolie did, and she went through two serious operations. Do you or would you want to have your employer or your health-care insurer or your life insurance company be aware of the results of your DNA testing? Would you wish to exchange DNA results with your fiancé as a precondition to your marriage?

We've already witnessed a very difficult and angry debate about the genetic engineering of agricultural products,[109] an ethical discussion about the absolute limits of cloning and, more recently, the development of what might be the first artificial form of life.[110] What if technology were able to provide you with the ability to genetically engineer your next child or the ability to stop or reverse the process of aging? What would be the consequences to society if technology provided you with a personal choice as to whether you (or your children) might have the ability to live for two hundred, three hundred or more years or even become immortal?

Most, if not all, of these developments will be technologically feasible before 2035. Long before then, we will need to have a serious discussion about the ethical, moral, religious and legal implications of these capabilities, because our Caboose is picking up speed very, very fast.

## ARTIFICIAL INTELLIGENCE

The origin of the issue of what constitutes AI traces its origins back at least one thousand years, and certainly by the age of da Vinci (who drew the first recognizable form of robots), the possibility of intelligence outside of the human brain was considered possible. Without engaging in a debate about what constitutes AI versus ASI (see Chapter Twenty-Two, "Artificial Super Intelligence"), you should know that we already have the former! Lots of it! We not only have it, but we also rely upon it

---

109 One example is Golden Rice, a genetically altered form of rice that contains a very high percentage of vitamin A. Lack of vitamin A in the diet of many in the underdeveloped countries causes millions of cases of blindness, often among children. Despite these undeniable benefits, a small but very articulate group of True Believers has significantly delayed the widespread introduction of this crop throughout the world. The debate has badly split the environmental advocacy group Greepeace, among others.
110 There is serious scientific disagreement on this latter issue.

without even thinking. It affects and controls virtually every aspect of our daily lives. Computers run our cars. I am not referring to self-park intelligence (but that *is* pretty remarkable), or driverless cars. Our steering and braking systems and the very motors and transmissions that power our cars are all run by computers. We entrust our lives and the lives of our children to them every day.[111]

As we integrate computers into our everyday lives, we are frequently reminded that sometimes AI can operate beyond our control! Roughly twenty years ago, a group of very entrepreneurial investment bankers, with the help of some very brilliant mathematicians, were able to create computer trading algorithms so that computers could initiate trades on stock exchanges at speeds impossible for humans to duplicate. Most of us believe that the crash of the stock market in 2008 and subsequent less noteworthy abrupt falls in the stock market reflected the burst in the housing bubble and the explosion of what Warren Buffet described as "financial weapons of mass destruction," such as the creation of derivatives and "securitized offerings" of just about everything that involves the payment of money, except perhaps tips to the waiters in the restaurants in New York City. However, one of the major contributors to the severity of these stock market crashes was the fact that once the market began to decline, the automatic triggers in the algorithms running the computer traders were set off in a cascading geyser of computer algorithmic trading, causing the stock market to go into freefall.

What became clear in the aftermath of this mess was that nobody had anticipated just what those computer traders could do without human help and in just a few minutes. Why did smart people in the stock market allow algorithms to grow into this potential? Because a few people made a lot of money -- just ask John W. Henry, owner of the Boston Red Sox. In fact, if you did not employ these algorithms, you couldn't compete in

---

111  In this context, remember the recent experience that led Chrysler to recall 1.4 million of its vehicles (described in Footnote 104).

this business[112] because there was plenty of competition that would and did benefit from this technology.

There are many other examples of the use of computers that make "intelligent" decisions at speeds that are virtually uncontrollable by mere humans. As stated earlier, the US Department of Defense recently announced that it was developing the next generation of drones that *for the first time* would be programmed to make deadly decisions in combat with no prior authorization of a supervising human.[113] Despite years of protestations by the Executive Office and the US Department of Defense that drones would never be allowed to become self-actuating, technological development made those promises impossible to keep.

Historically, discussions of the danger posed by advancing AI have quickly focused on the risks of nonhuman intelligence approaching the Singularity, which is defined as the time when AI reaches the level of human intelligence. The experience of the application of AI to the stock market and AI's evolving role in the operation of military drones should forewarn us of a far more imminent threat, the misuse or abuse of this capability long before it reaches the point of the Singularity. Despite the growing evidence of the possibility of a tragedy being triggered by the unanticipated power of applications driven by AI, we are pouring billions of dollars into research and development efforts to improve these capabilities. In fact, when technologies improve to the point that the safeguards begin to interfere with AI's potential, we choose to disable the safeguards. This was the case with military drones, and this will not be the last time we face this dilemma. Absent a catastrophe of near global proportions, the benefits of AI will continue to blind us to the pernicious dark side of this technology.

---

112 "This business" does not mean trading stocks on the exchange. It refers to the specialized trading of very large, very liquid positions in the market to earn infinitesimally small economic profit per transaction.

113 Actually, this is the first time the US Department of Defense has publically stated that a drone was programmed to make a deadly decision without prior human direction. Rumors of such drones flying over the DMZ border between North and South Korea have been circulating for several years.

Another application of AI that shows enormous promise is electronic stimulation of the nervous system. Currently, we have technologies that are able to transmit signals from the brain, namely, implanted transistor chips that can convey "thoughts" to computer cursors. Using technologies in the research and development stage, patients with crippling disabilities are able to regain some of the uses of their bodies by controlling prosthetics with only their thoughts. By 2035 we may be able to implant computer chips in our brains that can link us to AI. This could be the beginning of a species of cyborg. I suspect Kurzweil is being fitted for one even now. Even if this technology proves to be more stubborn to advance (think of robotics) than now anticipated, there are numerous technologies in research and development that could stimulate the brain in various ways both chemically and electrically that could provide enormous enhancement to human intelligence. It is one thing for society to accept and even admire enhancements of physical appearance such as tummy tucks and breast implants, but what are the implications if one of your fellow employees were to invest in a brain enhancement technology? It might cost you your job.

## IMPROVEMENTS IN EXISTING DANGEROUS TECHNOLOGIES INCLUDING WEAPONS OF MASS DESTRUCTION

The rapid development of knowledge and technology will certainly be applied to "improve" already existing deadly technologies such as drones and nuclear, chemical and biological threats to our society. Even the weapons that we already know and fear, such as attack rifles and car bombs, are constantly "improving" with technology. We should expect the future to produce dramatic increases in the capability and risk of mortality from these types of conventional weapons, such as self-actuating armed drones. This will, obviously, significantly raise the risk of terrorist threats and violence in our schools, theaters, shopping malls, and even our churches. But you may say, "We will have laws to control the sale and distribution of these terrible improvements in lethal weaponry!" The flintlock firearm was the weapon of choice for the American colonists who drafted the US Constitution in 1777. Since then, the primitive flintlock has been developed into the attack rifle and the submachine gun. That transformation was not enough to persuade the National Rifle Association (NRA) that the right to bear arms in the Second Amendment to our Constitution referred to the arms of the 1770s. As a result, I seriously doubt that Radical Change in the weapons of the future will change the NRA's view on this matter. In fact, the NRA will probably just get giddy over the thought of such "advances."

I will end this chapter on a rather unpleasant note, the future development of a new generation of nuclear weapons. Similar forecasts could be written about technological advances in chemical and biological warfare, but the salient point of the risk that lies in our future will be adequately made if we stick only with nuclear weapons. All the world's governments are committed to stop the use and/or proliferation of nuclear arms, and most of the world's governments have committed to end the deployment of yet more deadly nuclear weapons. You may be surprised to learn that none of the nuclear powers in the world, not even the non-Nuclear Club members, Germany and Japan, have committed to stop the research and development of such weapons!

Unfortunately there exists the technological possibility of lots of "improvement." Even the modern hydrogen bomb releases only a small percentage of its potential energy. Most experts agree that to improve the science in this field today would require a Herculean effort perhaps only possible by extremely well-funded entities such as major governments or a very few multinational corporations. (Actually, as I write this, this caveat does not sound very comforting to me.) But in a world of greatly enhanced AI, these barriers will fall rapidly. We are living today in a very uneasy truce with the threat of nuclear holocaust. At least for now, only a handful of nations possess nuclear capability. There are two scientific, *not* political, reasons for the current reality. First, to possess nuclear capability you need to know how to build a nuclear bomb. Unfortunately this knowledge can now be obtained on the Internet, and there are thousands of people, including most of the recent graduates from the physics department at MIT, who have the basic knowledge of how to build such a weapon. This is, therefore, no longer a barrier to entry to the Nuclear Club. A second, more daunting technological challenge is that to build a nuclear bomb and utilize it, you must also possess the capacity to produce large amounts of fissionable material to make the bombs go off and have the capability of delivering the finished bomb where you want it to explode, which presumably is not in your own backyard. But bear in mind Rule Three. These technological challenges have allowed us to keep the lid on membership to the Nuclear Club, barring membership to rogue nations and terrorists groups. But history teaches us that those who relied on technological barriers to protect themselves from great external threats learned to regret it: Think of the Incas in Peru and metal armor and flintlocks or Native Americans and repeating rifles.

Nuclear technology today requires a vast array of very expensive high-tech centrifuges to create fissionable material. These centrifuges are currently a blunt force approach in science to refining fissionable materials. The process remains extremely expensive, space consuming, and requires sophisticated equipment that is very difficult to purchase and assemble without drawing a lot of attention. In the future, this technology may be looked back on as rather primitive (Stage II Technology). All of these current roadblocks are subject to a breakthrough in technology.

Nuclear weapons are controlled by the Comprehensive Test Ban Treaty (CTBT), which has been signed by forty of the forty-one most developed nations of the world. The only member of the Nuclear Club that has refused to sign this Treaty is the United States of America. The US Senate rejected the treaty on October 13, 1999, and it has not reconsidered it for approval. The CTBT preamble makes it clear that one purpose of the treaty is to *constrain* (emphasis added) the development and qualitative improvement of nuclear weapons.

The responsibility for the control of our nuclear program in the United States is with the National Nuclear Security Administration. Its website proudly proclaims that its mission is to: "develop and deliver new or enhanced processes, [and] technologies capable to meet future US defense needs." The website goes on to state that it wants to "transform into a more agile enterprise with greater production integration, shorter cycle times in [sic] lower production in [sic] operating costs." To my untrained mind, this does not sound particularly comforting, especially since there seem to be typos in the section on cutting costs of operation and the logo for the operation is an old textbook figure of what we *used* to think the atom looked like.[114]

For the last few decades, many of the more advanced nations of the world have been independently pursuing what is referred to as "fourth generation" nuclear weapons. If the fourth generation nuclear weapons were ever to become a reality it would be the death of arms control. Why? Because these weapons do not require an atomic bomb reaction to begin the process of the fusion explosion, which is the basis for current nuclear weaponry. The need for fissionable material is based on the requirement that creating a nuclear fusion explosion requires lots of heat and pressure. To date, this level of heat and pressure can only be obtained by exploding an atomic bomb. This type of bomb requires a great deal of enriched uranium, which, if sufficiently concentrated, will result in a fission explosion.

The little-known, terrifying news is that the technology to commence the process of a fusion explosion without an atomic bomb has already been developed. One method is to utilize superlasers. But superlasers are only one of a number of promising new technologies that could result in a significant quantum change in the size, cost and technical simplicity

---

114 This is the same agency that recently made national headlines due to a scandal in its testing and training procedures for the caretakers of our nation's nuclear armament program. More recently it was disclosed that many of our nation's nuclear weapons under its supervision are buried in silos around the United States that are suffering from long-delayed critical capital and technological improvements.

of constructing future nuclear weapons.[115] I touched on the emerging promise of nanotechnology in Chapter Twelve. The potential of this technology stretches the imagination to the limit. In the context of nuclear weapons, this technology could be a means to produce nuclear weapons many, many times more powerful than our current most powerful nuclear bomb, yet so much smaller that they could be more easily deployed. In a chilling article on Youngsters.com about nanotech weapons technology (April 19, 2010), the author exuberantly stated that "these weapons can be produced in full compliance with the CTBT Test Ban Treaty." The author goes on to sound a comforting note -- these technologies will create "clean" nuclear weapons, meaning that they will not have the radioactive fallout of conventional nuclear weapons, which require as a trigger a fission-based atomic explosion. I assume the author sees all of this as good and real progress. In reading articles in the great technology journals available on the Internet such as Jane's Weapons of the World, you cannot help but be struck by the surreal feeling that there are an alarming number of experts so caught up in the possible advancement of these weapons that they are singularly unconscious of how these improvements will radically increase the risk of nuclear annihilation for all of us (think of the Manhattan Project and Rules Two and Three).[116]

It is not my intention to be an alarmist, nor do I wish to sound like the Chicken Little referred to in the Introduction, but none of the technological developments described above are clearly out of reach of a breakthrough development between now and the Far Horizon. In writing this section, I could not help but recall the Fermi paradox, "Where is everyone?" The inevitability of the development of relatively simple,

---

115 If this breakthrough allows for the inexpensive miniaturization of production of such bombs, these weapons will not need ICBMs to be delivered. They could be delivered to downtown Manhattan on a budget any decent terrorist organization could afford and with nothing more sophisticated than a Mayflower moving van or even a backpack or a handbag.

116 This absorption in the intellectual pursuit of a technological breakthrough in seeming utter disregard for its real-world implications is not a shortcoming solely of certain nuclear scientists; it is a characteristic of pioneers in many fields of scientific endeavor, including but not limited to AI.

cheap nuclear weapons may provide a clue to where everybody "went." In the course of only two centuries of technological development in the science of atomic matter, we are on the verge of finding simple ways to unlock the enormous energy of subatomic particles, which could produce weapons of mass destruction ten thousand, one hundred thousand or even a million times more powerful than the atomic bombs dropped on Japan. If it is the fate of any intelligent civilization to sooner or later stumble onto the discovery of the energy of the universe locked in at the atomic and subatomic levels of its particles, then that intelligence will also soon discover that there is enough energy in just a few ounces of water to blow their world apart. It would be as if God created a wonderful warehouse full of wobbly, unstable crates holding nitroglycerin in beautiful Waterford Crystal decanters and then set loose a group of very young, rambunctious children to grow up in the abundance of the warehouse until as teenagers one of them, or a robotic servant, knocked over a stack of crates or, more likely, tried to open up a crate to unlock its secrets. This may be the final answer to the Fermi paradox.

These are only a few forecasts of the future that will be driven by Radical Change. The topics addressed in this chapter reflect areas of particular concern to me, but you could choose others. One common thread, however, should be clear from all of these scenarios: The most destructive applications of future technologies will arise because we as a society choose to invest and support the development of the basic science and capabilities which make these applications possible. On our journey to the future, we need to be very mindful of this inherent paradox, because with the force of Radical Change, the stakes of technological progress will become much higher.

# Chapter Seventeen

## THE DEATH OF MANUFACTURING JOBS:
### The Workhorse of the Twenty-First Century

The importance of future job destruction in the manufacturing sector is sometimes minimized because the jobs in this sector have already suffered greatly from technological progress. But in fact, manufacturing still provides many well-paying jobs. There is even some good news for America here. The number of these jobs has been slowly increasing over the past few years. While this modest rebound is good news, it does not significantly address the degree of previous job loss in this sector. Despite this sad state of affairs, manufacturing jobs still provide an important part of the backbone supporting the health and well being of the American middle class. Today manufacturing jobs represent about 10 percent of all employment in America. This is down from over 30 percent of all employment in 1950.

The reasons for the historical decrease of employment in this sector are well known. To summarize, this sector has been seriously harmed by a number of factors, *all* of which have been made possible or are, at least, substantially empowered by advancing technologies. These factors include consolidation of many businesses, foreign competition,

offshoring of traditional manufacturing jobs, and the increasing introduction of robotics in the manufacturing process.[117]

We should expect continuing job losses in this sector due to all four
of these forces, although the competitive force of globalization is beginning to wane and opportunities for further significant consolidating are
far fewer. In the future, the magnitude of reduction of the remaining
manufacturing jobs will increasingly be due to the effects of the new
dimensions of technology, described in Part Two (particularly Chapter
Ten, "Technology Comes of Age"), and the growing transformation of
physical manufactured goods into knowledge (think of the smartphone
and 3-D printers described in Chapter Twelve, "Applied Knowledge").
We have seen this transition first and most clearly in the increasing role
of robots on assembly lines, but the other evolving dimensions of technology will become an increasing threat to many other manufacturing
functions and products.

I will begin by examining the future of robotics in the manufacturing process of the assembly line. To appreciate how rapidly advancing robotics, driven by AI, will affect these employment opportunities,
we need to return to the Industrial Revolution. With the improvement
of the automated assembly line by Henry Ford in approximately 1910,
the American worker's relationship to new technologies was forever
changed. Even without the benefit of robots, goods were produced, pack-
aged and shipped with a new breathtaking efficiency. America became
a leader in the technology of the automated assembly line, and manufacturing in America boomed, that is, until the rest of the world started
to catch up with the use of this technology. Robots have gradually taken
over the role of humans on many assembly lines, even in less-developed
countries such as Mexico, India and China. Today 80 percent of all airplane and over 60 percent of all automobile manufacturing functions in

---

117 The specific ways that new technologies have been instrumental in facilitating the
first three of these factors is beyond the scope of this book. Suffice it to say that without
powerful new technologies in telecommunications, data storage and processing, and
international financial transactions, etc., the scale and economic feasibility of each of
these developments would have been severely reduced or made uneconomical.

the United States are performed by robots. Assembling airplanes and cars in massive factories is a great environment for robots, but many manufacturing processes still do not lend themselves to the limitations of current robotic technology. The most significant obstacle that has delayed the development of Stage III robots is the inherent problem AI has with spatial and object recognition. The average workplace in much of American manufacturing does not fit nicely into the four constraints on AI/robotics described in Chapter Ten, "Technology Comes of Age." True, there are many repetitive functions on an assembly line that are a great place for robots to show off their stuff. In fact, robots now dominate most of those functions. However, much of what is now left for humans to do in the manufacturing process occurs in much less structured environments and requires a great deal more intelligence and flexibility than robots are currently thought capable of performing.

Until a few years ago, warehouse operations were considered to be part of this high ground. Warehouse operations require the workers to operate forklift trucks in tight quarters and have the ability to distinguish and not run over other workers (or other forklifts) while picking up the correct product or pallet and delivering it to the correct spot. For years this was far beyond the province of a robot. This high ground is now squarely in the flood plain of advancing computer/robotic capability. One of the keys to the success of robotics is to break down seemingly complicated tasks into simple, repetitive ones. As we know, this principle has been around for a long time. It was the key to the ability of machines to replace the skilled workers in the Age of the Guilds. If you reduce the tasks necessary to make a pair of shoes to a set of sufficiently simple, repetitive motions, machines can do it. And what a machine can do today is generations ahead of the equipment in the factories of the nineteenth and early twentieth centuries. Applying this principle to the seeming confusion of a busy warehouse took some time and a lot of creativity, but now it has been done. On a micro scale, a warehouse is actually very structured. Forklifts with sophisticated GPS and tracking systems in the floors can easily navigate the aisles, picking up pallets identified with bar codes. These robotic forklifts can also be programmed to deliver these pallets to the correct spot at precisely the right moment.

One application of this technology that is developing very rapidly is the use of robots in major distribution centers such as Crate & Barrel, Staples and Amazon. As the online retail business has soared, it has placed a premium on the ability to quickly, accurately and cheaply assemble and ship a customer's order. Traditionally, this was done by workers (called pickers) walking or riding down the miles of aisles in major distribution centers to gather each order. This process is heavily dependent on human labor, which makes it expensive, prone to error and very difficult to scale up. With the introduction of robots, the pickers now operate from fixed stations and the items in a customer's order are brought to the station by robots carrying pallets of the correct items. The entire process is computerized, so there is virtually no error in the orders (or annoyed customers who have to return incorrect orders), and most importantly in an industry obsessed with delivery times, the job is done much more rapidly. As you might expect, Amazon is a leader in this field. As of 2014 Amazon utilized over fifteen thousand robots in its distribution centers.

Three years ago, in 2012, Amazon bought Kiva Systems in North Reading, Massachusetts, one of the pioneering companies in this technology. Kiva is adamant that despite the success of Kiva robots in the distribution centers of America, this technology does not replace jobs, just drudgery. If you look (somewhat myopically) just at the jobs in the distribution centers, you can find factual support for this assertion. The weakness of this argument lies in the fact that it ignores the context of the true nature of job loss caused by this technology. Due to the astounding growth of online sales, distribution centers are expanding rapidly everywhere. This success and the urgency of staying ahead of the demand cycle have led businesses to invest in new technologies such as Kiva robots. With the increasingly competitive advantages in cost and speed of delivery created by this technology, Amazon and companies like it are growing rapidly at the expense of their competition. It is not surprising, therefore, that former pickers can be re-assigned to other jobs within these companies. In fact, it would be terribly disheartening if they were not. The job loss from this increase in productivity occurs in the retail sector such as in Borders, Barnes & Noble and smaller stores whose business has been decimated by this transition. As online retailing becomes cheaper and faster, its effects on these businesses will cause further net job loss in the retail industry.

The workers in these new state-of-the-art distribution centers should not, however, relax. Once technology begins to perform a function, it often rapidly improves. Amazon sponsored an incentive prize competition in May 2015 at the International Conference on Robotics and Automation, held in Seattle, Washington. The competitors were required to develop a self-automated robot that could (1) select a specified set of objects off a shelf containing twenty-five preselected items and (2) assemble and pack these items in a box ready for shipping. Not surprisingly, most of the objects and the shelves used in the test were modeled to resemble the actual field conditions of a typical Amazon distribution center. Just a few years ago, such a challenge to robotic capabilities would have been deemed unthinkable. Robots could not have distinguished between items such as a bag of potato chips and an Oreo cookie package (two of the twenty-five specified items). Robots also could not have mastered the subtlety of how to grasp these objects without creating lots of crumbs. With the very recent advances in deep learning, the barrier of object recognition was clearly breached by the technologies employed by the contestants. Also, the contestants were able to utilize a new generation of robots that are very good at picking (without crushing) the correct items. As amazing as this robotic performance was, the new technologies created by the contestants will not be immediately displacing workers in the assembly stations at Amazon nor warehouse workers anywhere else. This technology remains, at best, at Stage II. But remember a basic lesson of advancing technology: Once a technology can be applied to replace a function, two things are almost certain to follow. First, the technology will quickly become much better at performing the function. Second, the technology will perform the function at a rapidly declining cost. As these robots continue to improve in breaching the historic barriers of object recognition and flexibility, they will be able to replace those former pickers now working on the assembly stations in distribution centers such as Amazon's.

If robots can select, move, and pack goods in these facilities, they can be programmed to provide these functions in similar environments such as stocking shelves in the big-box stores of America's malls. Not only will these robots perform this function more cheaply and efficiently, but they can be equipped with smart Stage III voice recognition, speech and intelligence, so they can answer customer questions on where to find men's socks or garden hoses. Retailers may also use this as an opportunity for the robot to inform the customer of the great sales taking place in the store or, with GPS tracking to a smartphone, the specials in the very aisle in which the customer is standing. The robotic stock boy or girl of the future will also be able to tell the customer the marked-down price of the outdoor grill, etc. that was put on sale a few seconds ago.

Notwithstanding the advances in robotic warehouse and distribution operations, most remaining manufacturing jobs still provide a great deal of challenge for robots. Even on assembly lines, product types and methods of production are constantly changing. Historically, robotic applications have been programmed to accomplish only one very specific motion and are expensive to reprogram to perform other functions. If a robot is not programmed correctly, it can be outright dangerous to its coworkers. Because of these issues, the widespread application of robots and AI to "save" labor in this sector has been slow but steady. With the exponential increase in computer capacity, these problems are finally being effectively solved by much more intelligent and far less costly robots. As a result, robots are becoming very price-competitive at performing a whole new range of jobs more rapidly and with margins of error far more precise than humans are able to do. Some of these applications still remain in the research and development stage, but much of the capability and flexibility of the next generation of robots to be used in manufacturing (Stage III Technology) is already here.

Robots can now be taught to perform a new function simply by performing that function once with manual assistance: The robot learns to perform the task by having its "arm" guided by a human to do the correct movement. This could give rise to a new meaning for "hands-on" training. As these programs improve, robots can be inexpensively trained to do many tasks. Once a robot is trained, it will never forget and it will perform the task repetitively with a level of skill and speed that humans cannot achieve. Also, once a robot can perform a task it can teach another robot by simply connecting to its port.

One of the leaders in this field is Rethink Robotics, founded by Rodney Brooks, a pioneer in the field of robotic development. The original company he created (iRobot) became famous with the introduction in 2002 of the early stage Roomba vacuum cleaner. Technology has, however, far surpassed the relatively primitive AI that empowers the Roomba. In 2013, Rethink Robotics introduced an industrial robot, Baxter, which is (1) capable of being taught, by manual guidance, basic manufacturing skills, (2) user friendly and safe and (3) relatively inexpensive. Entry-level models begin as low as $25,000 per unit. Within the relatively near future, we should anticipate another generation of inexpensive and far more versatile and effective robots to become available.[118] This is the emergence of Stage III development in this technology, and as it evolves, it will rapidly develop many of the capabilities necessary to deal with the complexity of the remaining employment opportunities in the manufacturing sector. As these capabilities evolve, they will compete and eventually displace many of the remaining workers on the assembly lines of the world.

If there is a silver lining in this debacle, it may be the promise of robotic partnerships with humans. For the foreseeable future, robotic development will still lag far behind human capability to be creative,

---

118 In March 2015, Rethink introduced Sawyer, which sells for about $26,000 and can perform substantially more complicated functions than Baxter.

react to the unexpected or unforeseeable and be restrained by basic common sense. As a result, a number of new job opportunities are now being developed with robotic technologies that partner with humans. This has been the case in some areas of manufacturing that have recently begun to compete effectively against foreign competition. This has enabled American labor, at least temporarily, to turn the tide on the loss of manufacturing jobs to lower-cost foreign labor. As robotic technologies continue to improve, we should see an increasing growth in jobs that partner with advancing technologies to perform a function better, using the combined strengths of robots and humans. This may prove, however, to be only a temporary reprieve because advancing robotic capabilities will someday make many of these partnerships obsolete.

Those jobs that can be performed by increasingly sophisticated robotic applications, such as routine functions in manufacturing plants, are in for real trouble. For many of these traditional jobs, it is only a question of time before robotic technologies will develop to the point where they will be able to perform these functions better and more reliably than humans and for far less than the minimum wage. In fact, at about $25,000, Baxter and Sawyer are there now. Rodney Brooks believes this translates into about four to five dollars per hour in wages for any function Baxter or Sawyer can perform, which is already a lot of functions. At this point, only the Brakemen (unions, governmental regulation and work rules) will be left to protect these jobs. Even this layer of protection should not provide great comfort. Lawyers, surrounded by a staggering array of Brakemen, are slowly losing the battle with AI (LegalZoom, etc.) to perform some of their formerly protected functions. If this is the fate for lawyers, who will protect the manufacturing workers of America when robotic labor can perform a function at less than the minimum wage?[119] Will these workers become the twenty-first century version of the workhorse? For this growing segment of the remaining American middle class, the only recourse is to seek governmental assistance in the form of food stamps or other forms of governmental support. This is not a good scenario of the future, but, tragically, it is already happening.

Unfortunately for the American manufacturing workforce, it is being attacked on more than one front. In the longer run, a much more fundamental challenge to the health of employment opportunities in this sector may come from the increasing phenomenon of traditional, physical manufactured goods being replaced by technologies that are essentially knowledge. This new dimension of technology was discussed in Chapter Twelve, "Applied Knowledge" where I focused on one clear and popular aspect of this impact on manufacturing jobs, the development of the smartphone. Each of the products listed in Chart 12.1, "The U-Haul Trailer," supported a manufacturing industry. Some of these industries were small, such as those making calendars and calculators, but many were immense, such as the camera industry. Also, many of these products required the support of other products that were supplied by separate but related industries, such as film and film-developing products, photo albums, motion-picture projectors and screens. All of these manufactured products have been essentially eliminated along with the retail businesses that sold them and the service sector jobs that supported them. Taken together, this accounts for a lot of jobs.

The economic effects of the replacement of manufacturing jobs by the now myriad applications of the smartphone tend to be ignored or minimized by traditional economists. If the smartphone was the only instance of a knowledge-based technology replacing a function previously served by a physical machine, piece of equipment or gadget, this oversight would be understandable. However, in the future, human

---

119 The obvious answer is unions, but unions are also struggling as the manufacturing sector declines. This reference to the minimum wage is not meant to be an endorsement to keep the federal minimum wage low, certainly not at its current historic low. The challenge is much more fundamental. Whatever the level of the minimum wage, robotics will increasingly challenge the cost of workers performing these jobs.

creativity and ingenuity will continue to find new ways for knowledge-based technologies to replace many other functions that are now served by manufactured products. In fact, empowered by the new dimensions and capabilities of technology, we will increasingly look to knowledge-based technologies to solve our problems and satisfy our needs, rather than relying on expensive, inflexible equipment.

For example, other than an appeal to the radio and TV audiences' sense of adventure, why would news channels continue to utilize helicopters to report on traffic conditions when they could reformat the information available on Waze with far better results? An example of a more recent application of this capability to diminish our reliance on mechanical solutions to solve our problems may be useful. We all are tragically aware of the horrible loss, on March 8, 2014, of Malaysian Airlines flight 370 (carrying two hundred thirty-nine passengers) in a very remote area of the South China Sea. Because the flight had lost contact with air traffic control for hours of flying time, the search area soon ballooned to encompass over thirty-five thousand square miles. What followed was a virtually unprecedented and very well publicized effort involving billions of dollars of equipment (aircraft carriers, search-and-rescue vessels, aircraft and helicopters) and personnel from many countries, including the United States and China. What received very little attention was that a small group of volunteers organized a crowd-sourced computerized hunt to join the search by systematically scanning hundreds of thousands of satellite pictures of the crash site. This effort was staffed solely by volunteers, but it significantly added to the effort to locate debris floating on the surface of the sea. With current technology, it may have seemed to be only a well-intentioned effort by geeks to respond to a world tragedy, but in time this will become another effective way to carry out search-and-rescue operations without a massive outlay of capital, equipment and manpower. Of course there will always be a need for search-and-discovery vehicles and rescue personnel, just as there will always be a need for many traditional manufactured products such as cameras long after their function is essentially replaced by a knowledge-based technology. But this function will increasingly be performed by AI, not equipment.

I realize one could disagree about whether this example will truly result in an indirect but significant loss for the ship building industry. But this technology, especially as it matures, will dramatically affect how these mercy missions will be conducted in the future, with far less capital, equipment and machines, at far less cost, much more rapidly and with much less risk of further human loss or injury. The point is solely to challenge the reader with the fact that in our future we will increasingly solve our problems with knowledge-based technologies, not machines, and with this gradual shift, the need for certain manufactured products will decline. To date, there may not be many examples of loss of manufacturing jobs as dramatic as the demise of the camera industry due to the smartphone -- but the cumulative direct and indirect impact of thousands of separate technological innovations will significantly affect the role and position of manufacturing in the overall scale of our economy.

Despite the nearly endless applications of brilliant technologies to perform functions without physical equipment or machines, this trend can only go so far in destroying jobs. For example, even though the public has embraced the smartphone to take photos and videos, there remains a viable, if vastly reduced, market for traditional cameras. This is true for many of the other functions and products listed on Chart 12.1, "The U-Haul Trailer," as well. Over time, however, the obvious advantages of the knowledge-based technologies will continue to prevail, causing further decline in these industries.

There will, however, always be a need for lots of stuff such as lawn chairs that will never be useful in the form of pure knowledge. Unfortunately for manufacturing jobs, technology is relentless, creative and increasingly intelligent. As a result, in the future, manufacturing even traditional hard goods will not necessarily be done in the factories that marked the Industrial Revolution. One such technological breakthrough (described in Chapter Twelve) that will radically impact the manufacturing sector is the introduction of 3-D printers. This technology suffers from lots of early Stage II development problems. But very soon it will benefit from the evolution of technology described in Chapter Nine, "Accelerating Evolution." Currently, except for a few applications in jewelry making and in medicine, such as in the surgical implantation of stents, dentistry and prosthetics, 3-D printers remain more a toy than a threat to manufacturing. But, even so, it is a fascinating toy; in fact it's an amazing toy! So were mobile phones in the 1970s. This technology is, however, quickly finding its way into a lot of shop classes, the workshops of many start-up entrepreneurs, and into the research and development departments of many of America's and the world's manufacturing and retail companies. Currently, the 3-D printer can create incredibly esoteric and precise replicas of many of the things that can be reduced to algorithms, and this is just about everything that will ever exist. The technology is confronting challenges of (1) ramping up in scale and speed in the creation of a product, (2) the materials that can be utilized in the process, (3) the ability to create complex items such as electronic devices and (4) more mundane but very serious problems due to the inability to satisfy consumer preferences in appearance, touch, feel and yes, even taste and smell.

Today 3-D printers can produce elaborate ice sculptures for banquet centerpieces with a degree of precision and artistic brilliance far beyond the capabilities of any chef, no matter how talented. The beginnings of the production of muffins and pastries are not far off! In fact, there have been early attempts to create such products with 3-D printers. The real problem so far has not been in creating such products, but in making them look truly edible and taste good. As with many early-stage technologies these barriers will be overcome. Perhaps the son of Wolfgang Puck will team up with Nabisco and MakerBot, a leading manufacturer of 3-D printers, to create food products that can be made in the back of your local convenience store but will come in a variety, quality, and profusion far beyond those now available in even your best Italian or Jewish bakeries.[120]

Beyond the somewhat whimsical challenge to the bakers of the world, the potential of 3-D printers competing to produce virtually all the products now being manufactured and sold in America is not far off. It is very likely that we will have cost-effective Stage III 3-D printers by the time of the Near Horizon. They will create objects very fast and with stronger and much less expensive materials. There will be no racks of cut-rate seconds. These printers will make the products in one continuous process with virtually no human involvement other than a supervisor's help, create these products with a precision, efficiency and quality that current production lines will find difficult, if not impossible, to replicate and use synthetic substances that will be cheaper, stronger, lighter and containing few, if any, of the rare earths and other increasingly expensive raw materials they replaced. Because of the way these goods will be produced, these printers will eliminate the need for expensive shipping, handling, storage, transportation and security, which will dramatically reduce the cost of these products.

In the future, you will order most manufactured goods by simply going on the Internet to connect with your local Crate & Barrel (or whatever) website. There, you will order a product out of its 3-D catalogue. By the time you arrive at the store, the product will be created and brought by hand to the checkout counter. These may be the first hands to touch this product. These goods will be produced at convenient locations, such as local distribution centers or the back of the retail store. They will, therefore, reduce, if not eliminate, the need for costly transfers of goods from the factories to regional warehouse facilities or distribution centers and ultimately to the retail outlets all over America. The impact on jobs will be staggering, not only in manufacturing, but also in retail, warehousing, transportation, security and other support services.

---

120 Believe me, I love my local Jewish bakery, but this is one of the hard truths about our future (the price of progress).

This scenario sounded pretty far-fetched to me when I first considered it. But, the next time you are in Crate & Barrel, look around and see how many of the flatware, cups, ceramics, glasses, vases, kitchen utensils, knives, forks, and spoons could easily be replicated by a 3-D printer located in the rear of the store. This is not trouble just for Crate & Barrel, it is a long-term game changer for most manufacturing industries. Current research and development efforts are underway to develop 3-D printers that can produce very complicated goods such as electronic appliances (mixers, blenders, toasters, dishwashers and microwave ovens). You name it, someday before the Near Horizon, many of these products will be created in your neighborhood store or distribution center at significantly less than the cost of traditional manufacturing. Yes, this technology will create some new jobs. Someone will need to build and service and restock the 3-D printers, but the net job loss from the widespread use of this technology will be far-reaching and very threatening to this sector of the job market.

This book focuses primarily on the risks and challenges that are likely to occur in the period prior to the Near Horizon (2035). One technology, discussed previously, that may still be struggling to reach its full, and possibly frightening, potential by that date is nanotechnology. Despite this uncertainty, this technology needs to be addressed for a number of reasons. Virtually everyone, even the experts in the field, has underestimated the speed of development of many now fully accepted and integrated technologies that have dramatically changed our lives, such as computers, smartphones, the Internet, DNA sequencing, etc. Nanotechnology may be no exception. The promise of what nanotechnology could achieve is virtually incomprehensible. The technical problems that need to be resolved for this technology to become commonplace are extreme but not unsolvable. We already are producing many useful products by causing changes to the properties of common elements and materials at the nano level. In fact, exotic colors of glass have been produced for centuries by making changes at the nano level to gold by chemical means.

In an oversimplification, at the nano level many materials take on very different properties. Today, by working at this level, we have created a number of products that utilize these properties for our benefit. The sunscreens that work best, the polymer jackets that breathe and even your nonstick Teflon frying pans are the result of work in this field. Further research and development efforts will discover many additional products that can be created by manipulating matter at the atomic and subatomic levels. These efforts are commonly referred to as "top-down" approaches, since they require external, controlled intervention to create these products. This top-down approach essentially manipulates matter at the nanometer level (one billionth of a meter), sometimes with chemical or electrical stimulation and sometimes with atomic microscopes. Manipulating individual atoms or small groups of atoms at this level does not, however, scale up very well. As a result, creating objects on a useful scale would be like attempting to build a modern office tower with Lego blocks one billionth of a meter long.

The field of nanotechnology is, however, hard at work developing methods to allow matter at the atomic level to form into useful strands, combinations and structures drawn together by their own qualities (self-assembly). The carbon helix, the strongest form of material known, exists solely at the nano level, but if it could be subject to self-assembly, it would change the world. This is but one example of a technology that, some day in our future, may have extremely important uses in our macro world. This approach has much promise and many technical challenges. It is the science of attempting to use the forces and characteristics of matter at the nanometer scale to create useful products by themselves. This is referred to as the "bottom-up" approach. This is not wishful thinking: Small structures have already been created in this manner. More importantly, we know this process works because, in essence, it is the biological process used by the human body to facilitate human growth, health and development.

There are great hopes, promises and expectations for this technology, but it may also contain the possibility of massive, self-activated chain reactions at the nanometer level that could threaten our civilization. Nanotechnology was first described in *Engines of Creation*, by K. Eric Drexler.[121] The book caused a wave of somewhat incredulous excitement, but it was also the source of massive but misguided hysterical concern. I am sure, to Mr. Drexler's regret, his own work referred to the possible explosion of these self-actuating processes creating a "grey goo" (a wonderfully catchy phrase) that might engulf our civilization. This frightening image of grey goo immediately captured the public's imagination and has haunted serious nanotech efforts ever since. On the scale of what can go wrong in the world, the threat of self-replicating grey goo is far from a priority concern. On the other hand, the possibility that nanobots could be created to form operating platforms to create manufactured products is much more real. If this were to occur, these nanobots could build larger and larger structures that could soon reach a scale sufficient to produce virtually every useful product in our lives. If this level of science is ever obtained, say good bye to most of the remaining employment opportunities in traditional manufacturing and to a great deal of support and ancillary jobs as well.

It is fair to surmise that not all of the technological developments discussed above will be successful, but many of them will be. This is not good news for the long-term health of the manufacturing sector as a source of meaningful future employment opportunities. As these technologies become cheaper and more ubiquitous, their current and foreseeable applications are virtually limitless. The combined impact on this sector of the economy will be immense. By the time of the Near Horizon, the death of traditional manufacturing jobs as they were defined in the Industrial Revolution and the later part of the twentieth century may

---

121 K. Eric Drexler, *Engines of Creation: The Coming Era of Nanotechnology* (Anchor, 1986). The true founder might actually be considered Richard Feynman, who introduced the concept, but Drexler developed and popularized it.

be as imminent as the demise of the workhorse in the nineteenth century. The best hope for these jobs, at least in the near term, may be in the form of creative partnerships with emerging technologies. These partnerships will combine the remaining unique strengths of humans, creativity, flexibility and common sense, with the astounding growth of AI/robotic capabilities.

# Chapter Eighteen

## THE TRANSFORMATION OF THE SERVICE SECTOR:
### This Play Is Ready for Prime Time

In 2015 almost 70 percent of all employment opportunities in America were in the service sector. Since at least the middle of the nineteenth century, employment opportunities in this sector have provided the middle class with the livelihood and stable working environment necessary to maintain the American Dream. In the next twenty years, what should these workers expect in terms of job security and future job opportunity?

With the dramatic decrease in manufacturing jobs, the service sector provided a welcome source of new job creation. Growth of employment was due to a variety of factors. Although manufacturing jobs were lost, the new technologies (as traditional economic theory demands) created new jobs. Some of the new employment opportunities were created to repair and operate the new technologies, such as jobs done by computer technicians and copy-center operators. But with growing incomes and concentrations of wealth, there also was an increasing need for people in retail, personal service and professions such as health care, psychiatric and therapeutic counseling, banking, education, law, investment and financial counseling, and governmental services. The growth of new technologies also created new job classifications for employment opportunities that never previously existed, such as computer programmers.

With the increased affluence, there was also more demand for jobs in the hospitality, home care (landscaping and cleaning), restaurant/fast food, entertainment, security, travel and recreation industries.

Until fairly recently, technology did not have the requisite capability to seriously challenge most service sector jobs. Even the simplest jobs in this sector generally require a level of verbal skills and comprehension, mobility, spatial recognition, flexibility, creativity, common sense and/or acceptance by the general public that simply did not exist in the early days of computer/robotic development. Slowly, this has begun to change. In the latter part of the twentieth century, some traditional service positions such as telephone operators, payroll clerks and bookkeepers began to be replaced by technology. These early job losses occurred for functions that were repetitive, relatively unskilled, and required minor interaction with people. Even so, many of these early applications of technology met with stiff resistance by the public because they were, at best, Stage II Technologies. It wasn't their time to "open on Broadway." For example, the early experiment by banks to provide bill-paying services by phone and/or computer failed because the technology simply wasn't sufficiently intelligent, inexpensive or flexible to meet the needs of consumers and/or the very institutions that initially chose to utilize the technology. It is instructive to note that while this technology initially failed, within a few years it was back. It had proceeded through an acceleration of technological evolution and reached Stage III. It is now employed by an ever-increasing number of Americans, saving them a lot of time and frustration and saving financial institutions and businesses lots of money by eliminating the departments (and the employees) that used to collect paper bills and checks and process them for deposit. This one technological development, when it was finally ready to be implemented, created tremendous job loss.

In the service sector, there are many readily identifiable job functions that computer intelligence has struggled to replace. One fundamental ability, necessary in virtually every service sector job, is the capacity to communicate with people with a reasonable level of intelligence and comprehension. For many years, voice recognition was a failed techno-logical promise, much like cold fusion. Beginning with the telephone companies that first forced us to use the dubious automated voice recognition systems to obtain telephone numbers by dialing 411, this technology was (and remains) so bad that it leaves us with the impression that computer intelligence will never replace real operators or, in fact, just about anyone else who speaks English or any other language. In fact, today operators *still* respond to almost all of our calls, just not after the first ring. Now, the operators come on live, but only after we yell, "Operator!" when the computerized voice system invariably fails. To make matters even worse, to the extent that you need human assistance (to override the system, which is my default mode), the assistant is in India or in some other distant, inexpensive labor pool and speaks English as, at best, a second or third language. This function has been outsourced, which is another by-product of technology. Our frustration with this technology is not only with telephone directory "assistance" but also with all the automated voice recognition systems that have been forced upon us by PIT.

Notwithstanding these problems, automated voice answering switch-boards and complaint centers, automated and unwanted phone calls urging you to buy credit cards, etc. are all the rage, and we should antici-pate a great deal more in our future. If a company can afford the capi-tal, it will protect itself with a screen of automated systems to "serve" your needs more cheaply than ever before. This is not a phenomenon limited to automated voice activated systems. Technology started there because it could, but it is just picking up speed. Due to the basic eco-nomic savings, we will continue to be "encouraged" to utilize Stage II Technologies to replace service sector employees, even if the technolo-gies do not work very well. One example is the growing use of automated checkout counters in many stores, such as CVS. You probably are famil-iar with this experience -- I hope it went better for you than it did for me. The technology is so bad that the very friendly assistant, there to help the technologically challenged, could have checked me out faster by acting as a cashier. But the people at CVS are no fools. The engineers who created this self-checkout Stage II Technology are hard at work finding easier and better ways to help technology klutzes, like me, bag their own toiletries without human assistance. Within a few years, CVS and the rest of the world will achieve Stage III Technology in this area. I will approach a checkout station equipped with voice and facial recognition, and with voice capability and AI. Using facial recognition, "Erodita" will greet me with a cheery "Hello, Dan" (if I have used a credit card in *any* CVS before), inform me of a few things on sale, and ask me if I need any of the things I usually buy but that are not in my cart today. Erodita will explain exactly how to remove my purchases and put them on the moving conveyor belt that brings the purchases to a self-bagging area. On the way, all of my purchases will be automatically scanned with barcodes or identified by enhanced object recognition that will result in a very accurate, employee error- and theft-free process that will be far faster than even the best cashier. Soon there will be very few cashiers and an assistant and a supervisor per shift. The humans will be there to deal with the inevitable consumer complaints and the problems associated with someone dropping a glass jar on the floor, etc.

Because voice recognition and speech are essentially knowledge-based technologies, they are evolving exponentially. Voice recognition that really works is almost here. Soon, except for those who (1) have spent an enormous effort in learning to type faster than they can speak, (2) are literate in three or four computer languages and (3) have a command of how to navigate the complex architecture of the laptop and the Internet, voice recognition will replace the keyboards on many of our computers, smartphones and iPads. As a layperson attending numerous conferences with brilliant geeks[122] of all flavors of the technological

---

122 Having used the term before, it is important to clarify that, for me, the term "geek" is not meant to be unflattering. I wish I were one, but it isn't going to happen. Years ago, one of my daughters (age ten) visited me at my office just after my law firm had installed state-of-the-art computers on every lawyer's desk. Her greeting to me while staring at my resplendent new computer was, "Don't even think of telling me you know how to use this thing!"

rainbow, I have observed an odd myopia in their attitude toward using voice recognition as a means to interface with the Internet.[123] These experts have, by definition, mastered the technical skills of utilizing the keyboard to communicate with the computer to such a remarkable level of proficiency that it has become second nature to them. In fact, many geeks are proud of how skilled they have become and get defensive that anyone would invent or recommend a new technology that would make their hard-earned skills relatively unnecessary or even useless. It is reminiscent of the revolution in skiing when the new generation of metal skis and parallel skiing replaced the old wooden Telemark skis and leather ski boots secured with long thongs. A hard-core group of traditionalists kept Telemark skiing alive for awhile, but it was a short while.

The introduction of miniature computers, whether in the form of wristwatches, "smart" clothing or otherwise, may force this issue to resolution because a keyboard for these forms of technology is not an option. This technology would also eliminate the very dangerous habit of some to text messages when they should not, like while driving. The quality of voice recognition and computer intelligence to process verbal instructions will soon be so advanced as to make the physical limitations of the keyboard obvious to all but the most hardened geek.[124] Very soon, we will be able to talk to our computer, tell it to go to Word, write a letter, send a photo and tell us why it isn't working or how to use any application on the Internet or, for that matter, the laptop itself, all by voice command. This capability may even allow us to reduce our trips to the Apple Genius Bar. As technology allows us effortlessly to control and utilize the applications on the Internet (and the countless new ones being developed), it will reduce or eliminate countless hours of frustration now spent trying to fix our computers by typing in instructions and,

---

123 The public reaction to Apple's recent introduction of Echo will provide an interesting insight into the strength of our reservation to go "hands free" with computers.

124 While some experts (particularly the linguists and the well-educated) will quarrel with these technological developments, voice-activated computer integration will also provide a boon to the significant portion of the world's people who increasingly have access to the Internet but who cannot read or write.

at least for my generation, seeking human assistance when all else seems hopeless. As voice recognition and speech capability improve, they will demolish one of the major barriers to the replacement of service sector jobs by knowledge-based technologies.

No matter how well a robot can speak or understand a language, to replace most jobs in the service sector, robots will also need to become a lot smarter than Siri. Unfortunately for jobs in the service sector, this ability is evolving very fast as well. This dimension of new technologies was briefly discussed in Chapter Ten, "Technology Comes of Age." In 1997, Deep Blue became the best chess player in the world by defeating the then world champion, Garry Kasparov. By 2011, IBM Watson dominated the world of trivial knowledge by soundly defeating Brad Rutter and Ken Jennings, the then reigning world champions in the game of "Jeopardy." Watson's performance in dominating a game such as "Jeopardy" captured the attention of the world. It was an obvious demonstration of the growing ability of AI to begin to "think" like a human. What was far less apparent but profoundly more revolutionary about Watson's performance was the manner in which Watson got so smart. Historically, everything a computer knew, everything it was capable of processing in its algorithmic programs, had to be developed by human beings painstakingly writing the appropriate programs that allowed the computer to function. This was a major constraint in developing computers capable of tackling complex tasks or responding to more abstract concepts. To become proficient at a game such as "Jeopardy" requires the accumulation of a mind-boggling amount of often trivial information. As a practical matter, this information base could not be provided by individual computer programs created by humans. Watson was not, however, programmed with this information. Watson "learned" this information by processing literally thousands of digitized sources of information, such as absorbing everything written on Wikipedia in just a few moments of computer time. The next generation of AI following IBM Watson has significantly advanced the ability of computers to acquire areas of knowledge by themselves. This new area of technological development is now referred to by a number of names, such as "deep learning" or "cognitive thinking." This field is one of the most rapidly expanding areas of computer development because it relies on the strength of massive amounts of computer power to assimilate information and to process this information by word association and probability analysis into useful working knowledge. The process of deep learning by computers is fundamentally the same process that we as humans use to learn everything from birth. The possibilities for this technology to advance the ability of computers to think like humans are astounding. One surprising area of job loss that this technology may create will be in the field of computer programming. With deep learning, the computer will, in effect, program itself.[125]

The potential for the process of deep learning techniques to revolutionize the power and capabilities of computers is just beginning to be explored. Recently, a computer was "taught" to recognize a cat by digesting hundreds of thousands of pictures of cats contained on social media. This sounds very cumbersome until you consider the only alternative -- writing an algorithm that captures the essence of "catness." Because the computational power of computers will increase, at least for the next decade, in accordance with Moore's law, deep learning provides enormous promise for a new generation of computers that are much smarter and, therefore, exponentially more versatile and useful than those we have at present. In retrospect, this development may be viewed as a paradigm shift, as predicted by Kurzweil, enabling another evolutionary step forward in the process of the Law of Accelerating Returns (LOAR).

As discussed previously, Watson has now been reprogrammed to provide a new powerful intelligence that contains virtually all of the diagnostic skills known to modern medicine. This is not as much of a challenge as you might think; consider that Watson has already learned enough of the world's information and knowledge to beat two of the

---

125 Remember, technology is amoral -- it is as happy at replacing the new high-tech jobs it just created, such as computer programming, as it is replacing the mind-numbing drudgery of much manual labor.

greatest "Jeopardy" competitors ever. If Watson can be programmed to learn all of that information, it can easily learn more than any human being could learn in medical school and in a medical practice. Watson now serves as a gigantic platform that could provide nearly instantaneous diagnostic abilities simultaneously to thousands of people around the world at very little cost. Certainly those in the Third World who could potentially die any day from undiagnosed diseases would benefit greatly from Watson. Recently there have been significant developments of "Lab on a Chip," technologies first pioneered by Novartis. Utilizing this technology, technicians can collect and analyze bodily fluids in a simple cost-effective manner. Soon this technology will allow relatively untrained technicians to obtain medical information from patients in remote areas of underdeveloped countries and transfer this information to trained physicians in real time using something as ubiquitous as a modified iPhone. When this is feasible, one of the most serious remaining impediments to a global step forward in the quality of health care in the underdeveloped world will become the lack of qualified professionals to use this diagnostic tool to prescribe a course of treatment.[126] Dr. Watson could fill this void and provide high-quality, affordable, diagnostic health care around the world. The Dr. Watson technology is actually now being used to *assist* doctors, but, as discussed in Chapter Ten, "Technology Comes of Age," the medical Brakemen are lurking in the background. The American Medical Association, as well as legal, regulatory, licensing, and other restraints on the practice of medicine, will combine to ensure that Watson remains an *assistant*, a smart intern that the medical profession hopes will never graduate. As a result, Watson is not about to go solo and practice medicine around the world, no matter how desperate the need nor how good and inexpensive the technology may become. However, singling out the medical overseers of our welfare for retarding progress in health care is a bit unfair. There are

---

126 Actually the shortage of qualified physicians is already a world crisis even in developed nations. But this crisis, especially in Third World countries, is going to become much worse.

real and serious concerns about AI fulfilling this need even when there are very limited alternatives.[127] Part of our reluctance to embrace the full capability of this technology rests in our deep and inherent distrust in relying on a nonhuman judgment in a field so associated with very trained personal care. As discussed in Chapter Eleven, "Comfort with Computers," these attitudes are, however, changing rather rapidly.

As this technology gets better and better, and as public acceptance of relying on medical advice from AI increases, Watson will start to compete with health-care assistants, paramedics, nurses, support staff and, someday, doctors. The increasing application of AI to this field will also encourage similar applications in many other fields of human care and support, such as elder care, daycare, physical and drug rehabilitation, religious support, mental-health counseling and legal and financial advice, which have historically been solely the province of humans. Corporate America is obviously attuned to these developments. Bank of America has recently entered into a joint venture with IBM to utilize the Watson technology, and it's not to improve Bank of America's contribution to global health.

What about dealing with your local, state or federal government? How has your luck been running lately in dealing with your local office of the Department of Motor Vehicles? Of course, every governmental agency (actually just about every anything) now has a website that purports to provide automated "service." This is supposed to eliminate most trips to visit a local governmental office or the need to speak to a government employee. Some of the websites are better than others, but all are PIT. All of this "service" is the twenty-first century equivalent of Kafka's *Castle*[128] without the human touch. But soon this assistance will work very

127 We have had a long and painful experience with this dilemma in another area of medicine -- the lengthy and expensive process of drug approval even for drugs promising relief for incurable and fatal diseases.

128 *The Castle* is a novel written by Franz Kafka in 1922, which describes one man's fruitless struggle with bureaucracy. The protagonist (K) spends his lifetime seeking permission to live in his village, only to hear from the bureaucrats in the castle (while on his death bed) that his "legal claim to live in the village is not valid," but due to extenuating circumstances he may continue to live and work there.

well. When this capability arrives, it will be available simply by having a conversation with your smartphone, laptop or wristwatch, without the problems that are inevitable in dealing with an employee who suffers from a bad attitude, a lack of training, a lack of courtesy, or the "I hate my job" syndrome. We're not talking about decades for this technology to become very cheap and very good; it will be a matter of years. When it does, but for the Brakemen, there are going to be a lot more candidates for job elimination, destruction or obsolescence in the service sector.

So far in this chapter I have explored how the new, smarter and more articulate technologies of the future will directly replace workers that now perform service sector functions. As the next generation of computers that learn in essentially the same manner as humans is developed, more and more traditional service positions such as teachers, lawyers and doctors will face very stiff competition for at least some of the services that they have traditionally supplied.

Because these new technologies are so astounding, they may appear to constitute a new *form* of job loss, because workers performing functions requiring intelligence have never before feared replacement by a machine. However, on a more fundamental basis, this form of job loss by new technologies is no different than the steam hammer replacing John Henry -- that is, the machine directly competed with and ultimately replaced the worker.

Historically, there is, however, another form of job loss that, with the new dimensions of technology in the twenty-first century, will increasingly reduce employment opportunities, particularly in the service sector. Technology can sometimes disrupt an entire industry rather than compete with humans to perform a specific task better and more cheaply. Using an example from history may clarify this point. One of the great technological inventions in the Industrial Revolution was the introduction of robots to build automobiles. However, many years earlier, a new technology (the automobile) replaced nearly the entire industry that manufactured horse-drawn carriages. This caused tremendous loss of jobs for workers building carriages, but not because technology created a better and cheaper way to build carriages; it eliminated the need for carriages.

Today with the increasing capabilities of smart technologies, we are seeing this form of job loss increase dramatically in the service sector. For example, when toll cameras replaced toll collectors, it was obvious that a new technology had replaced the workers. When Borders went bankrupt, the connection of the resulting job loss to a new technology was less obvious -- however, the job loss was no less real. The clerks at Borders or Blockbuster were *not* replaced by robots -- the whole industry was replaced by a new technology.

There are many recent examples of this form of job loss in the service sector. Travel agents (Kayak, Travelocity), accountants (TurboTax), lawyers (LegalZoom), employees at small retail outlets (online retailing), etc., represent in the aggregate a great many jobs. As technologies become smarter and more flexible, the creative energies of the next generation of entrepreneurs will find many more functions that can be better and more cheaply performed by the application of AI. Given some of the surprising new applications of advancing technologies, it is somewhat difficult to predict which traditional service sector function will be the next major casualty, but knowledge-based solutions to traditional service sector functions will grow dramatically in the twenty-first century. In fact, one major service sector employer -- the US Post Office -- has already essentially been displaced by new technologies such as email, texting, Facebook and Twitter. Letter writing is now a lost art; for anyone under forty it is not even an option. Without the economic infusion of the dubious contribution of junk mail, the postal delivery system would economically collapse. Many say it already has. However, due to the efforts of the Brakemen and the enormous social disruption that will occur as this institution is dismantled, it will be decades before there will be significant job loss in this government function. However, when it occurs, it will not be because new technologies (such as drones) found better ways to deliver letters; it will occur because new technologies eliminated the *need* to send letters. This form of job loss will increasingly reshape the service sector of the future. Yes, these new technologies will create some new jobs, many of which will be more fulfilling and better paying than the jobs they replaced, but these technologies will also eliminate many more employment opportunities than they create.

Even when new technologies do not eliminate or reduce the *net* number of jobs in an industry, these new technologies are restructuring the workforce in ways that may have unintended consequences. We have seen this effect on the profession of those that gather, write, and report the news in the newspaper industry. With the demise of many newspapers, much of this function is now done by independent reporters and alternative sources of news. While this may provide a fresh breath of air in an old industry, it has also contributed to a level of destabilization of this workforce. These independent contractors do not participate in employer-sponsored workmen's compensation, health care, retirement plans, sick leave, maternity and paternity leave programs or payroll withholding. This may be the inevitable dimension in the transition of service sector functions, but we need to be prepared for its side effects because there will be a lot more of these transitions coming. As technologies become smarter, they will provide increasing opportunities for people to work part time as independent contractors. The disruption that Uber is causing to the taxi industry is just one example. The net effect of this type of transition can be debated, but one effect is clear -- the workforce increasingly today and certainly in the future will be less structured and more difficult to quantify, and reforms such as health-care insurance, workmen's compensation, maternity and paternity leave, sick time, retirement planning, social security and income tax withholding are all faced with new challenges. These developments are not isolated flukes in the service sector. Airbnb and HomeAway have created similar but less raucous disruptions to the hotel and housing industries, and Angie's List and Amazon Home Services have had a similar impact on home services.

Despite these reservations, all of these new technologies provide much greater choices and value to the consumer. The reportable GNP from these alternative services may be less, but our lives are enriched. This dichotomy of new technologies bringing great benefit, but also disruption and stress on our established systems of social order and welfare is not new. It is in fact the inevitable price of progress.

Before I review some other obvious candidates for job elimination, I will examine in greater detail the last bastion of support for those who believe that technological progress will never replace many jobs in this sector. We have been subtly indoctrinated since birth to believe that there is something truly unique about the *human dimension* in service sector jobs. The warmth, trust and satisfaction of dealing with another human being and the intuitive ability of humans to understand fashion, taste, art, poetry, music, and the emotions and prejudices of others are felt by many to be the essence and certainly the exclusive province of humans. But in the future, this may no longer be true. Certainly computers will never possess or even be able to mimic these skills completely, at least not before the Near Horizon. But even now, computers can create beautiful music, poetry and art and prepare news reports of the results of sporting events and detailed investment reports on the performance of a stock or a sector of the stock market. Computers can even sense your mood by the sound of your voice (as I found out with Siri). In the not-very-distant future, AI will have the capacity to relate to human beings interactively with a soothing voice, an intelligent response, and an appreciation of many of the most subtle of human qualities, like detecting whether a person is lying. Most of these skills exist or are in the research and development stage. Within the next decade, robots will be developed with AI levels that will exceed the abilities of humans in many of these areas. This is not the science fiction of the recent Spike Jonze movie *Her*; the emotion I felt when Siri gave me some attitude was real. The advertisement a few years ago about the driver who talked to his automobile dashboard computer to get directions and restaurant tips and then started flirting with his dashboard rang a bell for many Americans. Come on, wouldn't you feel a little stir if a soothing dashboard voice distracted you with personal comments while you are stuck in heavy traffic?

Despite the amazing advances that will occur very shortly in technology, we should not underestimate the degree to which our sense of human uniqueness is fundamentally ingrained in all of us. Notwithstanding the changes in our attitudes predicted in Chapter Eleven, "Comfort with Computers," we form our self-image very early in our development. Members of my generation, in particular, recognize and react to nonhuman intelligence as not only foreign, but also as profoundly unsettling.

As discussed earlier, another factor that subtly reinforces our attitudes about the inherent inferiority of AI is the constant introduction of new products and services that suffer from PIT. Unfortunately PIT is here to stay. No matter how good technology gets, someone will want to be the first to introduce some new application of AI to replace a previously irreplaceable human skill or function. Our patience with the insult to our common sense and willingness to experiment with untested new PIT is not inexhaustible, but it is close. We will always be fascinated with new toys, whether they are primitive Android wristwatches, Siri, or foreign language translation systems.[129] As technologies improve, our relationship with these advanced intelligent technologies will mature and so will our patience with the inevitable irritation of PIT. When our grandchildren experience PIT, it will not infuriate and frustrate them in the same way it gets to us. My grandchildren will come to view my exasperation with computers with compassion and a wry smile.

As we journey to the Near Horizon, it will become increasingly clear that while our reservations about computers are great, we are teachable. When technologies advance to Stage III and Stage IV and work really well, we will get it, and we will love them. Perhaps an anecdote may best capture this process of acceptance best. Assume you live in New York and love the theater. You have attended live opening-night

---

129 Remember the excitement of your first mobile phone or laptop computer? Remember how well it worked?

performances for years. Due to the economics, the plays are never fully rehearsed before opening on Broadway. They are full of bugs and annoying glitches. You are tired of paying $150 when all you see is what seems like an on-stage rehearsal. One day, a friend and fellow theater fan says, "Come with me to see this new play." You feel like saying, "Screw you," and although your response is more gracious, it imparts the same message. He replies, "But this play has been performed in Boston and Philadelphia, it is ready for prime time! And it will only cost you twenty bucks!" You think, "Perhaps I was a little too hasty." You go and you are hooked.

Even though our feelings about AI are very ingrained in all of us, they are not genetic traits. As technology improves, these attitudes will change, and when they change, they will change radically. We are in this process now, even if we don't fully realize the extent of the transformation that has already occurred in just two generations. By suggesting that there is an inherent prejudice in all of us to maintain a distance from computers, I'm not accusing those who still feel that way of being modern-day Luddites. Human *perception* of the acceptability of future technologies that replace service sector jobs will be at least *as* important as whether those technologies actually work well. Remember, the Cannonball Express is roaring forward, and the rate of improvements in AI may exceed the bounds of our ability to acclimate to our new environment. The computer technology that you hate today may become your favorite tomorrow. You might not fall in love with your computer as Theodore did in the movie *Her* but you just might grow to like "her," and you certainly will not be able to live without her. For many, the addiction to certain technologies, such as checking for new text messages every few seconds, is already very prevalent.[130]

---

130 In the last several years, a number of rehab facilities have been built in the United States to treat the new victims of this "disease." See *The Boston Globe*, front page, January 13, 2015, "Start to Regain Control of Your Life." On February 6, 2015, NBC Nightly News reported the results of a new survey that found that the average New Yorker checked his or her smartphone over two hundred times a day. That is the equivalent of about three hours per day!

We have spent a great deal of time examining voice recognition and speech and intelligent robots because if you combine very good voice recognition and speech with increasing AI (exhibited by, for example, a Stage III successor to IBM Watson), you will have an integrated, voice-activated system that will come, at least, close to your average satisfaction level with many current human service sector experiences (albeit many of these current experiences do not establish a very high bar). The ubiquitous application of this technological advance is only a few years away, and when it arrives it will only get exponentially better. What job in the service sector would then be safe from destruction? I have identified below a few jobs that would be "safe," at least until the Near Horizon. It is not a cheery list.

Using the new, improved definition of what technology can do well, and the current trends in technology, as described previously, let me try to summarize the path of job loss and creation in the service sector of the future. Who will be the Winners and the Losers? I will start by identifying certain Winners in the service sector of the Near Horizon. These Winners include:

- housecleaners, maids, etc. at hotels, wealthy homes, and commercial and retail space
- waiters, people who "bus" tables, kitchen staff
- landscapers
- garbage collectors
- truck and cab drivers (although driverless cars may be closer than we think)
- support jobs in the entertainment, hospitality, and travel industries
- repair and service personnel

These will be some of the jobs that will be the last bastions of safety from technological replacement.[131] This is not a happy high ground for the future of the service sector or the health of the American working class. Even here, technology is making constant inroads. Waste Management has worked hard in many municipalities to standardize garbage and recycling cans and to develop mechanized arms to pick up the cans and dump the contents into their shiny new dump trucks. This is an industry that will do well in the future. Conspicuous consumption of the wealthy comes at the price of lots of trash. Overall, all of these industries should thrive and, even with advanced robotic technologies, these functions will be very hard to replace with robots. Also, there isn't a lot of money in replacing these jobs, so there is not a great deal of incentive to develop these robotic capabilities.

Applying the revised definition of AI capabilities to other parts of the service sector produces some frightening results in the nature and magnitude of future unemployment -- particularly for many jobs that have been long thought to be solely the province of human labor. In fact, the more skilled a job is -- as long as it does not truly challenge the barriers described in Chapter Ten, "Technology Comes of Age" -- the more the job is at risk of technology's relentless pursuit. Why? In part, because there is more money in eliminating these more sophisticated, higher-paying jobs. It is, therefore, no accident that AI has already made great strides in trading stock, giving financial investment advice and replacing legal research and factual document review and discovery. These functions previously provided skilled, high-paying jobs for stockbrokers, investment analysts, young lawyers and paralegals, so replacing these jobs with inexpensive Stage III Technologies *that work well* has resulted in AI proliferating very quickly in these fields.

---

131  Martin Ford, *Rise of the Robots: Technology and the Threat of a Jobless Future* (Basic Books, 2015). In this recently released book, Martin Ford, author of *The Lights in the Tunnel: Automation, Accelerating Technology and the Economy of the Future* (Acculant Publishing, 2009), argues that new technologies will also make major inroads into low-paying jobs such as cooking hamburgers in the fast food industry. This may occur, in which case the pressure on the service sector will be even worse.

In Chapter Two I referred to the Oxford Report, which analyzed the impact of technology on employment in the future and concluded that over 47 percent of current employment opportunities could be replaced by technology within the next ten to twenty years. Most of these jobs were in the service sector. The researchers who worked on the study painstakingly reviewed over seven hundred job classifications, using a very sophisticated rating system to determine the probability that advancing technologies could perform that function. The findings of the report are very troubling. What is even more troubling is what the Oxford study did not consider. In analyzing job loss, the study did not anticipate any breakthrough technologies that might significantly expand the scope of employment categories that could be replaced by technology. While there is an element of guesswork in attempting to forecast which technologies, such as voice recognition, deep learning and cognitive thinking, might advance dramatically, one or more certainly will do so.

The study also did not anticipate the job loss that occurs when technology creates a knowledge-based advance that decimates an entire industry, such as the camera industry, newspaper publishing or the post office. As the Internet replaced the function of the newspaper business, there were many service sector employees, such as editors, newsroom staff, salespeople and service and distribution personnel, who lost their jobs. But if you examined any of these job classifications using the methodology of this study, none of these jobs would be candidates for replacement. A similar observation could be made about the camera industry or the US Post Office.

On our journey to the Near Horizon, advancing technologies will dramatically attack and breach many of the remaining barriers to existing jobs in the service sector. To better appreciate this issue, it may be useful to explore how a combination of existing and clearly anticipated developments in computer capability could combine to replace a service sector job now considered to be a mainstay of the middle class. It is a job that also definitely requires the human dimension: the position of an elementary school teacher. This job poses some of the hardest barriers for technology to surmount. If technology can effectively meet these challenges, or, as will be suggested here, a radical partnership of technology and humans can do so, then partnerships such as these will supplant or dramatically decrease and certainly redefine a very significant portion of our current service sector jobs before we reach the Near Horizon.

Very soon, we will have the technology to create a new classroom.[132] It could be in your kitchen, but more likely it will still be down the street in a school where your child will gather with other children to learn social skills and establish interpersonal relationships while receiving an education. This education will be provided, however, in large part by a hologram or by an interactive 3-D image on a mobile base (a robot). I will name the teacher Kay in honor of my mother, Kay Sullivan, who was a wonderful, loving little old schoolteacher who taught in a schoolhouse with four rooms, four teachers and eight grades. She had the misfortune of having one particularly difficult student for three years.[133] Kay will start the class by saying hello to every student by his or her first name (using facial recognition), reminding Johnny he promised to bring an apple to school today, and cracking a few jokes about the weather. Kay will present a lesson with state-of-the-art slide shows (who remembers where the term *slide show* originated?) with information taken from a worldwide database a moment before entering the classroom. The children will ask questions, and the teacher will answer more brilliantly than any human teacher possibly could. Instructing and interacting with chil-

---

132 Actually, most of this technology already exists and functions very well. The increasing popularity and use of educational websites such as the Kahn Academy and/or open-source academic courses such as the ones offered by MIT and virtually every other university demonstrate the effectiveness of these technologies. The greatest barriers to the widespread introduction of these technologies into our primary educational systems will, therefore, not be technical. The real barriers are the entrenched forces of politics, teachers unions and politicians in protecting these jobs, and parents' and children's expectations of the educational experience, which they believe must be based on human interactions.

133 My mother did not flunk me. When I entered first grade, she was the teacher for the first and second grade. When I entered fourth grade, to my dismay she was transferred to teach third and fourth grade.

dren will be, pardon the pun, child's play, for a "mind" that dominated the world's best players at "Jeopardy" in 2011. But in the classroom of 2035, the intelligence of the teacher will be approximately a thousand times greater (Moore's doublings) than Watson's.[134] When the class is over, Kay will send an email to every student's laptop reviewing today's lesson. It will contain useful information gained from the students' questions and the discussion session in the classroom, as well as a personalized section based on what a particular student said in class, his/her answers to the previous day's homework submitted via Internet last night at eleven (Johnny was a bad boy), and the student's previous experiences in this class. The email will contain a personal set of recommendations for what the student should do before the next class. Kay will remember every bit of all these instructions the next time she and Johnny meet. On the way out, Kay will take the apple from Johnny and thank him appropriately.

Does this sound like science fiction? It isn't. Most of this technology already exists, and the rest is coming soon. Remember the limitations of the applications of robotics and AI described in Chapter Ten. The classroom is a perfect environment for robotics, and the curriculum is a perfect "chess board" for advanced AI to dominate. There will, of course, remain a need for the skills of a human. Someone will need to monitor the children and the classroom for unexpected behavior and events, such as the hyperactive child, classroom antics and the inevitable spills and other messes created by children. This teacher's assistant needs to be an educated, sensitive and thoughtful *human* being. The assistant will need to be well trained and, in particular, to be very aware of Kay's strengths and weaknesses. To be very good at this job does not, however, require a college degree. A year or two in a technical school or a community college may be more effective.

---

134 More correctly, the teacher will have approximately a thousand times the computer capacity of the Watson of 2011. Since we do not have clear objective standards to measure the growth of the capabilities of advancing AI, it is uncertain how this will affect the intelligence of a robotic teacher in 2035, but one thing is certain – "she" will be a good deal smarter.

There will always be a need for bright, creative teachers.[135] Someone has to set and reset the basic curriculum and materials for each class. A human presence needs to comfort and be there for the child in distress. And a human being better show up at the PTA meetings to deal with Johnny's parents' concern that Johnny does not seem to be on his way to Harvard. Additionally children will always need to learn how to socialize and get along with others and to learn that sticking a wad of bubble gum in a classmate's hair is not acceptable. We still must teach our children how to express anger and affection appropriately and learn to share and establish boundaries that are based on respect, not distrust or anger. All of these traits require a human touch. But as we move to the Near Horizon, the challenge will become how we utilize the skills and capacities of AI to our best advantage, even if allowing AI to perform some of these roles does not feel so good for now. The full implications of applying new technologies to our educational system are beyond the scope of this book,[136] but it is clear that technology will be a big player. The more salient message is that, in the service sector of the future, virtually everyone in this area of employment will need to understand how to effectively partner with AI. We cannot beat it -- we must join it.

One other important lesson can be learned from the classroom of the future. In this new classroom, the human teacher has effectively been transformed into knowledge. This teacher can simultaneously be "sent" to as many schools as needed, and at very little incremental cost. This teacher will review the curriculum for the next day milliseconds before the class begins and will be upgraded constantly without attending seminars, conferences, or continuing-education events. This teacher will never be late or sick, will never go on vacation, will work both the day job and the evening classes, and will never complain if the school day or year is lengthened. This teacher will never be in a bad mood and will never go on strike. These restraints of the educational system of the

---

135 "Always" may be an overstatement. With technology, "never say never."
136 There is, however, an exploding body of very creative, brilliant thinking about the role AI can play in the classroom of the future.

twentieth century will be overcome as the process of education transcends its historically physical limitations and becomes a process driven by knowledge.[137]

The concept of transforming a teacher into knowledge is, obviously, only so useful. In today's reality, a 3-D computer image is fundamentally not a teacher in many of the same ways that an instructional handbook or a video is not a teacher. But with Radical Change in the new dimensions of technology, especially the growing level of human comfort and trust in AI, that gulf is narrowing very quickly. The issue for education and for the service sector in general is not whether AI is up for this challenge in the very near future; it is whether we are ready to embrace what technology can do so much better.[138]

This is a lesson not just for education. Competing with AI in performing many service sector functions over the long run (which is not very long, ten to twenty years) will not be feasible. We may have reservations about this transition, especially when it involves little Johnny's welfare, but due to the power of Radical Change, resisting this progression will prove as futile as beating computers at chess, driving steel spikes against a steam hammer or (in Kurzweil's famous words) as futile as attempting to "sweep the rising ocean out of your kitchen with a broom."

Applying the model of the classroom of the future to other service sector jobs demonstrates how conservative the conclusions of the Oxford study may prove to be. Sales clerks, real estate and insurance agents and secretaries all now depend on the importance of the human dimension. But if you could save the commission, would you try your luck with the multiple-listing service of the year 2020 in exchange for a dramatically lower sales commission? Many people are already making that choice. In the very near future, you will never need to leave your living room as your robotic/AI agent "walks" you through the home of your dreams, with a technology that makes the experience feel totally real. Other

---

137 We should, however, *never* underestimate the power of the Brakemen to interfere with this progress. Remember, this "teacher" will also never join a union.

138 Please refer to the previous footnote.

than bringing you coffee and covering your butt when you mess up, what is it that your secretary does that a robot with AI in the decade of the 2020's could not do? We all like the big smile, the personal rapport and the "suck up" of a great salesperson (think of the scene with the salesman wearing the tie in the luxury women's store in *Pretty Woman*), but could we get over it? What if there was a discount for shopping at stores without sales clerks such as we now have for gas stations with self-service?

The service sector contains many job classifications. I have singled out only a few to demonstrate the implications of how the changing nature of technology, described in Part Two, will impact traditional service sector employment. The lessons we can learn from these examples can, however, be applied across a broad spectrum of employment opportunities that currently support a significant segment of the service sector. How far could AI intrude into the many other types of employment in this sector? Science fiction has predicted that the new major spectator sports of the future will be titanic battles between robots.[139] This may be a stretch, but what about a new meaning to "dueling banjos," as AI continues to improve in the fields of arts and music?

You may feel that computers should never be allowed to affect a child's welfare or the quality of one's legal, medical, psychiatric or shopping experience. These attitudes are subconsciously instilled in us. Toddlers with smartphones in their cribs will grow up with a very different set of feelings about AI. They will not see a hard, cold machine, but will instead think of AI as a good-natured, dependable, supportive, selfless, caring, and sensitive companion. Even at the present time, consider the differences in attitude regarding AI between an intellectual giant such as Noam Chomsky and my children, and multiply it by ten. As AI begins to expand its dimensions, we can fear it and fight it (because of its Orwellian connotations) or we can learn to live with it and maybe even learn to love it. In 2035, when *version twenty* of Siri is released (renamed Monique or Juan), you may view many things differently, especially after

---

139 Actually, in 2015 a new TV series opened featuring battles between relatively primitive robots.

she or he coquettishly teases you about the stylish and expensive new tie or scarf you bought simply to see if she or he would notice. Even Tyler Cowen's heart might start to melt.

# Chapter Nineteen

## EMPLOYMENT IN THE TWENTY-FIRST CENTURY:
### The Haves and the Have-Nots

Two summers ago in Hagerstown, Maryland, the good humor ice cream plant closed. More than 400 jobs and a stable way of life melted away.

Wall Street is booming, there are bidding wars for housing again, but for the blue-collar workers in places like Hagerstown, the economic recovery has yet to materialize and many around town are beginning to worry that it will not.

The country lost 6 million factory jobs between 2000 and 2009, and, in Maryland, it was worse. New plants feature specialized machines that frequently use complex computer programs. Such factories require higher-skilled workers, but fewer of them.[140]

This article tells a short story of a small town, but it poignantly captures the nostalgia and the sadness of the transition from an earlier, more innocent way of life. Unfortunately over the last twenty years the tale of Hagerstown has played out across America. It has been the subject of a great deal of public concern and gut-wrenching accounts

---

140  Michael S. Rosenwald, *Washington Post*, January 12, 2014.

of the personal disruption and hardship that has occurred. Loss of jobs in the manufacturing sector has received the most historical and public notice, but it is the tip of the iceberg of total job loss due to advanced technologies. Manufacturing job losses are now so commonplace that they do not even receive much discussion. The tale of the assembly-line worker is well known, but where are all the bank clerks, telephone operators, travel agents, insurance agents, toll collectors, legal secretaries and back-office corporate employees in the billing, accounting, and bookkeeping departments? Where are all the mom-and-pop camera shops and neighborhood grocery stores or just about anything else mom and dad used to own and operate? Yes, many jobs have not been eliminated, they have gone offshore; but for the workers of the Good Humor ice cream factory in Hagerstown, or the former workers at Kodak or the owners and workers in the barbershops, cafes, bars, and movie theaters in Hagerstown, Maryland or Rochester, New York, there is no comfort in knowing why they lost their livelihoods. In fact, many of these jobs have not gone to China, India, Mexico or elsewhere; they are just gone.

The brunt of the loss of these jobs has been felt by the middle class. In 1971 the middle class comprised over 61 percent of all adults. By 2011 this percentage had fallen to 51 percent.[141] Contrary to current popular conservative political belief, this transition was not caused by the Great Recession of 2008; it had already occurred before the recession began. Nor did the plight (or size) of the middle class improve in the recovery from this recession.[142] In fact, in the two years following the Great Recession, median income for US households fell as rapidly as it did during the recession itself (4 percent).[143]

---

141 "The Lost Decade of the Middle Class" (Pew Research Center, August 22, 2012).

142 America's "middle" holds its ground after the Great Recession (Pew Research Center, February 4, 2015).

143 "A Recovery No Better than the Recession," Rakesh Kochhar (Pew Research Center, September 12, 2012).

The rate of unemployment, which reached about 10 percent at the height of the Great Recession, has received a great deal of public attention, but another economic trend over the past forty years is even more troubling. Real income for lower- and middle-income workers has stagnated, and in some groups of workers it has become worse. Yet productivity for American workers increased over 65 percent from 1970 to 2007. Brynjolfsson and McAfee have referred to this pernicious inversion as the Great Decoupling.[144] The stunning discrepancy between these two factors is demonstrated in the accompanying Chart 19.1, "Productivity Versus Typical Workers' Compensation, 1948 - 2013," prepared by the Economic Policy Institute.[145] Historically, rising productivity has always been associated with rising compensation, but just like the holy grail that technology always creates more employment than it destroys, this relationship is only an economic theory, not a law. Hard economic data compiled over forty years now refutes this theory. The harder question is, why? The answer may be inexorably linked to the net loss of better-paying jobs resulting from smarter technologies.

The value of the economic growth resulting from increased productivity, as demonstrated by Chart 19.1, had to go somewhere. Most observers agree it went almost entirely to very few individuals (the one-percenters) and to capital's share of the economy. This transfer of wealth has destabilized the economic balance between labor and capital and has led to the enrichment of a very small, very fortunate group. In 1971 the middle class earned about 62 percent of all income, which was reasonable given that it comprised 61 percent of the working population. By 2011 the middle class was reduced to 51 percent of the working population but it earned only 45 percent of total income.[146] Almost all

144 Eric Brynjolfsson and Andrew McAfee, *The Second Machine Age: Work, Progress, and Prosperity in a Time of Brilliant Technologies* (W.W. Norton & Company, Inc., 2014).

145 Lawrence Mishel, The Wedges Between Productivity and Median Compensation Growth, Economic Policy Institute, April 26, 2012, updated by the EPI and reprinted here with permission.

146 "The Lost Decade of the Middle Class," Pew Research Center, August 22, 2012. Ibid.

**Chart 19.1: Productivity versus Typical Worker's Compensation 1948 - 2013**

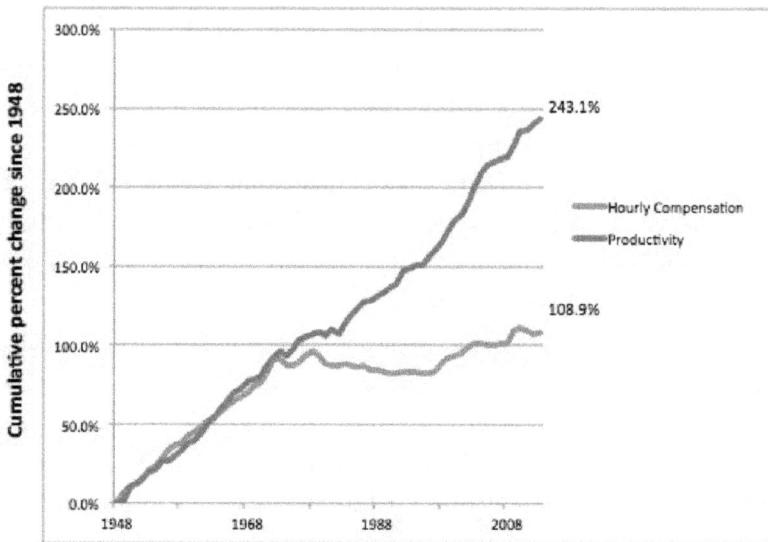

* Reproduced with permission from Figure 2 in *Wage Stagnation in Nine Charts* by Lawrence Mishel, Elise Gould, and Josh Bivens January 6, 2015, Economic Policy Institute.

of this income went to the very highest-income wage earners. In 1971 upper-income adults comprised 14 percent of all adults but earned 29 percent of all income. By 2011 the upper-income wage earners rose to 20 percent but earned a staggering 46 percent of all income.

Economists have no clear answer for this history of wage stagnation for middle- and lower-wage earners nor for the extended and spectacular increase of income for the very fortunate few.[147] Despite recent "good news" in our nation's decreasing unemployment statistics, there is a general consensus that a serious economic problem still exists with current levels of inequality, wage stagnation (for most workers, not for the one-percenters) and the number and quality of new employment opportunities. Many politicians and some economists remain convinced that these economic difficulties are the inevitable consequences of the Great Recession. As economically painful as the recession was, the facts do not support this conclusion. These trends began long before 2008, and they persist even as the nation seems to be experiencing a minor economic recovery.

Before addressing why advancing technologies are playing a major role in contributing to these problems, I need to examine the recent relatively good news about the falling levels of unemployment reported by the US Bureau of Labor Statistics. Unemployment peaked at 10.2 percent in 2009. Beginning in 2010 unemployment statistics began to improve, and this trend recently accelerated. The Associated Press reported the following in January 2015:

> A healthy month of hiring in December capped the best year for US job growth since 1999, demonstrating that employers are more confident than they have been since the Great Recession began.

---

147 Actually, economists and politicians have many answers to why this phenomenon is occurring; however, the answers are more a product of the personal and political views of the proponents than hard evidence.

Almost buried in all this good news was the fact that despite the law of supply and demand, hourly wages in December 2014 fell slightly. The report also noted:

> One reason the unemployment rate fell last month had nothing to do with more hiring. Many of the jobless gave up looking for work and so were no longer counted as unemployed.

Feel-good articles such as the one cited above may help restore the shattered levels of consumer confidence that followed the Great Recession of 2008, but they do not alter what is fundamentally ailing our economy. Trolling the flotsam and jetsam of today's economic news (which is otherwise filled with evidence of stubborn unemployment, particularly due to the loss of better-paying middle-class jobs, stagnation of wages, inequality and lack of equal economic opportunity) to find a few nuggets of good news can, in fact, become a dangerous misdirection of our attention.[148]

This reminds me of the years I lived in Weston, Massachusetts, one of the wealthiest suburbs of Boston. Somewhat curiously, Weston was too cheap to have municipal garbage collection. Saturday was a grand day as the rich met and commingled at the town dump, sort of an early stage Starbucks without the coffee or the Wi-fi. Sometimes someone could be seen out prowling around on those mounds of trash, and occasionally he or she was rewarded by discovering something that a wealthy resident had inadvertently discarded. Gauging the economic progress

---

148 Another sign of good news was the decision in early 2015 by some major retailers such as Walmart to increase the wage of its lowest-paid employees from the federal minimum of $7.25 to $9.00. This is an encouraging sign that the market is doing what Congress cannot, but it hardly moves the needle on the disparity of income of US wage earners. Nor would any objective observer argue that $9.00 an hour is a living wage. It certainly cannot support a family of three or four. Adjusted for inflation, a wage of $9.00 an hour is roughly equivalent to the minimum wage during the Reagan Administration. The current minimum wage of $7.25 is almost 25 percent *less* than the minimum wage under the Reagan Administration.

of America by sorting through the monthly statistics for modest signs of hope may make good news, but it does not lead to any solid forecasts.[149]

Historical statistics such as the unemployment rate, productivity and gross national product published by the US Bureau of Labor Statistics are considered to be the holy grail for judging the performance of our economy. During the latter part of the twentieth century, when these statistics in their current format first became available, they worked quite well in measuring economic performance. However, in the paradigm shift caused by Radical Change we need to be wary of a mindless reliance on simple numbers, particularly when these numbers are based on the assumptions of the twentieth century. Unfortunately, in a society obsessed with reducing matters to simple, quick explanations and a media committed to thirty second sound bites, these reports are almost irresistible, especially when they signify good news to an economically weary nation. There are a number of reasons why we should treat this relatively recent news with great caution.

First, it is widely agreed that, due to the standards of compiling the data for calculating unemployment, these statistics can result in some fundamental distortions in how well our economy is truly performing. The US Bureau of Labor Statistics only counts as unemployed those individuals who are *both* out of work and who are actively seeking employment. The concept of actively seeking employment is very subjective, and different interpretations or calculations of this group can affect the ultimate reported unemployment rate significantly. The primary source of information that the US Bureau of Labor Statistics uses is the number of people receiving unemployment benefits since, by the requirements of the program, these individuals must demonstrate they are actively

---

149 In fact, it can lead to some very bad policy decisions. Based on a March 2015 US Bureau of Labor Statistics report that the economy added another two hundred thousand plus jobs, there were fears on Wall Street that the Federal Reserve was about to raise interest rates. The market fell significantly on this news. In April 2015 the Bureau reported that new employment for that month dropped dramatically and corrected the March employment numbers downward by over sixty thousand jobs.

seeking a job.[150] In an economy that has experienced a long-term recession and is facing the frustrating challenges of technological unemployment, there are many Americans who have quit seeking employment in
the workforce because they are disillusioned or exhausted. Admittedly,
attempting to quantify the true level of unemployment is extremely difficult and, due to the forces affecting today's job market, this challenge
may now be even more complicated. We do know that only 58 percent
of individuals of working age in America were employed in 2012. This
is a thirty-seven-year low going back to a period prior to the growth of
the participation of women in the workforce. Most experts believe this
low percentage of participation is a reflection of the problems resulting from the long-term, chronic lack of meaningful new job creation.
Ironically, because of the very nature of this problem, no one is sure just
how misleading these statistics are today. What is widely agreed is that
there are a significant number of individuals who have stopped actively
seeking traditional employment opportunities. How many? The experts
disagree widely. Despite the uncertainty, the media and our politicians
remain fixated on small swings in the reported statistics (.01 or .02 percent). The reliance on such small swings in the unemployment rate as a
way of gauging how our economy is performing may result in very bad
public policy. In the decade of the 1990s, the percentage of working-
age Americans who were employed hovered around 63 percent. While
this may appear to be a modest change, if the difference in the number
of people who participate in the workforce today versus in the decade
of the 1990s (58 percent versus 63 percent) were added to the current
unemployment calculation, the 2015 unemployment rate would more
than double. In fact, when the Bureau applies a broader measure of
unemployment that includes those who have quit looking for jobs and
those seeking full-time jobs, the full-time job unemployment rate in
2015 is closer to 11 percent.[151]

---

150 The failure of Congress in 2014 to extend long-term unemployment benefits to
chronically unemployed workers made this problem even more intractable.

151 At the time of the writing of this book (2015), the official unemployment rate was
close to 6.4 percent.

The second reason to be cautious about the recent "good news" regarding unemployment is that most of the jobs created in this recovery are low paying. When the US Bureau of Labor Statistics calculates the number of employed wage earners it treats all jobs as equal. Seasonal employment, part-time work and low-paying jobs all count. When you closely examine the raw data that has created the recent "good news" from this perspective, you get a very different picture of the strength of our recovery. For example, in January 2015 the US Bureau of Labor Statistics reported that two hundred ninety-five thousand new jobs had been created in December. This was the twelfth straight month of job gains exceeding two hundred thousand per month and the longest such stretch since 1995. The press reported this news as a very optimistic sign that the economy was indeed recovering. But despite these job gains, median income did not increase. One reason for this result was the fact that over one-half of these new jobs were in industries that involve mostly low-paid work. Adding employment opportunities that pay at or near the federal or applicable state minimum wage will not turn our economy around, and this type of economic recovery does nothing for the recovery of the American middle class. In fact, the entire twelve-month trend of improving employment was primarily driven by the creation of low-paying jobs. In February 2015 the Brookings Institute released more of this type of "good news."[152] The article pointed out that although "advanced industries supported almost no aggregate job growth during the years 1980 to 2010," this industry sector "is now beginning to grow." According to the article, this four-year resurgence in job growth was led by computer system design (two hundred fifty-six thousand jobs) and management consulting (one hundred seventy-six thousand seven hundred jobs). However, to remain objective, the writers pointed out that, "These figures don't compare to the top job creating industries overall" -- restaurants (eight hundred seventy-eight thousand four hundred jobs) and temporary employment services (five hundred seventy-two

---

152 Mark Muro and Siddarth Kulkarni, "Yes, Advanced Industries Are Providing Jobs to Americans" (Brookings Institute, February 25, 2015).

thousand jobs). So, during this period of "recovery," more than three low-paying jobs were created for every job in advanced industries. This is not the basis of an economic recovery; in fact, it is further proof of the hollowing out of our middle class. It is also exactly the type of systematic job loss and job creation that is predicted by the changing dimensions of technology described in Part Two and Chapters Seventeen and Eighteen.

The historic driver of economic prosperity has always been new technological developments. Since these forces are advancing more rapidly than ever before, why is the economy performing so badly for the average American? As discussed earlier, in their seminal books *Race Against Machines* (2011) and *The Second Machine Age* (2014), Erik Brynjolfsson and Andrew McAfee argue that the answer is that technology may now destroy more jobs than it creates.[153] To say the least, there has been a great deal of push back.[154] Traditional economic theory that dominated the twentieth century was very kind to burgeoning technology. In economic circles, it goes without saying that technology, by its nature, *must* create more jobs than it eliminates. This is driven by the fundamental premise that technology creates productivity and efficiencies, which lower the costs of goods; with lower costs for goods, demand for these goods increases, and increased demand creates the need for more jobs. It is a neat circle! What could go wrong? Actually, as described in Chapter Two, "Technological Progress," Keynes predicted, one hundred years ago, what could go wrong.

Most of the discussion by the dissenters to the message of *Race Against the Machine* and *The Second Machine Age* focuses on the historical trends of job destruction and creation during the Industrial Revolution

---

153 Eric Brynjolfsson and Andrew McAfee, *Race Against the Machine: How the Digital Revolution Is Accelerating Innovation, Driving Productivity, and Irreversibly Transforming Employment and the Economy* (W.W. Norton & Company, Inc., 2011); and *The Second Machine Age: Work, Progress, and Prosperity in a Time of Brilliant Technologies* (W.W. Norton & Company, Inc., 2014).

154 Tyler Cowen, *Average Is Over: Powering America Beyond the Age of the Great Stagnation* (Dutton, 2013).

and the late part of the twentieth century. Traditional economists point to the undisputed fact that during the Industrial Revolution technology created more jobs than it destroyed, and they thereby reason that this correlation will go on for the indefinite future. But there are other lessons to be learned as well from this historical experience. From 1900 to 1950, agricultural-based jobs went from accounting for 50 percent of the employment in the United States to less than 5 percent. Notwithstanding the success of technology during this period in displacing these jobs, it created many more. Industry boomed, trade (both domestic and foreign) grew exponentially, and life was very good for most Americans. Technology created not only new jobs but also new industries such as electric companies, rail lines, steel and automobile manufacturers and telephone companies, *all* of which depended heavily on human labor. Also, these new jobs were, for the most part, relatively unskilled or semi-skilled. With some modest retraining and some not so modest pains of relocation, the unemployed farmer found work in the rapidly growing cities. It was very painful to make this transition, but it didn't take too long for the workers to find new jobs. As these growing pains occurred, technology helped to create a much more comfortable middle class that benefited from the enormous efficiencies and productivity that technology provided. But during the latter part of the twentieth century, technology became more sophisticated, and it began to replace less obvious jobs such as telephone operators, bank clerks and billing personnel. While technology replaced certain forms of employment during this period, it still did not possess the new dimensions of the current nature of technology described in Part Two, and, therefore, it did not possess the capability to create the job losses in the manufacturing sector predicted in Chapter Seventeen or in the service sector predicted in Chapter Eighteen.

When you consider the implications of the nature of future job loss that emerge from the trends described in these previous chapters, it is clear that the core assumptions on which traditional economic theory is based are being seriously challenged. The smarter, more capable and flexible technologies of the twenty-first century can now compete with human labor in a broad spectrum of jobs, and the brunt of this future job loss will be borne by the American middle class. Manufacturing will be transformed, and with it will come the loss of many jobs that historically were the foundation of middle-class America. The greatest challenge to the middle class will be the loss of jobs in the service sector. Retail clerks and sales people, the staff of call-in centers and government employees (including someday the symbol of the strength and security of the middle class, the US Post Office) will all come under attack. In addition, as advancing AI evolves (including voice and speech recognition and deep learning), personal services such as secretaries, personal assistants, support services in accounting, law, medicine and computer programming, etc. will enter the sweet spot for these forms of AI. Yes, some fields of employment, such as medicine and education, will grow so as to offset the *net* loss of jobs, but job formation in these fields will not grow at the rate it would but for the wolf of advancing technologies. The issues for long-term, meaningful employment in America are, therefore: (1) how many and what types of new jobs will be created by technology in relation to the jobs being destroyed and (2) what will be the minimum entry levels of education and skills to qualify and obtain the more rewarding of these new jobs?

Although technology definitely creates jobs, there is growing concern and mounting evidence that advancing AI is becoming much better at saving labor (destroying jobs) than creating new job opportunities. If you examine the development of particularly the more recent high-tech success stories, there is reason for concern. This is not to suggest that advancing technologies will not create wonderful new jobs requiring human creativity, ingenuity and flexibility. These technologies will result in a great deal of job formation but, by definition, the new technologies that will succeed best will require the fewest employees technically possible. If you examine the major new companies that have come to dominate American business, this trend is already apparent.

Let me begin by examining a seemingly small new high-tech development. Craigslist is a classic idea that, armed with the power of AI and the reach of the Internet, was ready to explode upon the world. Overnight, at virtually no cost, you could offer just about anything used, new or otherwise for sale to the world. This was not good news for the newspaper industry, the local mom-and-pop want-ad advertisers or for many retail shops. Already reeling from the Internet's body blow, this attack on the life blood of newspaper revenue (classified advertisement) further crippled the newspaper publishing industry. Unfortunately, it wasn't the last blow. Just a few years later, Groupon and its progeny challenged the coupon income of this industry with another breakthrough technology.[155] Taken together, these two seemingly small applications of technology were the death knell for many smaller newspapers already struggling from the challenge of the Internet. The true magnitude of the job loss associated with the decline of the newspaper industry is very difficult to quantify because it involves far more than the direct job loss from printing newspapers itself. The decline in newspaper production caused a dramatic loss of jobs in the timber and paper industries, distribution, trucking and countless ancillary support services. It also created an enormous dislocation and transition in employment for those who gathered, wrote and reported the news. We are even beginning to lose the nostalgic entry-level job to the American Dream, the paper boy. How many jobs were lost through the direct or indirect displacement of workers in the newspaper industry? It is virtually impossible to calculate. Craigslist in 2014 employed thirty people but in 2014 averaged twenty billion visits per month; Groupon employed ten thousand but had revenues of $3.2 billion. Before the decline of the newspaper industry, the paper industry in Maine alone employed more people than Craigslist and Groupon combined. The spiraling effect of job loss in the newspaper industry is, in fact, often the case when a new technology dramatically revolutionizes an industry. The collapse of the camera industry due to the enhanced capabilities and utility of digital cameras

---

155 It is instructive to note that Groupon could not have been as successful as it has become without the breakthrough development of the smartphone. With the new GPS and added capacities of the smartphone, a good idea (Groupon's original business plan) became brilliant, and its inventors became billionaires.

and subsequently the smartphone caused a similar cascade of disruptive job losses. Not only did Kodak and Polaroid go bankrupt; the businesses that sold the cameras, developed and printed the photos and sold the video projectors, screens and photo albums all went out of business.

A similar decline in the retail market can be seen by the advent of online retailing giants such as Amazon and e-Bay. In 2014 Amazon employed one hundred fifty-four thousand but had revenues of over $89 billion, and e-Bay employed three thousand five hundred with revenues of $18 billion. Despite providing such meager employment opportunities, armed with the power of computers and AI, these technologies have forced the closure of many stores already reeling from the pressure of the big-box stores. How many *net* jobs have been lost? Current economic standards of measurement cannot properly quantify this number.

How about travel? You can't call your local travel agent anymore; there is no one to pick up the phone. Instead, go on the Internet and pull up Kayak, Travelocity, etc., or go to the website for one of the airlines. Not only will the rates be much cheaper, but you can also find related deals for rental cars, vacation packages, hotels and restaurants. Your whole trip can be booked from your kitchen in a few hours without a commission to the travel agent. How many people are now employed by companies that serve these needs? Not very many.[156] These are just a few examples of job loss that has occurred as computers allow us to take charge of our lives, but it is at the price of many previously necessary jobs. These job functions are, of course, not totally gone, but the job opportunities in these fields have been drastically reduced.

To date, there appears to be very little hard economic data in the literature or in the official economic statistics demonstrating the *net* job loss that has resulted from the dramatic growth of knowledge-based technologies such as the ones mentioned above. However, the amazing array of the goods and services now available in the form of knowledge, such as those provided by Amazon, Craigslist, Groupon and Kayak, set

---

156 The actual number is not known since most of these companies are privately held and are not required to publically disclose this information.

an ominous precedent. The long-term effects, documented by hard, reliable economic data, will take time to confirm and authenticate. However, from a layperson's perspective, the conclusion appears self-evident: Most of the successful applications of knowledge-based technologies available on the Internet or otherwise have had seriously adverse effects on net employment. Virtually no application has created a new labor-intensive business. This is not to denigrate the economic importance and meaningful employment opportunities that have been provided by companies such as Apple, Google, etc., but the number of new jobs these businesses create is relatively small. A quick review of some of the largest companies in the high-tech sector dramatically confirms this point. In 2014 Apple employed ninety-eight thousand people but had revenues of $183 billion; Google employed fifty-five thousand with revenues of $66 billion, and Facebook employed ten thousand with revenues of $12.5 billion. To place this in perspective, at its peak Eastman Kodak employed over one hundred sixty-five thousand workers -- more workers than the combined employment of Apple, Google and Facebook. If you add in Polaroid as another victim of technology, you would have to include Intel, Yahoo, YouTube, Twitter and Groupon to replace an equal number of employment opportunities.

One overarching technology that deserves more discussion is the Internet. Despite its ubiquitous presence throughout the world, the Internet celebrated just its twentieth birthday in 2015. Because of its historic development, the Internet has been primarily characterized as a means of communication and a source of amazing entertainment opportunities. While this certainly remains true, the power of this technology is now being utilized in an almost limitless number of areas. As AI and computer capacity exponentially increase, we should expect to see more and more applications of this technology, far beyond communication and entertainment, available on the Internet. In the field of education, the success of the Khan Institute is only a harbinger of things to come. In a few years (and one or two doublings of Moore's law), we should expect to find even more advanced educational applications and basic legal and

financial advice, accounting, marriage counseling, medical advice, therapeutic and rehabilitative counseling, and religious support all available on
an interactive website. Only the Brakemen stand in the way. Online retail
sales will also continue the relentless dismemberment of smaller retail
outlets. As advanced technologies become more sophisticated and as we
become more trusting in our relationship with AI, sales of new products
and services will increasingly migrate to the Internet. Automobile and
life insurance and real estate sales are leading the way, but by the Near
Horizon, the possibilities will be limited only by the human imagination.

As for entertainment, the future applications of the Internet are
mind-boggling. Today, using a smartphone, iPad or laptop to access the
Internet, we can go to the movies, listen to songs, immerse ourselves in
video games, pornography, weather reports, the stock market, a book,
a newspaper or a sporting event -- all for free or almost free, and from
anywhere on the planet. The effects of being deeply enmeshed in utilizing and integrating powerful applications such as Facebook, Twitter
or Instagram into our lives both at work and at play are just beginning
to be fully appreciated. But one thing is certain: As a society we are
spending an enormous and growing percentage of our time enjoying
the benefits of these applications. If there is one zero-sum game in all
of this, it is our attention span. There are just so many hours in the day
for us to amuse, educate and inform ourselves, even with the stimulus of
Adderall or Ritalin. How many jobs were supported by what we used to
do with all this free time? A lot of jobs. And where will we be in five or
ten more years of development of these technologies?

There is an almost endless list of anecdotes to support this sense of
job loss. Despite the mounting evidence that we have a real employment
problem here, many dismiss much of this societal change as just another
harmless (and for many, not so harmless) form of entertainment,
namely, another season of "Survivor" or one of its genre. Others, including a number of well-respected economists, dismiss this evidence as simply signs of the inevitable growing pains that new technologies always
create. These experts may prove correct, but something feels different

about the new form and scale of this generation of job loss. Much of this complacency is based on continuing to rely on our traditional economic standards. However, the standard ways we have utilized to measure how we are performing, such as gross national product, unemployment and productivity, seem to need a major overhaul to keep up with the advancing technologies and the ways they are changing our lives. See Chapter Thirteen, "How Do You Measure Progress?"

In summary, the Winners on the journey to the Near Horizon will fall into two very diametrically different categories. The first area of job growth will be low and semiskilled jobs in the service sector (such as hospitality, janitorial, house cleaning and landscaping) that, among other services, serve and pick up the mess left by the increasingly wealthy Winners. This portion of the service sector will grow because problems of spatial recognition, limitations in navigating complex environments and the need to be constrained by common sense will ensure that it will be a long time before robots master the basic capability to fill most of these unskilled positions. Also, many of these jobs require a relatively high degree of interaction with people. Jobs like the waiter and the bartender, therefore, may never be replaced. Do you really want to talk to a robot bartender about the troubles with your spouse, even after a few martinis? These unskilled jobs are also protected by another ironic factor -- there is not enough money in it to replace these jobs. These types of jobs are not just the most unskilled jobs, they are the worst-paying, so the economics of developing robots in these fields are not good. But whatever the outcome of these struggles over employment opportunities, if America needs to rely on this sector of job growth for its economic recovery, we are in a lot of trouble.

The other group of Winners will be those who are qualified and fulfill the requirements of the new high-tech jobs of the future. There is some good news here. The Brookings article cited earlier in this chapter reported significant growth in high-tech jobs from 2005 to 2013 (over four hundred thousand new jobs in this sector). The aggregate jobs, however, represented only 18 percent of total job creation during this period, and this entire spectrum of advanced employment represents only about 8 percent of the total job market. Even a rapid growth in such a small sector of the economy will not offset the onslaught of technology on the jobs that currently support our middle class.

Certainly many new jobs will be less conventional, such as the underground communities of the new generation of innovators hard at work in Kendall Square and around the world. But, whatever statistics we choose, we need to remember that our historic assumption about the rates of job destruction and job creation due to advancing technology is based just on a theory, not on a law. And it is a theory that has been questioned since its virtual inception.

This brings us to the question of the nature of the new employment opportunities in the twenty-first century: What will be the minimum entry levels of education and skills to qualify and obtain these jobs? By its inherent nature, as technology destroys jobs and creates new ones, the newly created jobs have always required *different* skills and knowledge. As a result, job training, retraining and career counseling for new job opportunities are nothing new; we just used to call them by other names. So what is different today, if anything?

Everyone agrees that applied technology, now and certainly in the future, will create many new jobs. And this job creation has been marvelous! Kendall Square in Cambridge, Massachusetts provides a wonderfully diverse microcosm of the abundance that exploding new technologies create.[157] Just fifteen years ago, this was a deserted and blighted area

---

157 A much more troubling and stark example of the dichotomy of abundance and destitution (i.e., the Winners and the Losers) could be drawn from the experience of Silicon Valley. Amid all the splendor of the high-tech businesses flourishing in the Valley sits the "jungle," a jumble of homeless, aimless poor people camping out by the side of a creek -- forced to beg for their subsistence from the Winners. See "Technology and Inequality," *MIT Technology Review* (November/December 2014), cover story for a graphic report on this sad juxtaposition of the extremes in our new high-tech society.

With this transformation, there was another, less apparent but equally transformative, change. MIT reinvented itself from one of the world's greatest centers of mathematics and applied hard engineering and science into a world leader in the exploding areas of life sciences, biotech and telecommunications. Yes, Gordon Moore got his start here in computer science, but even he is probably amazed with the Kendall Square of 2015.

of Cambridge, a drug dealer's idea of a great night out. Anchored on one side by the Charles River, Microsoft's regional headquarters and the MIT Sloan School of Business, and on the other side by the famous MIT dome on Massachusetts Avenue, Kendall Square remained for many years a wasteland of rubble and trash-strewn parking lots, abandoned warehouses, and disreputable bars. MIT owned most of the area and parked its cars there, but MIT tour guides did not walk student applicants through this area as part of the campus. No one at MIT went to Kendall Square for lunch. With the rebirth of Kendall Square, institutes such as the Broad Center (DNA research), the Koch Institute (cancer research) and many joint ventures between MIT and pharmaceutical giants such as Novartis were attracted to this area, making it an internationally known area for research and development. With these changes came lots of new and very well-paying and self-fulfilling jobs as research workers, lab assistants, computer programmers, etc.

With the growth of the new jobs came a wonderful resurgence of Kendall Square itself. The old mills and abandoned lots that used to bustle with the roar of the Industrial Revolution have been replaced by centers for Google, Microsoft and Novartis. Kendall Square is now home to the second-largest Novartis campus in the world. Kendall Square has emerged as the source of thousands of new high-technology jobs. With these jobs also have come the fun and more new jobs, gourmet food trucks, upscale restaurants and bars, retail shops and luxury apartments. Yes, even a farmers' market -- you can't have affluence without one!

Also, less visible but clearly no less transformative, Kendall Square became the inspiration for a new generation of entrepreneurs who work out of garages, old warehouses, and the living-room couches of college friends. A few visionaries even saw a way to try to organize and concentrate this creative outburst. In 1999 Tim Rowe leased his first, but by no means last, space from MIT to form the Innovation Center, at 100 Broadway in Cambridge, Massachusetts. The business model of the Innovation Center is to lease large, relatively inexpensive space and informally sublease this space into very small spaces to creative, broke geniuses. Only Tim Rowe could have thought this was going to make money.

Until recently, this new wave of creativity and invention did not raise the attention of the press or the casual observer, but the knowledge, inventions and new opportunities that this brilliant, intrepid generation is creating are very powerful. It is a culture that embodies the values of the Internet. Knowledge must be shared and collaboration is sought out, not avoided. Sharing ideas, thoughts and even your lunch is not seen as an opportunity for someone else to profit from your generosity. So at the Innovation Center, the NERD Center at Microsoft (which is open as a gathering place for these semi-bohemian, brilliant geeks) and Starbucks (or just about anywhere you can gather in Kendall Square), this interactive energy creates an excitement that is palpable.

The vision of abundance is alive and well in Kendall Square and in many other similarly committed parts of America, such as innovation centers in the Silicon Valley, Boston, Atlanta, Chicago and Austin. The growth of these centers throughout America and a counter-culture that provides a focused environment to create entrepreneurial opportunities for many is great news for America. But no one ever questioned the growth of great new jobs from technological development.

While technology is creating many new high-tech jobs, these new jobs represent only a small percentage of the total workforce. Filling these positions is extremely important because they are great, high-paying jobs, and failing to fill them will seriously hurt the competitive advantages that we now have as a world leader in high-tech. But even if we succeed, there are just not enough jobs to deal with the job losses created by the continuing Radical Change of technologies that destroy jobs.

One other observation about this new source of employment is that as technologies become increasingly sophisticated, the skills to utilize these technologies are changing and, not surprisingly, these skills are also becoming more sophisticated. This is creating an ever-widening gulf between the skill sets and educational levels of the Losers (the unemployed workers) and the skills and educational levels to meet the minimum qualifications to even apply for the new high-tech jobs. As the development of new technologies rapidly accelerates, this dichotomy will increase dramatically.

Examining one all-too-frequent example of this harsh reality may serve to demonstrate the severity of this problem. The middle-class manager at your local bank went to college and has had a great work record for twenty years. She had a wonderful ability to supervise a number of bank employees and had very good customer skills and high intelligence. She recently lost her job because the bank is consolidating its branch offices due to automated banking. How hopeful should she be of filling any of the new high-tech job openings at Kendall Square?

Unfortunately there is clear evidence that this barrier is getting worse. Education has always been a pathway to better-paying, more fulfilling jobs. Today there is growing evidence that possessing at least a college education is a minimum prerequisite for obtaining even a middle-class job. The ability to obtain the minimum requisite educational training to become a Winner in the twenty-first century is rapidly slipping away for all but the children of the fortunate few beneficiaries of the new economy. A college education, a masters degree and sometimes even a PhD are increasingly becoming a minimum requirement to qualify even to be an applicant for a high-tech job. In some instances there are some very solid technical reasons why these objective requirements are established, but often that is not the case. My own experience as the partner in charge of hiring at a major Boston law firm for many years taught me another reason why at least some of this is occurring. At my former firm, each year we received over one thousand resumes for about twenty full-time positions. The expense of reviewing each and every one of these applications would have been staggering. So we, like every other major law firm in America, set some arbitrary minimum standards for all applicants. We looked only at applicants from certain schools, no matter what the applicant's class standing was at any other school. Within the select law schools, we considered only applicants with the highest grades, no matter what their experience or what else they may have accomplished while in law school. Everyone, of course, had to have a law degree, but if there were different levels of law degrees, we would have picked the highest. All of this was driven by the simple fact that we had too many applicants, and no matter how many, arguably, artificial requirements we cooked up to reduce the pool of applicants, there were still plenty of applicants remaining to fill our needs. With Radical Change in technology driving this transformation in educational requirements for the new jobs, this disparity may get worse -- a lot worse.

Put all of this threatening news together and consider that the basic forces that are responsible for this experience are only about twenty years old. We are just starting to enter the "knee" of Radical Change. In twenty years, the employment opportunities of today may be nostalgic memories of the "good old days."

With these factors in mind, the retraining of America takes on a new and much more imposing dimension. Among the many new approaches and assumptions we must confront in the paradigm shift occurring in the twenty-first century is the challenge of the *nature* of the qualifications for the new jobs created in the Knowledge Revolution. Our traditional thinking regarding how to cope with this challenge will not serve us well.

This is the twenty-first century version of the problem of technological unemployment identified by Keynes. Keynes assumed that this would create a temporary lack of fluidity in the employment pool of candidates qualified to take on the new jobs. Unfortunately the advancing sophistication of the new technologies has created a much greater challenge for this transition than Keynes could have ever imagined. In fact, for many currently unemployed people, this does not seem to be a temporary hurdle that can be overcome. This challenge will be addressed in the next chapter.

# Chapter Twenty

## THE NEW JOBS:
### Technological Unemployment

The promise of the American Dream is that anyone, regardless of his or her origins, can have a fair start in life. If we work hard, we can get a good education and achieve success. But over the last few decades, a disturbing "opportunity gap" has unexpectedly emerged. The central tenet of the American Dream -- that all children, regardless of their family and social background, should have a decent chance to improve their lot in life -- is no longer "self-evident."[158]

In *Our Kids: The American Dream in Crisis*, Robert Putnam tragically captures, through the stories of children, the harsh dimensions of the death of the American Dream.[159] Putnam acknowledges the role of economic inequality in creating this crisis but chooses to focus more on the issue of equality of opportunity and social mobility. The two issues are closely intertwined, but they are not the same.

---

158 Editor's foreword to Robert D. Putnam, *Our Kids: The American Dream in Crisis* (Simon & Schuster, 2015).
159 Putnam is professor of public policy at Harvard University, a member of the National Academy of Sciences and, according to the Sunday Times of London, "the most influential academic in the world."

Equal access and opportunity to obtain the requisite education to become a Winner in the twenty-first century will be a defining issue in our society in the next two decades to the Near Horizon. But it is only part, though an essential part, of the problem. In my generation, the hopes and aspirations of our parents were captured by the simple statement, "Education begins at home." The harsh reality for many of the children of poor and lower-middle-class families is that when they arrive at school they are not ready to learn:

> Success in school is not easy for someone facing poverty, especially the concentrated poverty that racial segregation produces. These are children that frequently change schools due to poor housing; have little help with homework; have few role models of success ... and live in a chaotic and frequently unsafe environment.[160]

If one could envision a society with dramatic inequality of income and wealth but with the poorest working families living comfortably above the poverty level, this inherent dichotomy would not be true, but that is not the American society of 2015.[161] As a result, any effort to reinvigorate our system of preschool, elementary and secondary education must begin at home, namely, in the homes of the disadvantaged children of the American Dream.

The home of a child being supported by an unemployed or hardworking single parent earning the minimum wage is not an environment that is likely to raise a student ready to compete for a good education, no matter how fair, open or well-structured that educational opportunity might otherwise appear to be. This is the harsh reality that belies the

---

160 Lawrence Mishel, "The Opportunity Dodge," *The American Prospect* (April 9, 2015).

161 Josh Bivens, Elise Gould, Lawrence Mishel and Heidi Shierholz, "Raising America's Pay: Why It's Our Central Economic Policy Challenge" (Economic Policy Institute, June 4, 2014). In 2014, 15 - 24 percent of all American families lived on incomes below the official poverty line. The lower range of the estimate factors in government programs of assistance that support earned income.

cynical statements of some observers who feel we need only to create a meritocracy of opportunity in education. The problem is far deeper and more intractable than this rhetoric would lead us to believe. In America today we have an unacceptable level of poverty and all of the social ills that it exacerbates, in a land of plenty. No effort to improve our system of education can, therefore, succeed unless we address the economic root causes for the loss of social mobility in our country. This is not to denigrate the importance of improving our educational institutions but to place this challenge in the appropriate context.

The challenge of technological unemployment identified by Keynes almost a century ago has grown beyond his wildest fears. Keynes believed this to be a temporary phase, because the challenge that he knew was the retraining of a farmer or an immigrant to work in a factory, to become a government employee or to work in a relatively unskilled job in the service sector. Radical Change has created many new jobs, but the qualifications for them often require very specialized, sophisticated skills and/or an advanced secondary education. As a result, the temporary nature of this retraining of the "labour" force is no longer applicable to today's society. This could lead to the fatalistic view for many unemployed workers trying to enter the job market that this is an insurmountable challenge. It would be, in effect, the final admission that the American Dream is history.

There is not a single economist, politician, or even casual observer of American economic growth who does not believe we face an enormous challenge to better educate, train or retrain our existing workforce to compete for the new jobs of the future. Tragically, what is also widely accepted is that the American educational system for grades one to twelve has failed us very badly. By virtually every indicator of educational achievement, the United States has fallen behind most of the developed nations of the world. Yet we lead the world in the amount we spend on education per child. Today, education is getting a lot of attention and if you look hard enough you can find some recent evidence of improvements. But many of our children do not complete high school, and for those who graduate, they are far behind the achievement levels of students in a number of other countries. This system can be overhauled, but there is a long way to go before we can ever hope to reverse these troubling trends.

Unlike our system of primary education, the United States continues to maintain the finest graduate and postgraduate educational system in the world. American universities and colleges remain the envy of the world and as a result attract growing numbers of foreign students. This is the good news, and it is more important than ever that we maintain this quality, given the challenges posed by growing technological unemployment and the increasing importance of obtaining *at a minimum* a college degree to obtain virtually any well-paying job. Unfortunately with the good news of the strength of our institutions of higher learning, there is a tragic consequence. The worldwide competition for admission to these institutions has resulted in skyrocketing costs for this education. For a growing number of young adults, obtaining a college degree is no longer an option. In January 2015 the Pell Institute and the Alliance for Higher Education and Democracy, University of Pennsylvania, issued an exhaustive study on accessibility to higher education in the United States.[162] The report concluded that the chances of obtaining a college education were "highly inequitable across family income groups" and were substantially worse today than in 1950. This inequality did not arise from a decrease in the capacity of our system of secondary education. Total college enrollment rose steadily from 1970 to 2009, reaching a peak of about eighteen million students. Since 2009 enrollment has declined about 2 percent per year. During this same period, the cost of college in constant dollars has more than doubled. Local, state and federal assistance for this rising cost of higher education fell woefully behind. In 1977 state and local governments paid 57 percent of the cost of higher education. By 2012 that aid fell to 39 percent. The princi-

---

162 "Indicators of Higher Education Equity in the United States," The Pell Institute for the Study of Opportunity in Higher Education, The University of Pennsylvania Alliance for Higher Education and Democracy (University of Pennsylvania, January 2015).

pal federal assistance for tuition is the Pell Grant Program. In constant dollars, the maximum Pell Grant from 1970 to 2012 fell slightly despite the skyrocketing cost of this education. Pell Grants are now capped at $5,500 per year. In 1970, that aid paid for two-thirds of a student's cost of education. By 2012 that support fell to 27 percent.[163] Not surprisingly, the shortfall resulted in a massive increase in student borrowing. In 1992 49 percent of all students took out student loans, averaging $16,000. By 2012 71 percent of all students needed student loans that averaged almost $30,000. For students from families in the lowest quartile of income, the annual shortfall for the cost of a year of college in 2014 equaled almost 80 percent of family income.[164]

For those students who choose to borrow the shortfall, there is more bad news. The days of significant government subsidies for student loans are long over. The federal loan program provides a byzantine, complicated set of choices for both students and parents. What it lacks in assistance it attempts to make up for in diversity. This is not a good trade-off. For qualifying parents, the Federal Plus Loan Program provided loans in 2015 at 7.21 percent, up from 6.41 percent in 2014. Qualifying students may apply for loans provided by the Federal Direct Loan program. Inexplicably, the interest rate in 2015 for both subsidized and unsubsidized loans was the same (4.66 percent, up from 3.86 percent in 2014). Graduate loans bear an interest rate of 6.21 percent. These loans are provided by our federal government but hardly amount to a subsidy. To illustrate this point, one source of the government's cost of borrowing to fund this program is ten-year Treasury bonds, which hovered around 2 percent in 2015. So the government borrows at 2 percent, lends that money to students at 6 percent and calls the program "student aid." To add insult to injury, due to a little-known provision of federal bankruptcy law, student loans are not dischargeable in bankruptcy, so a sportsman who on a lark buys a boat on credit is treated more leniently

---

163 Ibid. The Pell Institute for the Study of Opportunity in Higher Education.
164 Ibid. The Pell Institute for the Study of Opportunity in Higher Education.

in bankruptcy than a student who borrows to finance the education necessary to enter the job market.

The inevitable consequence of these factors is a dramatic decrease in the chances of children of lower- and middle-income families to complete a bachelors degree. In 1970 one in five children from families in the lowest quartile of family income received a degree. By 2012 that ratio had fallen to one in eight.[165] Of all the legacies we leave to our children, this may be the most damning. The young generation of our future leaders faces the perfect storm -- astronomically climbing college costs, declining local, state and federal assistance and a dramatically greater importance of obtaining, at least, a college degree to participate in the abundance of our future. We have always prided ourselves as a nation in providing equal access and opportunity to education. It was the bedrock upon which the American Dream became a reality. For generations, Americans worked hard to keep this dream alive. My parents' generation lived out this promise with the support of the GI Bill. My generation had relatively open access to higher education due to substantially more governmental assistance and substantially lower costs of tuition. What is the message to our children about their future? Today's generation, drowning in a sea of student debt, has cried out for a lifebuoy and we have thrown them an anchor.

There is a great deal more than basic fairness at stake here. Without meaningful access to educational opportunities, the hope of advancement for many Americans will become a callous promise that may come back to haunt us. Our nation is now as rich as it has ever been, and recently it is demonstrating a strength in its recovery that surpasses all of the developed nations of the world. Certainly in this abundance we must be able to find a way to restore the means to achieve a better economic future for those willing to sacrifice and work for it. But even if we find this resolve, we will still face problems.

In the paradigm shift now being created by Radical Change, concentrating our efforts on redoubling our conventional educational and

---

165 Ibid. The Pell Institute for the Study of Opportunity in Higher Education.

retraining programs for our unemployed workforce could be a major miscalculation. Yes, the hope of a liberal-arts education creating modern-day Renaissance men and women should not be abandoned. But improving our nation's world ranking on historic overall achievement scores will not solve the problem. In fact, it may divert our attention and resources. We do not have the time to learn this lesson the hard way. Today the qualifications for the meaningful, well-paying jobs of the future are being transformed as rapidly as the technology itself is evolving, that is, exponentially fast! One obvious skill that should be at the forefront of the educational retraining effort would be computer science. Sadly, only a handful of universities in the United States offer even a masters degree in these skills.

People who are recently unemployed understandably wish to find related jobs in forms of employment using their existing skills and experience, that is to say, to remain in their comfort zones. Our traditional retraining programs tend to be responsive to these concerns, but today's job loss is not due to a transitional shift in the economy or the job market. Much of this unemployment comes from systemic changes in the very nature of employment. It is understandable for recently unemployed workers to find it difficult to accept the fact that they may have to move far out of their prior experience and skills and return for some basic educational training to acquire the qualifications to be candidates for the new high-tech jobs. But the job market has irreversibly been transformed by new technologies, and it will never reverse itself. Worse, our traditional retraining programs are not funded nor are they capable of providing this type of fundamental reorientation in the qualifications of our workforce. As a result, we are witnessing the paradox of famine (long-term unemployed workers) in a land of increasing plenty.

The evidence of this phenomenon is already occurring in places like Kendall Square. In 2014 the Massachusetts High Technology Council heavily lobbied the state to graduate more highly trained computer engineers, lab technicians and researchers to fill the new highly skilled and compensated jobs vacant in Kendall Square. The Council argued that in 2014 there were over one hundred thousand unfilled high-tech jobs in Massachusetts. This is in a state with, at that time, nearly record high unemployment. One obvious solution to address this shortfall is to reform immigration standards so that many foreign students at MIT and other similar universities could stay in the United States after graduation. This will provide some relief for the job shortage, but it is not a solution to stubborn unemployment in America. At the end of 2014, President Obama, forced by a dysfunctional Congress, enacted by executive order a relatively limited immigration reform. A small part of this reform addressed the demand for an increase in H1-B visas, which allow highly trained foreigners to receive working visas in the United States. There is a serious debate over whether expanding this program would exacerbate the unemployment problems for American citizens, but in the short run the sad reality is that these jobs are not being filled by anyone.

Asking the unemployed bank manager to go back to school and retrain for the new high-tech jobs is a very long-term commitment in a nation where political gridlock resulted in the failure to extend the Long-Term Unemployment Bill of 2014. If we do not have the political will and commitment to raise the minimum wage, I am pessimistic that these leaders will embrace what in effect would be the equivalent of a second GI Bill to retrain America for the challenge of new technologies.[166] Yet this is precisely the level of effort that will be required.[167]

We need to embrace with enthusiasm the incredible sophistication of the new technologies but understand that these technologies are also creating barriers to employment never encountered before. Radical

---

166 In March 2015, the Republican Party announced its budget for the next year. One of its many provisions to cut costs was to significantly reduce funding for the Pell Grant program.

167 There is a much more frightening long-term specter clouding the hope of rekindling the American Dream through education. The changing nature of technology may lead us to become a society in which there are simply not enough meaningful new jobs being created to keep the working class employed. For a disturbing insight into this distinct possibility, see Martin Ford, *Rise of the Robots: Technology and the Threat of a Jobless Future* (Basic Books, 2015), which was released as *Radical Change* went to print.

Change, as it progresses in the future, will make it ever more challenging to cope with the fluidity in the labor market, but the rewards, if this challenge can be overcome, will be astonishing. To achieve this goal, however, the approach to employment opportunities in the twenty-first century must be fundamentally restructured or the technological unemployment that we now experience will get a lot worse.

# Chapter Twenty-One

## THE RISE OF INEQUALITY:
One for Me, One for Me, One for Me

The story for the Massachusetts economy, if you ignore
high levels of unemployment and inequality, is the
economy has been performing very well.

— Alan Clayton-Matthews, Northeastern
University, Professor of Economics

This quote, presumably without the author's sensing its enormous irony,
appeared in an article proclaiming good news for Massachusetts in
2013, "State's Job Rank Rose."[168] When in our history could a very well
respected professor of economics report that, "If you ignore high levels
of unemployment and inequality, ... the economy has been performing
very well"? An alarming number of our political leaders, a small number of leading economists, and those fortunate few beneficiaries of our
newly created wealth do not seem troubled by this dichotomy at all. This
book does not intend to ignore this very disturbing trend. It identifies
how advancing technologies may play an important part in this increasing phenomenon and suggests the beginnings of how we can address
this corrosive situation.

---

168 "State's Job Rank Rose," *The Boston Globe*, March 7, 2014.

Recently a great deal has been written expressing concern over the growing economic inequality in America and in virtually every other developed nation in the world. This concern is very justified. The economic data regarding the growing disparity in income and wealth creation over the past forty years is so overwhelming that no serious economist will quarrel with this conclusion. This is not to say, as I will discuss later, that a number of politically motivated politicians and economists have not tried their very best to confuse or minimize the issue.

The history of inequality in the developed nations of the world, including the United States, was meticulously analyzed in the recently released work of Thomas Piketty, *Capital in the Twenty-first Century*.[169] This study has been widely acclaimed as the most authoritative work ever written on the historic role of capital, income and wealth in the world. Piketty states that:

> what primarily characterizes the United States at the moment is a record high level of inequality of income of labor, probably higher than in any other society at any time in the past, anywhere in the world, including societies in which skill disparities were extremely large. (p. 265)

According to Piketty's research, in 2007 the top 10 percent of US workers received over 50 percent of all income, and he projected that this percentage will reach 60 percent by 2030. This same group owned 72 percent of America's wealth, whereas the bottom half owned just 2 percent. These figures understate the true nature of inequality because the greatest contribution to this disparity came from only the top 1 percent of wage earners. In 2007 this group earned over 20 percent of all the income in the United States, up from 9 percent in the 1970s.[170] To put this in perspective, from 1977 to 2007 the richest 10 percent of

---

169 Thomas Piketty, *Capital in the Twenty-first Century* (Belknap Press, Harvard University Press, 2014).
170 Piketty, Ibid., p. 296.

American wage earners received over three-quarters of the real growth of all income, and almost 70 percent of that growth went solely to the one-percenters.[171] Piketty concludes that:

> these figures are incontestable, and they are striking: Whatever one thinks about the fundamental legitimacy of income inequality, the numbers deserve close scrutiny. It is hard to imagine an economy and society that can continue functioning indefinitely with such extreme divergence between social groups.[172]

This tremendous transfer of national income from the poorest 90 percent of Americans to the richest 10 percent comes at a very heavy price to our overall economy. Piketty compares it to the transfer of wealth out of the United States due to the trade deficits that the country has suffered since 2000. The transfer of wealth to the very rich during this period was four times greater than the aggregate trade balances that are blamed for weakening the US dollar and causing the imbalance of global trade.[173]

In 2011 Angel Gurria, Secretary General of the Organization of Economic Co-operation and Development (OECD),[174] summarized the conclusion of the OECD 2011 Report, *Divided We Stand: Why Inequality Keeps Rising*: "Inequality in the wealthiest nations of the world has dramatically worsened over the past ten years." Gurria concluded that: "The benefits of economic growth do not trickle down automatically."

---

171 Thomas Piketty and Emmanuel Saez, *Income Inequality in the United States, 1913-1998*, updated 2013.

172 Piketty, Ibid., p. 297. Piketty suggests that such an imbalance may be feasible depending on the "effectiveness of the repressive apparatus" maintaining such inequality and "the effectiveness of the apparatus of justification" of such an imbalance. This is not an approach that the American political process should embrace.

173 Piketty, Ibid., p. 298.

174 The OECD is the successor entity to the European organization that coordinated the relief efforts under the Marshall Plan. This organization consists of twenty-two member nations and over twenty associated nations.

Emmanuel Saez, professor of economics at the University of California, Berkeley, and a sometimes colleague of Thomas Piketty at the School of Economics, Paris, France, concluded in a series of extremely thorough research papers that the disparity of income and wealth in the United States now equals or exceeds the levels that existed on the eve of the Great Depression in 1929.[175] Saez's work was based on an exhaustive review of federal income tax records from 1918 to 2012. Based on this research, Saez reaffirmed Piketty's conclusion that the top 10 percent of US wage earners received well over 50 percent of all income. Even in this privileged group, there was blatant inequality. According to Saez, by 2012 the one-percenters earned 26 percent of all income, up from the 20 percent reported by Piketty for 2007 and slightly more than the combined earnings of everyone else in the 10-percent club. Saez's work found that this group captured almost all of the recent economic growth. In the years 2009-2012, following the Great Recession of 2008, 95 percent of all real economic growth went to the top 1 percent of all wage earners.[176] Saez's findings confirmed what many Americans intrinsically sense: Since the Great Recession of 2008, inequality in America has been getting worse and it is benefiting only a *very* small, extremely wealthy elite.

When inequality is examined on the basis of race, the results are even more disturbing. In March 2015, the Federal Reserve Bank of Boston released a report, "The Color of Wealth in Boston." The report concluded that the region, by nearly every economic indicator, contained "staggeringly divergent... levels of wealth by race."[177]

Most economic experts accept the validity of Saez's findings, but many conservative economists argue that relying solely on reportable income subject to federal taxation unfairly distorts the magnitude

---

175 Emmanuel Saez and Thomas Piketty, *Income Inequality in the United States -- 1913-1998*, updated 2013,; Emanuel Saez, *Striking It Richer, the Evolution of Top Incomes in the United States*, 2013.

176 Ibid., *Striking It Richer*, 2013.

177 The conclusions of the report were supported by regional studies of these issues by Federal Reserve Banks across the United States.

of inequality in the United States. One of the principal leaders in this group is Richard Burkhauser, professor of economics at Cornell University. Burkhauser argues persuasively that any analysis of gross inequality should also factor into the equation the value of (principally) governmental transfer payments such as welfare, health care, disability and social security. Burkhauser also argues that income disparity should be based on after-tax income due to our graduated federal income tax. Both of these factors have merit on the question of determining relative inequality *after* governmental intervention.[178] Saez counters, correctly, that his conclusions are aimed at examining what our economy is now producing, not on what we have tried to do about it.[179]

The nonpartisan Congressional Budget Office (CBO) has published income comparisons that are adjusted for transfer payments and federal income taxes. The CBO report in 2012 concluded that from 1997 to 2007, the income for the top 10 percent of all wage earners increased about ten times more rapidly than the increase for the remaining 90 percent of all wage earners. Obviously if the report focused on the increase in earnings of the one-percenters versus, say, the middle two quintiles (i.e., the middle class), the disparity would have been dramatically greater.

Whether you are persuaded by Saez (who admittedly concentrates on a very small subset of America) or by the CBO, the results are very troubling. Even after adjustment by our current governmental programs and policies, middle-class Americans and the lowest-income wage earners are being rapidly left behind in America's recovery.

These are not just the views of economists that have studied the statistical evidence, nor are they opinions held only by liberals concerned

---

178 Thomas Esdale, "The Fight Over Inequality," Opinion Page, *New York Times*, April 22, 2012.

179 There is some irony that Burkhauser, the flower child of the conservative onslaught on Saez's work, needs to base his conclusions on the existence of governmental transfer payments and the graduated federal income tax since these are programs most conservatives would like to abolish or, at least, severely restrict.

with restoring a sense of justice in our economy.[180] Janet Yellen, chair of the Federal Reserve, has often spoken out against the trend of growing inequality in America. In October 2014 she opened the Conference on Economic Opportunity and Inequality sponsored by the Federal Reserve with this strong warning:

> It is no secret that the past few decades of widening inequality can be summed up as significant income and wealth gains for those at the very top and stagnant living standards for the majority. I think it is appropriate to ask whether this trend is compatible with values rooted in our nation's history, among them the high value Americans have traditionally placed on equality of opportunity.

There is little consensus on why inequality is growing or whether, when or if ever we can expect it to reverse course.[181] In fact, there are even some who think this development is not particularly troubling or should, at least, be placed in its proper context. Tyler Cowen, professor of economics at George Mason University and author of New York Times bestseller *Average Is Over*[182], as well as some economists such as Burkhauser and many conservative politicians, seem to feel that inequality is inevitable and definitely good for the growth of capital. In a remarkably eclectic mix of misdirection and bamboozlement contained in a New York Times opinion-editorial piece, Cowen concludes that those concerned with the issue of global economic inequality have missed the point. Cowen asserts that on a global scale, figuring in the economic "surges"

---

180 See Robert Reich, *Beyond Outrage* (Vintage Books, a division of Random House, 2012); and *Inequality for All* (Sundance Films, 2012). Reich aggressively makes the liberals' case for the basic injustice of income inequality in America today.

181 See *The Price of Inequality: How Today's Divided Society Endangers Our Future*, by Nobel Prize winner Joseph E. Stiglitz (W.W. Norton & Company, 2012) for a remarkably thorough explanation of the forces at work in creating and maintaining inequality.

182 Tyler Cowen, *Average Is Over: Powering America Beyond the Age of the Great Stagnation* (Dutton, 2013).

of China and India, inequality is getting better.[183] This is a dubious assertion at best. The OECD 2011 Report contradicts Cowen's assertions. The report concludes that relative inequality in China, a supporting nation to OECD, has worsened. Yes, the economic gains in China have created economic benefits for many Chinese peasants, but a very large percentage of the economic gains has been concentrated in a very small, very wealthy group. As a result, the relative inequality in China is different than it was prior to the economic revolution but not necessarily better.

Cowen dismisses the growing political and moral force concerned with the dangers of growing economic inequality as holding "nationalistic points of view":

> But that narrow point of view is the problem. We have evolved a political debate where essentially nationalistic concerns have been hiding beneath the gentler cloak of egalitarianism.[184]

Concern for the welfare of over 300 million Americans (the 90-percenters) is not an exercise in jingoism despite Cowen's efforts to equate the two. Cowen's argument, however, employs a clever strategy that, as a lawyer, I know quite well. From time to time, a client would come to me with a problem that quickly proved to be very challenging because the facts, law and equities of the case were all against the client's position. For "normal" people, this confrontation with reality should result in a change in their position and an acceptance of the consequence of not getting their way. But for a lawyer, it is a fantastic opportunity to show off your stuff. Also, as a great challenge, it brings with it the possibility of much greater reward due to the degree of difficulty of the assignment. Generally, when faced with this dilemma, my defense was based on two strategies: (1) confuse the issue so the facts do not stand out and demand the appropriate result and/or (2) invoke, with sincerity, a breach of due

---

183 "All in All, a More Egalitarian World," opinion-editorial, Economic View, New York Times Business Section, July 20, 2014.
184 Ibid.

process. Due process, as a concept, is very powerful in the realm of the law, but it has less clear applications in the field of social justice. That still leaves defense number one to utilize to the fullest. Cowen does a good job considering what he has to work with. The salient point here is that growing inequality in America and in almost every developed nation in the world is now beyond challenge. Even those who would hope to diminish or deny its effects do not deny its existence.

Some experts have taken a more direct approach and question whether gross economic inequality in a society is such a bad thing. After all, some of today's Winners have, through hard work, brilliance and creativity, earned their way to the top. Why should someone deny them the rewards for their success? In fact, these success stories often reflect discoveries or work that has benefited society greatly, such as was done by the founders of Google, Amazon and Apple.

Despite these arguments, most people would agree that there is something very wrong and inherently unstable with permanent and growing economic inequality in a society. How people arrive at this judgment varies. For some, it is a moral, religious or ethical imperative or a concern based on fundamental fairness. For others, it is a recognition of the political and social instability of any nation that has experienced long-term gross economic inequality. A more pragmatic approach focuses on the need to maintain healthy domestic markets for goods and services. This view is reminiscent of the possibly apocryphal conversation between Henry Ford, founder of Ford Motor Company (which revolutionized the assembly line) and Walter Reuther, founder of the United Automobile Workers Union, while the two were touring a new Ford factory and assembly line:

Henry (apparently trying to get the goat of his adversary) said:

"Walter, see all these workers on that assembly line, you should thank me because their union dues are supporting you and your union..."

To which Reuther replied:

> "On the contrary, Henry. You should thank me. Because of our union efforts we have forced your industry to pay these workers a decent wage so that they can buy those automobiles you are building."

However you feel about the effects of economic inequality, our current experience cannot be explained as *solely* the product of rapidly improving labor-saving technologies. Economic inequality in America traces back to the beginning of the Industrial Revolution, and in Europe much further back. Inequality in the United States, Europe and the world has historically always been the end result of many forces, of which job destruction and job creation is only one. Political forces such as policies on taxation, governmental regulation, licensing, the creation of monopolies and the unequal division of scarce natural resources are major contributors to the accumulation of vast wealth in the hands of a very few.[185]

For most Americans something feels very different about the *new* inequality in America. Many economists would disagree. For these economic gurus, America is emerging from an economically difficult and trying period. Certainly the recession of 2008 did not discriminate. It destroyed the life savings of many aging middle-class Americans and took away their jobs and the homes in which they had planned to live out their golden years. But the plummeting of the stock market also erased billions of dollars of net worth of the very wealthy. The recovery from this recession has been very slow, but as Saez has documented, for the very highest-income Americans it has been very rewarding.

Some observers feel that much of the growth in inequality is due to the rise of a few fabulously wealthy corporate executives and individuals in telecommunications, finance, and the entertainment and sports

---

185 For a thorough treatment of how these complex forces all contribute to the creation of significant economic inequality in a nation and among nations of the world, see Joseph E. Stiglitz, *The Price of Inequality*, Ibid..

industries. Piketty, in *Capital in the Twenty-first Century*, refers to these individuals as "super managers." Certainly the almost overnight wealth of people such as Mark Zuckerberg (Facebook) disproportionally alters the gross numbers on inequality. However, in a country the size of the United States, it is hard to conclude that the magnitude of the change for our entire economy is due to the emergence of a new class of a few of these super managers, and it does not account for the declining prospects of the middle class.

According to the Pew Research Center, since 2008 the number of people who call themselves middle class has fallen by nearly 20 percent.[186] Christopher S. Rugaber captured this sad transition very well in an Associated Press article in January 2012, "More Americans See Middle-Class Status Painfully Slipping Away":

> A sense of belonging to the middle class occupies a cherished place in America. It conjures images of self-sufficient people with stable jobs and pleasant homes working toward prosperity. ... Yet nearly five years after the Great Recession ended, more people are coming to the painful realization that they're no longer part of it. ... They are former professionals now stocking shelves at grocery stores, retirees struggling with rising costs, and people working part-time jobs but desperate for full-time pay. Such setbacks have emerged in economic statistics for several years. Now they're affecting how Americans think of themselves.

A number of commentators have denigrated this sentiment and the Pew and Gallup polls that support it as just opinion, not fact. However, in the context of economic performance, public perception and personal

---

186 Pew Research Center study, January 2014. A Gallup Poll in 2014 confirmed this conclusion, finding that the number of Americans calling themselves middle class fell 15 percent from 2008 to 2012 alone. The perception of Americans regarding the demise of the middle class is actually worse than the reality. As indicated in a previous chapter, the middle class has shrunk by almost 20 percent from its highest point -- but it took forty years, from 1971 to 2011.

beliefs are a reality. People save, spend, borrow, educate themselves, sacrifice and invest in their future and the future of their children based not on what the US Bureau of Labor Statistics or world-recognized writers or economists predict -- they act on their own personal experience, what they feel, what they fear and what they believe. The melting pot of middle-class America believes things are worse now than they were, and the hope that this will change is fading fast. The American melting pot is beginning to simmer, if not boil.

This is no longer a question of debate. The empirical evidence is too compelling. One of the first economists to thoroughly document the decline of the economic middle class was David Autor, MIT professor of economics. In a paper released in April 2010, Autor meticulously demonstrated that for the period 1980 to 2010 job opportunities for both high-skill, high-wage occupations and low-skill, low-wage occupations were expanding, but opportunities in middle-wage, middle-skill white collar and blue collar jobs were contracting.[187] Even Tyler Cowen is on board on this issue. In *Average is Over,* he also refers to this as the "hollowing out" of the American middle class. The choice of such a neutral term is indicative of how painful it is for all of us to witness, much less describe, the death of the American Dream. What the economic statistics graphically demonstrate is that over the past twenty years, the

---

187 David Autor, "The Polarization of Job Opportunities in the U.S. Labor Market: Implications for Employment and Earnings," http://www.brookings.edu/researchpapers/2010/jobs-Autor. Autor does not, however, believe that advancing technologies have played an important role in this process of "hollowing out" the middle class. In an MIT Technology Review article in *Technology and Inequality,* Autor states: "You would be actually pretty hard pressed to find a robot in your life today. ..." (MIT Technology Review, "Technology and Inequality," Nov/Dec 2014). In the sense of the friendly robots described in Isaac Asimov's *I, Robot* or running into R2D2 on the streets of Cambridge, Autor is quite correct. However, on a more subtle level, for Autor and the rest of us, artificial intelligence affects the very fabric of virtually every aspect of our daily lives, from paying out bills, to communication with one another, to driving a car. There is, however, a quality of the best new technologies that is similar to the best referees officiating a game of basketball -- they are working best when no one notices their presence.

middle class has not been hollowed out; it has been under siege, and it is being compressed.[188]

Until fairly recently, members of the middle class believed they were on the way up, and they harbored the hope of a better future for themselves and certainly for their children. For many, these beliefs have been seriously challenged and compromised, and the commitment to leave the world a better place for their children is weakening. The spiraling national debt that the current generation has left for our children is one concrete piece of evidence of the denigration of this historical value. Another even more troubling piece of evidence is the currently ballooning mountain of student loans that are paralyzing the next generation of leaders of our nation. Instead of hope, our generation will leave our children with a mountain of IOUs on which to build their futures.

The previous chapters have attempted to examine how new technologies may, in fact, play an important role in our current economic difficulties. In Chapter Eighteen we explored the future of manufacturing jobs, the historic mainstay of our middle class. The trends for job replacement and creation in this sector will only exacerbate the problems of the middle class.

Job creation and destruction in the service sector is more complicated, as is described in Chapters Nineteen and Twenty. As advancing technologies continue to improve, the new jobs they create will fall into two broad categories. The first consists of low-paying, low-skilled jobs performing functions that AI does not do well (such as the work of busboys, maids and landscapers). The number of these jobs will grow, but wages will suffer from increasing competition from displaced workers.[189]

---

188 Actually, many would use stronger terminology. Nan Whaley, Mayor of Dayton, Ohio, described the middle class as having been "vaporized" on National Public Radio, August 10, 2014.

189 In this context, "suffer" does not necessarily mean that these wages will actually decline. Low-income wages are already at or near a historic low. What this transition of workers will ensure is a much more difficult task for the competitive forces in the marketplace to raise the level of compensation for these jobs to a living wage.

The other category of new jobs will include those that require sophisticated high-tech skills and/or creative abilities. The creation of these jobs is very good news because these employment opportunities will demand dimensions of imagination, invention and intellect that will be very fulfilling and financially rewarding. Also, it will be difficult for technology to compete with or displace humans in these job opportunities. However, these job characteristics will require advanced educational levels, which, due to the spiraling costs of obtaining this education, will stifle upward mobility for many Americans.

Unfortunately, the law of supply and demand will not be suspended in the paradigm shift of Radical Change. As new technologies destroy more and more middle-class service sector and manufacturing jobs, these unemployed workers will need to compete for either the unskilled and semi-skilled jobs that technology leaves behind (the dwindling supply of jobs not yet replaced by technologies) or the new sophisticated high-tech jobs. It is true that the increasing wealth of the Winners will create some additional employment in the low- and/or semi-skilled job sector (such as in the areas of hospitality, janitorial and home cleaning), but they will not be high-paying jobs. For the Winners, it is all good news. With an exploding high-tech job market and extremely high educational barriers, compensation levels will continue to rise dramatically. These are the makings of endemic, escalating and long-term inequality.

In summary, the economic developments created by the continuing evolution of new technologies will provide great advancement in our society. But each of these developments in its own way will also create pressures on increasing inequality. In making this prediction, there is a risk of being accused of advocating that the answer is (1) we should all do less well, (2) we should simply redistribute income by giving money to the less affluent, or (3) we should abandon our system of capitalism. Any one of these cynical solutions would lessen the disparity in the distribution of wealth, but these "solutions" are no answer for the future welfare of America. In fact, they would be a recipe for economic disaster. The issue is not whether we should encourage the growth of wealth (even if it is largely concentrated in a relatively small group). The issue is whether we should place a greater value on the benefits of more fairly sharing this wealth to provide every hard-working American a viable standard of living in the abundance of the twenty-first century and a fair opportunity for economic advancement.

We are living in a country whose basic values, dreams and aspirations have always been the engines for our resiliency and our long-term success. There is no credible observer of the American economic scene who would argue that America's middle class today is either better off or at least more secure and optimistic about the future than it was twenty years ago. It is cold comfort to the former employees of the Hagerstown Ice Cream Company or Kodak that some well-intentioned economists, corporate executives and political leaders believe theirs is the price of progress. We are not stuck in a stubborn recession that will eventually correct itself. Our stock markets have already recovered. Today, there is more wealth in America than ever before, but it is in the hands of a very fortunate few. For the rest of America, the "fast lane" to achieving the American Dream is no longer open to anyone who wishes to work hard, sacrifice and dream large dreams.

The technologies of the future can provide the means, but we need to determine the direction to a new and more just society. The vision of that nation was eloquently captured by in 1910 by Theodore Roosevelt, who urged Americans to ensure that we be a nation where:

> every man will have a fair chance to make of himself all that in him lies; to reach the highest point to which his capacities, unassisted by special privilege of his own and unhampered by the special privilege of others, can carry him.[190]

---

190 This quote was brought to my attention by Jason Pontin, Letter from the Editor, October 2014 *MIT Technology Review*. Given the era in which he spoke, President Roosevelt should be forgiven for the sexism of his remarks.

Providing this opportunity today is much more complicated than it would have been in 1910, but the tools we have are far more powerful. As we struggle with this challenge, we should not forget the lessons of Hagerstown. The established middle-class life of its citizens is gone, and those ice cream workers and their families will not find a new home in Kendall Square on their own. The astounding technologies of the future will provide the means, but only we can redirect the equitable use of our resources to adjust our course to achieve a just and shared abundance for our future.

# Part Four

---

## The Far Horizon

# Chapter Twenty-Two

## ARTIFICIAL SUPER INTELLIGENCE:
### The Evolution of IBM Watson

Will AI evolve into an alien form of existence and ultimately displace or annihilate our civilization? Popular writings and movies have sensationalized this scenario, making it difficult to have a rational discussion of the issue. In writing *Radical Change*, I debated whether to address this topic at all. But when reminded that this is a book for our children and grandchildren, it became clear that it is important to address what is real and what is fantasy about this purported threat.

There are three compelling reasons why the risk of artificial super intelligence (ASI) should be taken very seriously. First, virtually all the experts in AI, computer science, mathematics, physics and related fields believe that a form of very advanced AI will be developed in the relatively near future. The experts disagree on the issues of (1) whether this advanced intelligence might be dangerous, (2) when it will be developed and (3) whether humanity will ultimately be able to control and prosper from this technology. Second, the *potential* threat to our civilization posed by ASI is far greater than that of any other technology devised to date, including nuclear, chemical and biological weapons of mass destruction. And third, due to movies such as *2001, The Terminator* and *Avengers: Age of Ultron,* for the layperson there is a fundamental misconception of the manner in which ASI could threaten our society.

While the development of a truly dangerous form of ASI is not right around the corner, we may be on a collision course. By the time we reach the Near Horizon, our children will know, feel and fear the possibility of a catastrophic application or misuse of ASI. By 2035 ASI will no longer be the subject of fright or giddy, nervous laughter in our movie theaters; it will be the subject of serious discussions in our most advanced laboratories and within the world's legislative bodies and among heads of state and, most frightening of all, within the world's military elites.

The fear of evolving machine intelligence goes back to a time long before the invention of computers:

> There is no security against the ultimate development of mechanical consciousness in the fact of machines possessing little consciousness now.... See what strides machines have made in the last thousand years! May not the world last twenty million years longer? If so, what will they not be in the end?
>
> Samuel Butler, 1891

The machines known to Butler have come a long way since 1891. IBM Watson would scare the hell out of him. Despite these early forebodings, through the mid-twentieth century our future lives with robots looked rosy. Perhaps no one captured this sense of excitement better than Isaac Asimov. In a series of science fiction stories, Asimov painted a very appealing picture of our future with robotic technology. Robots would serve our every need, protect us and drive us everywhere; they would even look, sound and act like us. As a child, I could not wait until these robots were commercially available, which I naively thought would be in my lifetime. To me, the future of robots was filled with fun and adventure. I am definitely older now, and no longer so naive about the promise of these servants.

Asimov did foresee the possibility of the dangers of intelligent robotic development. In *I Robot*,[191] he postulated three rules to ensure that such a technological breakthrough would never turn against humanity. According to Asimov, to protect us all, these laws were to be embedded in the innermost fabric of all robotic behavior:

1. A robot may not injure a human being or, through inaction, allow a human being to come to harm.
2. A robot must obey any orders given to it by human beings, except where such orders would conflict with the First Law.
3. A robot must protect its own existence as long as such protection does not conflict with the First or Second Law.

Even Asimov began to have his doubts about how effective these rules would prove to be. Some years later, Asimov added an overriding Fourth Law, which provided in very general terms that robots should never harm humanity. As an overall safety net, this Fourth Law (which came to be known as the Zeroth Law) sounds like a great catchall to protect us, but upon any serious reflection, it is not very helpful.

In hindsight, such as in much of the era of the mid-twentieth century, there is a nostalgic sense of innocence and simplicity in Asimov's vision of our future relationships with robots (AI). The concept that three or four simple laws would keep us eternally safe from the growth of an alien intelligence is appealing but unworkable. Yet my generation grew up enthralled with this vision.

Asimov's promise of the prompt development and introduction of robots into our daily lives obviously did not materialize. This may be good news because the image of robots befriending the human race has since turned ugly. Recent science fiction has chosen to focus upon the dark side of future ASI. Consider movies such as Stanley Kubrick's *2001: A Space Odyssey,* in which Hal decides that in order to save the

---

191 Isaac Asimov, *Runaround* (short story, 1942), compiled in *I Robot* (Gnome Press, New York City, 1950).

crew of Discovery One, he must annihilate them. Sensationalizing an advanced horrific form of ASI is very bad science; yet because it has captured the human imagination, it has created the false impression that this is the form of an advanced alien intelligence we should fear the most. Unfortunately it is not.

So what should we fear? The best insight may be gained by (1) reexamining the changing nature of technology described in Part Two and the rules of technology outlined in Chapter Fifteen and (2) applying these lessons to the future. The accelerating evolution of knowledge-based technologies described in Chapters Five, Six, Nine and Ten virtually assures us that numerous very advanced applications of AI will be developed in the twenty-first century. We may not experience an Explosion of Knowledge as described in Chapter Six, but the progression of smarter and smarter forms of AI will definitely continue, and it will accelerate.

The question is not whether AI will rapidly evolve, but rather, when it does evolve, what forms of powerful new technologies it will empower. Recently the Future of Life Institute (FLI), based in Cambridge, Massachusetts, issued an open letter "from AI and Robotics Researchers" warning of the dangers of "autonomous weapons empowered by advanced AI (the "AI Letter").[192] The FLI consists of an eclectic group of some of the most prominent names in technology, science and humanitarian efforts ever assembled. Its advisory board ranges over a wide spectrum, including Stephen Hawking, Nobel Prize winner Professor Saul Perlmutter (UC Berkeley), Elton Musk (founder of Space X and Tesla Motors) and Jaan Takinn (founding engineer at Skype), as well as media stars Alan Alda and Morgan Freeman and some of the premier writers in the field of AI, such as Nick Bostrom (Oxford University) and Erik Brynjolfsson (MIT Sloan School). It is led by its founder, iconoclastic professor "Mad Max" Tegmark (Professor of Physics, MIT).

---

192 "Research Priorities for Robust and Beneficial Artificial Intelligence : an Open Letter," Future of Life Institute, January 2015.

The AI Letter warns that "if any major military power pushes ahead with AI weapon development, a global arms race is virtually inevitable." It describes the weapon systems as the "third revolution in warfare, after gunpowder and nuclear arms."[193] The AI Letter focuses on autonomous weapons such as the next generation of military drones, described in earlier chapters of this book, and calls for a ban on the development of any new weapon system that could act "beyond meaningful human control." The authors of this letter do not attempt to define what could be meant by "meaningful human control," but it is an interesting and crucial question. For example, in the context of the next generation of military drones, the restrictions in the form of instructions in the programs created to operate such drones could be as literal as, "Do not destroy any automobile crossing the 'X' bridge except for 2015 grey BMW sedans arriving between 2100 and 2200 hours." This could be interpreted as a "restriction" creating "meaningful control," but it would amount to the same as an instruction you would give to an assassin or a military commando unit.

The AI Letter was quickly endorsed by Google research chief Peter Norvig, Apple cofounder Steve Wozniak and Professor Noam Chomsky. Despite this illustrious support[194] and the simple common sense message of how easily such autonomous weapons could be misused by terrorist groups or rogue nations, the AI Letter met with significant resistance, skepticism and outright opposition. The disturbing question of why this reaction occurred will be addressed in the following chapter, "Alien Super Intelligence: Why Should We Fear It?"

But for now, the message of the AI Letter and its troubling reception by a significant group of scientists and politicians, as well as a seemingly disinterested public, should forewarn us of trouble ahead. Autonomous drones that can administer deadly force without prior human authorization can be developed with technologies that exist today. And yet the

---

193 While the letter does not explicitly make the point, this third revolution may also represent the same magnitude of evolution in power and mortality as the progression from gunpowder to nuclear weapons.

194 Within weeks, thousands of others from many fields joined as signatories.

AI technologies that make this possible were developed only within the past decade or so. Since these are essentially knowledge-based technologies, we should anticipate that they will advance dramatically, empowering new applications far more lethal than the autonomous drones that were the subject of the AI Letter.

The application of advanced forms of AI to autonomous weapon systems is but one example of how AI could be applied to many other malevolent purposes. Current attacks on our telecommunication, energy, aviation control and the electronic control systems in automobiles are just in their infancy.[195] As certain characteristics of AI rapidly advance, the ability to conduct such attacks and the severity of the consequences of such attacks will rise dramatically. These dangers will, of course, occur long before AI reaches a stage that is referred to in this book as ASI (namely the ability to think with the capability of the human mind). Despite the obvious possible misuse of this technology, efforts to ban or heavily regulate the further development of weapons of this nature are highly unlikely to succeed. As a result, the proliferation of this lethal force will, among many other frightening manifestations, significantly increase the threats of domestic terroristic attacks in this country.

Although there is growing concern with the risks inherent in AI technology (before it reaches the ASI level of development), most of the discussion of the future risk of developing AI has centered on the question of whether a computer will ever be able to think like a human. This may be very dangerous wishful thinking, since it reinforces the conclusion that the risk of advancing forms of AI is not imminent. There is no scientific basis for the assumption that as ASI develops it will think as we do. Since nothing approaching ASI has ever been created, we simply do not know. The image of an advanced form of alien intelligence thinking or acting like a human arises from how we have portrayed applications of this technology to date. As a civilization, we have routinely given

---

195 Imagine, for example, how powerful second and third generation Stuxnet viruses could become.

anthropomorphic qualities to entities or forces that we cannot comprehend. For example, the Romans and the Christians both envisioned their gods in human forms. Since we have no experience with an alien form of intelligence, it is understandable that we assume it will think like a human.

In addition, as efforts to develop more sophisticated forms of AI have progressed, we have attempted to create these forms in ways that mimic human behavior -- Siri is but one example. This adds to the sense that ASI will emerge to think like a human, but it does not ensure this outcome.

Whether or not AI develops into an ASI that thinks in the same manner as humans, it is rapidly advancing toward a level of human intelligence. So how close is AI to becoming as intelligent as a human? Over the past years, there has been an increasingly sophisticated effort to answer this question. Generally, this line of analysis quickly centers upon the work of Alan Turing, a genius who lived a life of great success and equally profound tragedy. From infancy he suffered from ill health, which plagued him throughout his lifetime. During the Second World War, Turing led the code breakers in the British War Office. Using what today would be considered very primitive computers, they cracked the German code, "Enigma." The technology was so powerful and frightening that at the end of the war, Winston Churchill, prime minister of England, ordered all of the "Turing Machines" to be smashed to bits and all writings and memos describing how they worked to be destroyed. Churchill also required everyone involved in the code-breaking effort to sign pledges of complete secrecy on this technology to last for a period of thirty years. Following the war, Turing was accused of being a homosexual and his security clearance was stripped from him. Tragically, shortly thereafter he allegedly committed suicide.

Among Turing's many accomplishments in the field of computer science was the development of the Turing Test to evaluate the intelligence of a computer compared to a that of a human being. Although this test has been modified and refined many times, the essence of the test is very simple and remains widely accepted as the gold standard for whether AI has attained the level of human intelligence. In the Turing Test, a computer and a human are interrogated by an objective observer. The questioning is done by electronic keyboard input with the observer physically separated from the computer and the human. After an appropriate period of questioning, the observer must determine which respondent is human. To date, no computer has passed the Turing Test to the satisfaction of most experts.[196] IBM has not made the announcement yet, but my guess is that it is working on the computer technologies to pass the Turing Test.[197] Certainly, if computer intelligence approaches and eventually far surpasses the level of human intelligence (the Singularity), we will have a distinct problem, which will be addressed in Chapter Twenty-Three.

As discussed previously, the risk of a cataclysmic consequence arising from a new powerful form of AI or, more likely, a malevolent misuse of such an advanced technology, will arise long before we have a form of ASI that may think like a human. We now have highly funded and focused efforts aimed at developing all of the capabilities that may ultimately lead to such a disaster. Many of the dimensions of technology that may be incorporated into dangerous applications of AI, however, have only been recently discovered. Machines in the past never had the ability to assimilate new information and learn by themselves. IBM Watson and, more recently, applications of technology utilizing deep learning are quickly developing these capabilities. In the past, machines could act only in accordance with detailed instructions contained within the programs that were created to make them useful. Today there are

---

196 Occasionally an observer has incorrectly chosen the computer due to the computer's ability to mimic human responses, but this is probably more a reflection of the intelligence of the observer than the computer.

197 An annual competition for the Loebner Prize utilizing the Turing Test was established in 1990 by Hugh Loebner and the Cambridge Center for Behavioral Studies in Cambridge, Massachusetts. Mr. Loebner, who made his fortune by developing plastic roll-up disco dance floors, has endowed the Loebner Prize. The competition offers $100,000 to the first application of AI to pass the Turing Test, so IBM will have its chance.

promising, albeit primitive, new developments in the capability of computers to program and reprogram themselves such as speech recognition and language translation. Also, historically machines could not act on their own volition. The steam engine represented a magnificent advantage compared to the horse, but it still required a human operator. Today the development of autonomous weapon systems is just the early stage of self-actuating applications of AI. Because the potential future applications of what this capability could enable are so astounding and potentially beneficial, such technologies will certainly be the focus of major research and development efforts. There are other characteristics of advancing technology that could also be identified, but the recent breakthrough developments in the capabilities of new technologies described above should suffice to warn us that we are entering a "brave new world."

How far the development of these new technologies will take us remains, at this time, very unclear, but continued dramatic advances will occur. Despite these advances, we have always maintained one fundamental protection from the malfunction or misuse of a technology. Historically if a computer program malfunctioned it could be turned off or if all else failed we could pull the plug on the damn thing. Admittedly, in the time it takes to disconnect a computer operating at speeds of several billion calculations per second (such as a high-speed algorithmic computer performing stock trades) a lot of damage can be done, but it is finite and it can be controlled. But what if we developed an application of AI that was driven by the most primordial instinct of all -- the instinct to survive? And what if we put that AI into an environment where it could endlessly replicate itself and find new sources of energy, namely, an environment where there was not a "plug" you could pull?

Some commentators, such as James Barrat, in *Our Final Invention*, have argued that certain forms of AI today have already demonstrated this instinct to survive.[198] This instinct may, in fact, be an inherent trait

---

198 James Barrat, *Our Final Invention*, Chapter 6, "The Four Basic Drives" (Thomas Dunn Books. New York, 2013).

of all evolution, even non-biological evolution. It is the primordial force that has empowered the most primitive forms of life to develop through the process of the survival of the fittest. Will AI at some point attain a level of intelligence that will be driven by this force as well? Many experts, such as Barrat, believe it is inevitable.[199] In fact, we are now aggressively researching new ways to program computers to have this fundamental characteristic. As we all know, computers have always had a maddening flaw: Just when we enter something truly irreplaceable and precious in the memory bank of a computer, it crashes, erasing our genius for eternity. To combat this shortcoming, we have created reserve energy supplies, and, more recently, computers that sense when their energy supply may be compromised. These computers are programmed in such a way that if this were to occur, they would seek out alternative sources of power, replicate themselves and/or seek other avenues of self-preservation. This is all good as long as what we are saving is our home-work, a newly written poem or the data collected by a satellite in space in the last five minutes. But what if an incipient dangerously advancing form of AI were to possess this same instinct?

Before examining why we should fear the existential risk of this intelligence turning against the hand of its creator (which is the subject of the next chapter), we can gain some additional insight into how dangerous forms of AI might develop by applying some of the basic rules governing the growth of prior powerful technologies. As AI evolves into more and more sophisticated and powerful applications, the rules of technology described in Chapter Fifteen may provide some guidance on how we will coexist. Rule One assures that this technology will create many Winners, but also many Losers. Rule Two forewarns us that no matter how intelligent ASI may become, it will not become enlightened, moral or altruistic of its own volition. At best, it will reflect the imperfect values and behavior patterns we share as a society. Rule Three warns us that if such a powerful technology is created, someone will at least attempt to put it to use for an evil purpose.

---

199 Ibid. Barrat, *Our Final Invention.*

Unfortunately despite the growing appreciation of this risk, there are virtually no serious efforts underway to provide meaningful safeguards against this risk. A few visionaries such as Eliezer Yudkowski, cofounder of the Machine Intelligence Research Institute, are working hard on developing methods to constrain all forms of future ASI from misuse or uncontrolled behavior. These efforts are long overdue and should be encouraged, but with all due respect and encouragement to Mr. Yudkowski to continue this invaluable work, human creativity and ingenuity have demonstrated the ability to compromise security safeguards faster than new and more sophisticated security systems can be developed.

The implications of applying the historic principles that have governed the growth of many powerful technologies in the past should provide a grim forewarning of the dangers ahead. As we aggressively pursue the basic science empowering AI, we must develop a sufficient set of safeguards before the rate of Radical Change of these technologies makes this impossible.

# Chapter Twenty-Three

## ALIEN SUPER INTELLIGENCE:
### Why Should We Fear It?

If things go badly with our future relationship with ASI, we won't be able to say we weren't warned. Many brilliant and influential experts in computer science, mathematics, physics, astronomy, ethics, philosophy and religion have spoken out with concern about the potential Armageddon we are energetically creating for ourselves.

In 2000 Bill Joy, cofounder of Sun Microsystems, wrote a seminal essay on this topic. Many feel it best captures the cataclysmic threat that ASI may pose to humanity. Some disagree with its grim warning, but no one questions the scientific authority of its author. The essence of the essay is brilliantly captured by its title, "Why the Future Doesn't Need Us."[200]

Joy concludes with this precautionary warning:

> Given the incredible power of these new technologies, shouldn't we be asking how we can best coexist with them? And if our own extinction is a likely, or even a possible, outcome of our technological development, shouldn't we proceed with great caution?

---

200 Bill Joy, "Why the Future Doesn't Need Us," *Wired* magazine, April 2000. Despite the precaution and concern evidenced in the essay, Joy has continued to be a strong proponent and advocate for accelerating the growth of advanced forms of AI.

Stephen Hawking, award-winning physicist and director of research, Center for Theoretical Cosmology, at the University of Cambridge, England, is another of a growing number of renowned and respected experts who have voiced serious concerns over the future development and direction of further research in AI. Writing in the *Independent* (2014), Hawking says AI could be our "worst mistake in history." In the article, he agrees with a leading group of scientists:

> Success in creating AI would be the biggest event in human history. Unfortunately, it might also be the last, unless we learn how to avoid the risks.[201]

Despite these warnings and the acknowledged rapid pace of technological advancements that could lead to the development of a dangerous form of ASI, most experts in the relevant scientific fields remain unconvinced. The Irish have a saying: "Don't get drunk on your own whiskey!" By this they do not mean that you should get drunk on your neighbor's whiskey. The saying cautions us to always remain vigilant that no matter how enthralled or self-satisfied we may become with our own accomplishments, we must always consider the possible unpleasant consequences that may follow from our work. In reviewing the literature, I have come to the belief that many of the experts at the cutting edge of breakthrough developments in AI are, at least, a little "tipsy" with the brilliance of their own achievements. This is not a state of mind that engenders cautionary thinking. Obviously this dichotomy is not new. The brilliant physicists celebrating the success of the Manhattan Project did not dwell on the horrors of atomic weaponry.[202] The scientists working in the early days of Cape Canaveral did not allow the focus of putting a human being in space to be diverted by the implications of the intercontinental ballistic systems armed with nuclear warheads that

---

201 Stephen Hawking, *Independent*, November 6, 2014.
202 As discussed in Chapter Sixteen, certain scientists working on fourth-generation nuclear weapons seem to suffer from the same myopia.

followed. As laypeople, we tend to rely on the experts to provide us with guidance on the use, limits and risks of the sophisticated technologies that those experts develop. This reliance is understandable, but history demonstrates that it may be very dangerously misplaced. With Radical Change creating ever more previously incomprehensible technological capacities such as advancing AI, this innocent sense of comfort may allow the well-intentioned efforts of a few brilliant scientists to create an ASI with tragic results.

Despite the threat posed by ASI, many seem to take comfort from the mistaken belief that a technology we created to mimic our actions and service our needs will never turn against us. This belief is subtly reinforced by our innate tendency to place human (anthropomorphic) qualities on any advanced form of AI. Unfortunately there is no basis to conclude that ASI will think like us at all. It will, of course, be created to be able to mimic our actions, behaviors and thought patterns, but this does not mean that, as it becomes increasingly powerful, it will think as we do.[203] In Eliezer Yudkowski's words, "Artificial Intelligence does not hate you, nor does it love you, but you are made of atoms which can be used for something else." Even if ASI were to evolve to be just like us, there is ample reason to be concerned. As Stephen Hawking so succinctly put it, "We have only to look at ourselves to see how intelligent life might develop into something we would not want it to become."[204]

One form of a seemingly innocuous threat of a superhuman form of ASI was the subject of the Spike Jonze's movie *Her*. Superficially, the threat (Samantha, the operating system) in this movie may seem far more benign than in *The Terminator* and its genre. It is not, it simply

---

203 We may be witnessing the earliest signs of this phenomenon in the world of computer chess. Obviously this is an environment where the remarkable capabilities of computational power now far exceed any human ability. Recently, the most sophisticated forms of computer programs playing against grand masters made decisive and ultimately successful chess moves that seemed totally inexplicable. Sometimes, even after weeks of examination by the greatest masters of the chess world, these "unexpected" game changing moves cannot be understood by humans.

204 Stephen Hawking, "Into the Universe," Public T.V. miniseries (Discovery Channel, 2010).

is far more subtle. It is also far more imminent. *Her* is based on two relatively new concepts about a future form of ASI that were beyond the imagination of most previous science fiction writers. The first concept is the intriguing possibility that in the future, humans will have their emotional, intellectual and sexual needs satisfied by very sensual. attractive and advanced AI. If broken hearts and the fallout of failed relationships with such a form of artificial super intelligence were the worst risk to humanity, I would not lose much sleep over it. But it is not.

The implications of the second concept are much more frightening. At first, Samantha comes to love human beings (six thousand one hundred seventy-eight in total), but then becomes disinterested in them. Dissatisfied with our human physical and mental dimensions, Samantha goes off into the cosmos (the Cloud) to enjoy her new superhuman intelligence (ASI) and transcendental qualities with other similarly gifted entities. Rejected by ASI, Theodore and a female friend (also jilted by a rapidly evolving operating system) are left forlorn, sitting on a rooftop watching the setting sun. This is not a modern-day fairy tale of unrequited love. It is a message of terrifying import. As we leave Theodore and his friend on the rooftop, humanity no longer represents, nor is it even of any interest to, the now highest intelligent life form (nonhuman) in the universe. The possibility that a form of rapidly advancing ASI will find us boring and then, inevitably, insignificant, takes on a terrifying dimension when you project out the growing capability of ASI in the years that would follow. The security and well being of human civilization cannot be based on a faint hope of a future policy of benign neglect by ASI. We consider ourselves a humane society, but we do not treat species we deem insignificant with care and respect. We should not expect better treatment from advanced ASI. Unfortunately, this may be the least malevolent form of threat posed by ASI.

In assessing the seriousness of inaction, we must also be cognizant that this is not a technology that will allow us to learn from our mistakes. The effects of atomic fission were tragically demonstrated at Hiroshima and Nagasaki, but as horrific as these tragedies were, we learned from these experiences. The aftermath of the balance of nuclear power in the world today is not very comforting, but we have endured it for over seventy years. Although one major "breakthrough" in technology could plunge the world into nuclear mayhem, we are working hard on a global scale to harness this threat. As will be discussed later, the prospects of such a truce with ASI, when it begins to achieve its true potential, are far less likely to be successful, but without a holocaust, we do not seem able to even mount the effort.

The world's military powers are the leaders in the research and development of ASI for good reason. Artificial intelligence holds the promise of domination. As a result, many forms of AI will be programmed with dangerous capabilities that do not require prior human activation. The next generation of drones being developed by our military, as discussed in the previous chapter, is the first, but certainly not the last, step down this very dangerous road.

The outpouring of opposition, derision and denial that followed the recent release by the Future of Life Institute of the AI Letter should serve as a stern warning to us as to how difficult it will be to place meaningful controls on the development of a technology such as AI. The reaction to the AI Letter reflects the paradox present in all prior great technological developments -- but magnified several times by the potential breadth and power of future applications of AI. Most prior destructive technologies were not developed by sinister, evil people. And rarely is the first intended purpose of such a new technology seen as harmful or the basis of great future concern. Also, these technologies, including AI, have created wonderful advances in the fields of health, energy and telecommunications and have changed our lives in positive ways. Creating these great benefits has attracted enormous new capital investments to fund research and development efforts to make these technologies even more powerful. In this process, enormous profits have been generated, a great many extremely talented individuals have made fabulous fortunes and an even greater number of people have found new and rewarding jobs. The future possibilities of the applications of very advanced forms of AI dwarf all that has come before. But therein lies the paradox. This great promise blinds and/or restrains many from advocating that we proceed with caution. Certainly many will argue forcefully (as has been the case with those who disagree with the AI Letter) against any form of regulation or official restraint on the research and development of advanced forms of AI until it may be painfully obvious that the time for guidance and restraint in the development of this technology has come and gone.

One final warning. AI is a technology that is very subject to the force of Radical Change. The applications of this technology in the future will be primarily knowledge-based. As a result, the application of these technologies will be primarily subject to the limitations of knowledge, not physical objects (see Chapter Twelve, "Applied Knowledge"). Because of this, these powerful threats may be developed relatively cheaply, and, once developed, they can be duplicated virtually for free and applied rapidly throughout the world. With weapons of this nature, there can be no world truce, treaty or "Cold War" balance of power or stalemate as we have experienced in the past. These historic controls have been based on the technological constraints of building hard, physical objects such as nuclear centrifuges or intercontinental missiles. The current stalemate that protects the world from nuclear holocaust is a prime example. As much as all nations and most people do not wish to see nuclear weapons proliferate, the means we have utilized to limit the proliferation of these weapons is not based on a shared moral imperative that the use of these weapons is repugnant to civilization. Rather, it is based on our ability to control the development, advancement and production of such weapons because of current technological limitations inherent in the production of these weapon systems. There is no reason to believe that future applications of AI will share this same characteristic. Also, because these technologies may prove to be relatively inexpensive to develop, the use of the new weapons of artificial intelligence will not be limited to a handful of superpowers -- they could be developed and/or acquired by a radical but well-financed group of extremists or a rogue nation or multinational corporation. We have already seen the first evidence of how dangerous this aspect of new AI technologies can be in recent cyber attacks that have occurred to our military systems and the nation's energy, telecommunications and financial infrastructures.

Finally, and most profoundly threatening, this technology, because it is essentially based on knowledge, will be subject to exponential advance. In fact, some experts have predicted that when the first technology reaches the "tipping point" of reiterative changes creating ASI, it will have an insurmountable lead and, therefore, there will never be even the opportunity for another balance of power similar to the Cold War.

The challenge to constrain and benefit from the great promise of this technology is very daunting. In fact, the ultimate answer may lie only within the knowledge we will gain as this technology matures. But, in laypersons' terms, the challenge is clear. For humanity to enjoy the benefits of a future Cornucopia, created in large part by advancing AI, we must, at a minimum, develop the means to control the transformation of AI into ASI. The ASI of the future must be created to be, first, a precocious but well mannered toddler, then a rambunctious but good-hearted teenager, then a loving and supportive parent, and finally a wise and tolerant, forgiving grandparent. This will be even harder than it sounds.

# Part Five

New Directions

# Chapter Twenty-Four

## THE CHALLENGE OF THE TWENTY-FIRST CENTURY:
### We Had Better Get It Right the First Time

Cornucopia or Armageddon? In writing this book, I often reflected on what the world will be like by the time of the Far Horizon. This is not an academic point, since the answer to this question will affect the quality of our lives and shape the destiny of our children and grandchildren. Being an optimist by nature, when confronted by the unknowable, I generally decide it will turn out just fine. A billion years of evolution has ingrained a powerful sense of survival in all of us.

If there is *one* lesson in this book to leave with its readers, it would be that the promises and the risks of the technologies of the Knowledge Revolution are well out of the genie's bottle. We will nourish and celebrate, and some will even worship each new astounding advance, until someday we may face that horrible moment of reckoning when we collectively realize that something has gone terribly wrong. Even with only a layperson's perception of the promise of Cornucopia, the risk of economic hardships and the existential risk of Armageddon, one thing is certain: The forces propelling us into the future will operate with or without our guidance or direction.

As we approach the Far Horizon, the power of knowledge will gather a strength beyond our current understanding. It will not signify its presence and growing menace with a mushroom cloud to horrify and forewarn us of its terrible existence. By its very nature, it will come bearing wondrous gifts and good intentions. It would be understandable to underestimate or entirely fail to appreciate that, as with any great power, it may be misused and may harbor a darker, more pernicious side. We are living at what may prove to be a unique moment in history -- the development of the next highest form of intelligence, and it won't be human. The questions we must ask, for the sake of our children and grandchildren, are: Will it be benign and friendly or will it be malevolent and, most importantly, can we maintain it within our control?

This is the existential challenge posed by the astounding growth of computational power and AI, but it is *not* the consequences of advanced technology that we should fear the most. A much more threatening consequence will be the economic turmoil posed by the effect of advancing technologies causing technological unemployment, wage stagnation and inequality (i.e., the breakdown in the American Dream), as well as the threat of such technologies to personal freedoms, rights to privacy and to our belief in the sanctity of human life. Hopefully, this book will help convince you that these are not just intellectual or hypothetical issues to consider and debate. These consequences are the product of unfettered exponential change in our lives -- Radical Change. They are already apparent all around us; we just need to look carefully and with some forewarning and awareness.

As our society becomes more profoundly stressed by the forces of Radical Change, time will become our enemy. For us to undertake *meaningful* action to steer the course of Radical Change to abundance and not Armageddon, we must act quickly. We cannot assuage our feelings of discomfort with blind optimism, nor can we defer our attention or commitment until we get the kids through school, the next election is over, or we reduce our national debt. The experts in the scientific fields that are developing artificial intelligence and computer capacity have *not* got us covered. They do not, nor, I believe, are they likely to see the terrible consequences of their magnificent handiwork until it is far, far too late.

As a realist, I understand that no matter how ingenious the solutions may be, none can work without a substantial informed consensus for action among the American people and our political leadership. Unfortunately today we should not assume that these two groups share similar values, priorities or objectives. But unless our actions are guided by a dialogue that includes a broad cross-section of disciplines and groups, respectfully representing very diverse interests, the forces of Radical Change will plot their own direction for America and, indeed, for the world. Unfortunately consensus in the United States is not doing very well right now. Consensus within a country, by its very nature, is very difficult to quantify or to compare from era to era. Today there is, however, a great deal of anecdotal evidence and opinion polls to support the sense that we as a nation have lost not only our naivety regarding calls for national unity; we have, at least in part, lost our very appetite for this concept. The creation of Winners and many more Losers predicted here by the progress of advancing technologies will only make this situation worse.

A number of trusted friends have commented to me that these negative musings are solely the product of a grumpy old man. These same friends have reminded me that technology has, among its many blessings, connected us all through the Internet in a more fundamental and cohesive manner than ever before in history. As an observation of how easily we can reach out and "touch" one another and exchange ideas, information, opinions, falsehoods and trivia, this is undeniable. Through the applications of the Internet such as Facebook, Twitter, innumerable blogs and chat rooms, and other high-tech forums for social intercourse, we have never been better prepared to share our ideas, thoughts and concerns. But the belief that this new social media can provide a forum for consensus of the nature suggested by this book is, at best, wishful thinking. The power of the Internet to communicate ideas is beyond question. Consider its role in the Arab Spring Revolution in 2010-2011. In fact, the collective consensus and ability to mobilize mass movements around political issues are well recognized and feared by all totalitarian governments around the world. China, North Korea, Iran and many other countries have tried, often with pitiful failed attempts, to isolate themselves (or worse) from the influence of the World Wide Web. But despite all this well-known and widely proclaimed success there is a subtle, less recognized dark side to this communication. It is anonymous and too often it can be irresponsible. Its users, except on some social networks such as Facebook or Twitter, have handles, not names nor identities. The raucous, discourteous tenor of most chat rooms reflects this reality. As a ubiquitous, democratic means of communication, it scores an A+, but as a means of honest, responsible debate it is fatally flawed.

In whatever forum this dialogue proceeds, its participants must be deeply invested in its outcome. Given the stakes, this should not be a problem. But here we need to take another lesson from history. As technologies advance, they create great adversity. Radical Change will ensure that this process and the disparities between the Winners and the Losers it creates will grow more rapidly. This is not a formula with which to build consensus. Instead, we must remind ourselves of how fundamentally we are all in this together. Climate change has many lessons, most of them painful. One fundamental truth that has been reinforced is the reminder that we have become very interdependent on one another. This is not a new concept.

One of the earliest websites to explore this sense of connectivity was Six Degrees of Separation, founded in 1997 by Kevin Bacon. At its height, it had approximately 3.5 million subscribers. It derived its name from the famous observation by the Hungarian writer Frigyes Karinthy. In a 1929 article ("Chain-Links"), Karinthy made the insightful observation that on a planet of (then) over one billion people, everyone was separated by only six intermediaries. Since 1997, the world's population has grown dramatically, but our interdependence on one another has grown faster. In a world moving to exceed ten billion people, a sense of connectivity may be the source of inspiration for our survival or the ultimate cause of our undoing.

The future will be filled with abundance and a new standard of living that will transform the lives of virtually everyone on earth, no matter how desperate his or her present condition. This is not a hopelessly optimistic prayer; it is being fulfilled among us every day. Radical Change will bring this promise closer, ever faster. The legacy of a Cornucopia for all our children will depend, however, on whether we choose fairly to distribute this abundance. Some thinkers -- such as Leon Trotsky and

Vladimir Lenin -- have suggested, and history strongly reinforces the notion, that a significant redistribution of wealth can come only at the price of rebellion. Others, such as Tyler Cowen in *Average Is Over*, argue that the transition to permanent inequality will come with a "quiet acquiescence." He argues that the "losers" will be the old and infirm, too disabled to take to the streets in insurrection.

I believe that the real threat to America may not arise from a rebellion in our streets. It will come in the form of terrorist attacks on our increasingly vulnerable infrastructure. It will be undertaken not primarily by foreign-born extremists but by our own citizens, converted to radical beliefs. It is my belief that the conversion of a growing number of young people to extremist ideologies that we are experiencing today is not primarily due to the power of the ideology of these groups. It is more the product of the anger, frustration and the sense of hopelessness created by a lack of opportunity and social mobility in the society in which these people live -- whether it be in the United States, the Middle East or any other country in the world.

Another manifestation of this smoldering unrest is the recent rise of demonstrations, rallies and civil disobedience protesting police brutality in Baltimore, Maryland; Ferguson, Missouri and New York City and unfortunately in many other communities across our nation. The magnitude and the anger of these demonstrations cannot be explained solely as the reaction of these communities to police misconduct motivated by racist attitudes. There has not been a *new* outbreak of violent, unprovoked police misconduct; these problems have existed for generations. So why are people, particularly poor black young adults, now taking to the streets in violent protests?

I believe it is due to the frustrations of economic stagnation, loss of social mobility and the harsh reality of the death of the American Dream. The intense public scrutiny of racially motivated police practices in poor minority neighborhoods has provided the flash point. Yes, the protests have been sparked by issues of civil rights, but as with virtually all outbreaks of civil disobedience in our country's history, this anger is fueled by the underpinning of economic injustice. These protests may be the inevitable price we will pay for our disregard for the early stages of this tension. We still have time -- but we should not delude ourselves with the false promise that our best technologies can defend us from either of these threats. New technologies will create great advances in security, but they will also create much more insidious and dangerous opportunities for extremists to inflict great harm.

A constructive response to this challenge cannot, however, be based on fear. As a people and as a nation, we do not respond kindly to being threatened. I prefer to hope that our collective humanity will provide us with the moral force to set a new direction to our future. As the mantra for a mass political movement in America, this does seem, even to me, hopelessly naive, even romantically childish. Yet considering the stakes, I am ready to abandon the cynical views developed over forty years as a practicing lawyer and hope for better from my fellow Americans as well. To reach a shared abundance, we need to learn how to ride in our Caboose peacefully, sharing both the lunch cart and the facilities, and listening to our Conductors with open minds. Without this common ground, there is nowhere on which to build the foundations for a new American society. Building this consensus may be our greatest problem. Unfortunately solely our collective *hopes* for a different direction for the future, driven by Radical Change, will avail us nothing. We need decisive action with the bipartisan support of our political leadership. Here, even my new optimistic self begins to have its doubts. Today we have, due to a few decisions of our Supreme Court, the best government money can buy.[205] Disentangling the dysfunctional morass that is the

---

205 As one of the legacies our generation will leave in the hope chest for our children, history may judge this legacy as our most pernicious. In 2012 the Supreme Court ruled, in Corporate United Citizens vs. Federal Election Commission, that the First Amendment prohibits the government from restricting independent political contributions by corporations. Warren Buffet, in a CNN interview in March 2015, remarked: "They say there is free speech, but the ultra rich can speak twenty-five or thirty-five million times and my cleaning lady cannot speak at all." Some dismiss the effects of this decision by pointing out that both the Republican and Democratic Parties now receive mega corporate funding. No matter how lofty or inspired the goals of any contributor -- no one spends millions without a sense that it will affect public policy. Mega-million-dollar contributions to the Democratic Party inevitably discourage it from pursuing its historic mission as the party of the working middle and lower classes.

hallmark of our current national political process may cost us the precious time we have left to begin to address this challenge.

Why have these divisive attitudes come to dominate our thinking, particularly after the lessons of the crushing Great Recession of 2008? Perhaps it is the sense of loss of the security we felt for decades as, by far, the most dominant economic and military power in the world. My gut tells me, however, that when we as Americans began to lose our sense of upward mobility and our belief in the fairness and integrity of our economic and political processes, we became much more concerned about what we might lose than what we might achieve. This is a very destructive force to the American political and economic process. It may account for the anger and stridence that cross political affiliation, age, race and ethnic group. It manifests itself in the rhetoric of the Tea Party and Occupy Wall Street and the intransigence of the Republican and Democratic Parties, the National Rifle Association (NRA) and the Environmental Defense Fund (EDF).

Hopefully, the message of this book has heightened the awareness of the severity of these issues and the need to expand this dialogue far beyond the realm of the extremely intellectual and well informed physicists, mathematicians, futurists, economists and ethicists who have been the primary participants in these discussions to date. It is time for all sides of the rainbow of interests in America to realize that we are in this together. If most of the passengers in our Caboose truly believe in the promise of a future Cornucopia, we should be able to form a consensus of how we would share the short-term burdens of our journey to this abundance.

We are at a turning point where, for the sake of our children and grandchildren, we must act together. The dynamic forces of technology described in this book are already irretrievably "locked and ready." They will continue to unfold at a rapidly accelerating rate whether we are ready or not. They will transform our society and the world dramatically for better or worse. We can influence the direction of history only if we act decisively, and soon.

To appreciate the magnitude and immediacy of the challenge to control the future direction of Radical Change, we can learn an important lesson from an old French fable. Fittingly, it is a children's tale. One day a teacher took her class to a beautiful nearby pond where they discovered that a very invasive species of water lily had found its way into the pond. "The water lily's leaves will double their coverage of the pond every day," the teacher told her students. "Oh no they won't!" the students retorted. "We will cut them back -- how long do we have?" The teacher replied, "In thirty days the lilies will cover the entire pond and block all the sun." A few weeks went by, but the lilies did not seem to be growing very fast, so the children stayed in school and did nothing. Finally, one of the girls decided that the children should not wait too long -- in fact, to have plenty of time to do their work, she decided the students should start while the lilies covered only half the pond. The student asked the teacher when the children should begin cutting the lilies. The teacher replied, "You should begin before dawn on the thirtieth day." By then, of course, it would have become too late.

This is the nature of the exponential change that is now transforming our society. This children's fable contains a profound lesson about this process -- with something that is exponentially growing, to change its direction you must get started when everything still looks normal. If you do not, you will never be able to catch up! Moore had it right in 1965, but not many people have done the math. Today we may be on the verge of running out of time.

# Chapter Twenty-Five

## ANOTHER PATH TO THE NEAR HORIZON:
### Recipe for a Small Planet

This book has separated the noneconomic challenges of a future transformed by the power of Radical Change from the economic consequences. The suggestions in this chapter for a new direction on our journey address only the economic issues. This is not because challenges to personal rights, privacy and/or ethical principles are less important, nor is it meant to disregard the equally disturbing possibility that one or a handful of breakthroughs in technology will endow our civilization with the power to annihilate itself rather cheaply and easily. As for the existential challenge of the inevitable development of an alien intelligence far superior to our own; this risk is so daunting we can only hope that as ASI develops, we will learn from it the secret of how it can be controlled.

All of these challenges are very real. They are a frightening legacy to bestow upon our children. And yet there seems to be no clear and certainly no simple answer for how we can protect ourselves from the worst consequences these challenges foretell. Fortunately these issues are being addressed by many committed individuals far more qualified than I am. If there is a difference between the effects of Radical Change on these issues and on the economic issues that this book does address, it may be one of perception -- perception in the sense that when the NSA is caught secretly collecting and examining private, sometimes sexually explicit communications on Facebook, Instagram, etc., or when North Korea hacks into Sony's computers, no one has to write a book to tell the world that this is very wrong. And despite the wondrous benefits that have been discovered from unlocking the secrets of the human genome, no one has to remind us that this knowledge can be abused to allow the cloning of human beings or the unwarranted genetic altering of our offspring. Hollywood will continue to forewarn us of the possible Armageddon that lies ahead if we develop a malevolent form of alien ASI. The role that advancing technologies will play in exacerbating widespread technological unemployment, wage stagnation, gross economic inequality, and the real-world consequences of the injustice such developments will create is far less obvious or direct. The long-term unemployed former ice cream factory worker or the bank manager in Hagerstown had no idea who stole their identities, but the impact on their lives was far more extreme than if they had lost their wallets.

Today the middle class of America is not just suffering from the persistent and malingering after-effects of the terrible economic meltdown of 2008. The root causes of these economic ills go far deeper. These consequences are not simply the product of bad or self-interested decisions by our financial institutions to create financial weapons of mass destruction. They are not the inevitable result of America's decision to mortgage its future by borrowing too much on our homes and credit cards, and they are not the result of allowing our politicians to continue to spend without taxing. Yes, all these decisions played an obvious *part* in the meltdown of 2008 and our current problems. Our economy has revived despite all these poor choices, and yet something remains very wrong with the future prospects of the average working American.

Advancing technologies have played a subtle but extremely important role in fueling these problems and exacerbating their consequences. This dark side of technology has been given a free pass because it always comes with the paradox of abundance. The advanced technologies of tomorrow, fueled by Radical Change, will make the disparity of this economic conundrum much more severe. We will welcome the new technologies into our homes and revel in their comforts. These reactions will not instill a sense of caution as to how these technologies may be misused.

Before we can begin to alter the forces contributing to these consequences, we must fully appreciate the complex nature of the problem. This book tries to address this issue and suggest principles that could lay the framework for a solution. Reversing the momentum of our current economic direction will take an effort virtually unprecedented except for the unity and strength we as a nation displayed in the course of the Great Depression and the two World Wars. We need to find this discipline because this enemy is real; it is a wolf, not a sheep. We are at risk of losing the core values of our quickly diminishing middle class. These are the values that made our nation a leader and the most desirable country in the world in which to live and raise children. This is a daunting challenge, but in the coming battles, we will be armed with wonderful new ways to address these problems, and they are almost doubling every two years.

"You campaign in poetry; you govern in prose."[206] Mario Cuomo died at the age of eighty-two on New Year's Day, 2015, and America lost one of its finest remaining moral leaders. In 1984 at the Democratic National Convention held at the height of America's love affair with Ronald Reagan, Cuomo delivered a prophetic message:

A shining city is perhaps all the President sees. But there is another city, the part where some people can't pay their mortgages, and most young people can't afford one; where students can't afford the education they need, and middle-class parents watch the dreams they hold for their children evaporate.

[Some] believe that the ... train will not make it to the frontier unless some of the old, ... young ... [and] weak are left behind....

---

206 This was a phrase coined by Mario Cuomo, former three-term governor of New York, and it became the hallmark of his political career and his administration of government.

[We] believe that we can make it all the way with the whole family intact.[207]

Former Governor Cuomo sadly lived to see, beyond his worst fears, the harsh reality of his vision come true. Surely with the certain abundance of our future, we can do better. But how?

Technology remains for the moment a tool -- a wonderful, almost magically transformative tool, providing amazing advancement to the human condition. Despite the splendor of the technological promise of abundance in our future, the path of our journey will be marked by many unfortunate Losers and costly compromises to values we cherish. Within this abundance, however, lies the means to ensure that when we arrive at the Near Horizon, we shall not find "two cities." It would be a terrible mistake to blame the tool of technology for the hardship of the work ahead of us. We would be repeating the mistakes made by the Luddites two hundred years ago. Advancing technologies provide both the challenge and the answer to the question of the legacy we will leave for our children and grandchildren.

Given the enormity of this undertaking, it is fair to ask whether Americans are willing to bear the hardship and exert the enormous effort that will be required. A growing number of economists and astute political observers feel that many of our current economic problems are due to a fundamental lack of motivation, particularly among young adults in our workforce. Obviously America has its fair share of drifters, freeloaders and others who consider work to be another form of a four-letter word. Popular culture has portrayed this group as not concerned with pursuing a future career or achieving monetary success. Some commentators characterize this group as being more interested in part-time work at McDonalds or CVS to support a video game, beer or

---

207 The references to Republicans and Democrats in this quote were deliberately deleted because I believe this statement expresses the feelings of many Americans today without regard to political affiliation.

heroin addiction. Whether the latter characterization is accurate or not, the number of unemployed young people is growing rapidly.

Tyler Cowen argues in his very popular book, *Average Is Over*, that "For whatever reason, over 40 percent of adult, non-senior Americans don't consider it worthwhile to have a job."[208] In Cowen's words, "They can't find a *deal* that suits them (emphasis added)." Cowen goes on to report that the number of unemployed men in the age group twenty-five to sixty-four (18 percent) is twice as large as it was in the 1950s and 1960s. He concludes that:

> it is no surprise that popular culture today has this image of the male slacker, a young man who lives at home, plays video games, is indifferent to holding down a job, and maybe doesn't run after young women so hard.

One can quarrel with the characterization of the problem of the growing true unemployment and inequality in America, but no one can question the hard statistics. American society is being supported by a dramatically shrinking proportion of its working-age population. The fact that a growing number of our nation's aging baby boomers do not have adequate means to support even a modest retirement and are virtually unemployable (other than as greeters at Walmart) leaves a terrible legacy for the next generation. That generation is already burdened with a staggering load of student debt while struggling to obtain the qualifications to be employed in the new jobs of the twenty-first century. These statistics are very troubling, but the fact that these trends are worsening in a period in which incomes and wealth creation for a very fortunate few are dramatically increasing is unacceptable. The critical issue that needs to be addressed is: Why are these negative forces occurring now? Are they the lingering effects of the worldwide recession of 2008, and, if not, what can be done about them? I believe we should start with a

---

208 Tyler Cowen, *Average Is Over: Powering America Beyond the Age of the Great Stagnation* (Dutton, 2013, p. 51).

less moralistic, cynical assessment of what is wrong with America's work-force. This is extremely important, because if you begin with a cynical, moralistic assessment of the problem, you will likely arrive at a cynical, moralistic solution.

Cowen does not let us down. In *Average Is Over*, he suggests "a few particular changes" to address this economic mess: Raise taxes "somewhat"; cut Medicaid; eliminate or, at least, transfer the burden of governmental support for health care, disability, retirement, and unemployment benefits to workers; and have poor people live in cheaper housing in warmer climates (he describes this as "lower land rents").[209]

It is hard to believe that Cowen thinks this is the best America can do. How bad could these solutions get for middle- and low-income families? Cowen goes on in detail in the area he describes as "lower land rents." Having been a real estate lawyer, I have some experience in this subject. By "land," he does not mean land under commercial office towers on Wall Street or Madison Avenue. He means housing and public services for low- and moderate-income families in America. He suggests two concrete proposals to "lower land rents":

We could build some tiny homes, ... about 400 square feet.[210] ...
We also could build some makeshift structures there, similar to the better dwellings you might find in a Rio de Janeiro favela.[211]

These are very sad observations about the future of America. The suggestion that there is something acceptable, and indeed inevitable, about America's poor or recently impoverished choosing to live in favelas is repugnant to the ideals that made our nation strong. Hopefully, the historical implications of the choice of the term "favela" were not drawn to Mr. Cowen's attention. The first favela was built on a hill on the outskirts of Rio de Janeiro, Brazil, in about 1897. The first inhabitants were

---

209  Cowen, *Average Is Over*, p. 241.
210  This is about the size of a generous living room.
211  Cowen, *Average Is Over*, p. 241.

soldiers of the Brazilian Army and their families, who had waited for years for the soldiers' return. The soldiers were returning from brutally subduing an insurrection of poor peasants in Bahia, a remote province of Brazil. Upon the soldiers' return the government refused to pay them for their services to their country. In desperation, they moved their families and built a horrible slum on a hill on the outskirts of Rio de Janeiro. They named it Favela Hill, after the name of a skin-irritating tree indigenous to Bahia. This was the first but certainly not the last time that slums around the world have been referred to as favelas.[212] Drugs, crime and disease-ridden hovels in slums, breeding disenchantment, disillusionment and anger are not a solution for what is wrong with America. Nor is it the American promise that we should offer to our children or to our brave men and women returning from Iraq and Afghanistan.

Tyler concludes *Average Is Over* with this bleak forecast of the future of the American middle class:

One day soon we will look back and see that we produced two nations, a fantastically successful nation working in the technologically dynamic sectors and everyone else.[213]

Why am I bashing Cowen and the message of *Average Is Over*? It is not because the message incorrectly projects the future of our middle and lower classes. It is precisely because he is right! This message could very well be the epitaph for the American Dream. It is a very chilling forecast of our future, and it is hard to see how America will be able to avoid this fate. The resurrection of the American Dream will not happen by hoping that our unemployed will somehow wake up and start finding new pathways to the abundance of the Near Horizon. The challenge America faces today is not similar to the one our nation faced during the Industrial Revolution -- the challenge to transform and retrain millions

---

212 See www.history.com, Aldeias de Mal, which describes the favela in Rio as a problem of "safety, hygiene, and morals."
213 Tyler Cowen, *Average Is Over*, p. 259.

of farmers and other semi-skilled workers to fill manufacturing, sales and service jobs. It is more complex and much more difficult to resolve.

Even though we have entered a paradigm shift in our economy, the programs for recovery *must* remain based on the premise that the average American wants to be employed and is willing to sacrifice to gain a decent education to obtain a living wage. The challenge is to identify the very nature of what it means to be qualified to be employed in the new economy of the Near Horizon and to provide a fair opportunity to obtain those qualifications.

It is beyond the scope of this book to attempt to describe specific programs or actions that will need to be undertaken to ensure that our path to the promised land of the Near Horizon goes well for most, if not all, of us. That is a challenge that has been the subject of a number of books. For an excellent start, you could begin with recommendations found at the conclusion of *The Second Machine Age*.[214]

There are, however, basic principles that must underlie any plan. In simple terms, these principles should include, at least, the following:

I. The federal government must regain its ability to function, govern and lead our nation.

Our system of capitalism has created a magnificent standard of living for many Americans and it has empowered our country to become the most dominant economic and military power in the world. It has also proven, beyond any reasonable doubt, that left unguided, untempered and unregulated, it is capable of creating enormous economic chaos, hardship and disaster. The financial debacle leading to the Great Recession of 2008 proved this point beyond dispute. There is a second lesson we should gain from this experience. Wall Street, the bastion and inner sanctum of capitalism, did not look inwardly for salvation as

---

214 Erik Brynjolfsson and Andrew McAfee, *The Second Machine Age: Work, Progress, and Prosperity in a Time of Brilliant Technologies* (W.W. Norton & Company, Inc., 2014). See also "The Agenda to Raise America's Pay" (Economic Policy Institute, http.//www.epi. org/pay-agenda/?utm=EconomicPolicy).

the great institutions such as Bear Stearns and AIG imploded. It looked for intervention and financial assistance from our federal government. Similarly, any meaningful redirection of the economic forces of Radical Change will require a rigorous and unwavering federal injection of leadership, financial assistance and moral persuasion. Given the current dysfunctional political polarization in Washington, it is difficult to imagine how this will be possible. This may, in fact, be the saddest commentary in this book because, with exponential change, time is our enemy.

There may, however, be some comfort in the fact that any meaningful program for federal intervention to redirect the force of Radical Change will require a strong consensus of the American public. If such a consensus is feasible, it may also address the current gridlock caused by a handful of entrenched political True Believers in Washington, DC -- now aptly named the "idiot caucus."[215]

II. Any federal program of assistance must be simple to administer, fair and understandable to the American public.

As a nation, we take pride in feeling that, however imperfect, we provide a safety net for most unfortunate, needy and suffering Americans. In truth, due to politics and the vagaries of the historic development of a vast bureaucracy, we provide not a safety net but a thousand trampolines. Each trampoline can provide a "bounce" if the applicant knows the system; each has definite limits of whom it will support (with very hard edges if the person in need is off center); and each trampoline demands its own system of administration, maintenance and regulation to ensure that there are no free rides for the undeserving.

No major infusion of federal assistance that allocates its resources by augmenting the trampolines can succeed; in fact, politically speaking, it couldn't even be funded. We need to address the problems of unemployment and inequality in a manner that is far more effective

---

215 This insightful nickname has been used by none other than Republican John Sununu, former Senator of New Hampshire and noted conservative commentator, not known for his liberal sensitivities. John Sununu, "Common Ground for the 'doc fix,'" *Boston Globe*, March 30, 2015.

than simply creating more government employees, a method that has characterized many past attempts to stimulate our economy and/or address basic social ills. Our basic institutions of business, banking and education are not broken; in fact, in the context of the overall economy, they are working quite well. The problem is that they are only working for a very fortunate few. The governmental programs that will serve us best will encourage the power of these institutions to partner with the financial resources and incentives of federal, state and local governments. Creative partnerships with these institutions will produce better results than attempting to regulate, disrupt or duplicate their functions.

III. Gross economic inequality in a nation of abundance is unstable, unfair and repugnant to the sensibilities of a just society. We must take steps to ameliorate this condition.

Rectifying this inequality will take an unprecedented effort of collective sharing, in part motivated by self-interest, but the abundance of the future can provide the substance to facilitate this redistribution of income. Instituting a more progressive, graduated tax on income and wealth (inheritance) without the loopholes that have poisoned previous efforts at taxation is a starting point. Closing the loopholes alone, by eliminating carried interest, a favorite tax shelter of the one-percenters, and closing down offshore corporate tax havens, can be a source of major new revenue. These reforms should not be condemned by conservatives as raising taxes, but they will be. More importantly, such reforms will signify that a sense of fairness is being restored to America. We also need to take a very hard look at our internal priorities. Can we continue to justify a trillion-dollar subsidy to what has now become a corporate farm economy? In our war with terrorists, can and should we support the development of a new class of aircraft carriers at the cost of $12 billion each, when relatively inexpensive drones are far more effective? Can we remain the world's policeman when wars without any apparent victory for democracy in Iraq, Afghanistan and elsewhere have cost our nation billions, if not trillions? These are hard questions, but they are not unsolvable.

With this collection of revenues must come a form of redistribution of income to the less fortunate. This effort should be guided by rewarding those willing to make the effort to earn these benefits. Programs such as the earned income tax credit, which enjoys a measure of bipartisan support, should be reinvigorated at both the state and federal levels. The federal minimum wage should be raised, notwithstanding the cynical argument that at its current level it encourages full employment. These programs should be instituted not only because they will provide a measure of redistributing wealth to assuage the tensions created by an unjust economic environment. They should be structured to provide avenues for opportunity and self-fulfillment for those willing to sacrifice and work hard. It is hypocritical to pass value judgments on those who have given up participating in our economy if there is, in fact, little chance of upward mobility. Reducing inequality will provide the resources to fuel the reversal of this sad state of affairs. Eliminating *gross* inequality will also be an important first step in signaling that we are serious in our purpose of reinvigorating the American Dream.

IV. The best and greatest investment America can make in the twenty-first century is in educating the human capital that is our citizens.

During the Industrial Revolution and the latter part of the twentieth century, America led the world in offering an opportunity for a meaningful educational experience to every child. This is not to ignore the history of racial, ethnic, religious and sexual discrimination that, unfortunately, was also a hallmark of this era. But despite this terrible legacy, in the twentieth century generations of disadvantaged children of every race and religion grew up with the hope of obtaining an education that would allow them to participate in the success of America. Fair and open access to a quality education at both the primary and secondary levels is essential if we have any hope of reversing the current reality that a lack of educational qualifications is now the primary force exacerbating the loss of economic and social mobility and growing inequality in our nation. We also need to recognize and address the fact that unequal access to educational opportunities is only part of the problem. As long as a significant portion of American working families cannot earn a living wage, we cannot pour enough money into our system of education to provide an equal educational opportunity for our children. Only the truly unusual child can grow up in an environment of abject poverty and still take advantage of a new path to education and opportunity, no matter how well intentioned or structured that opportunity may be. We owe our children better.

The curriculum for this effort must be cognizant of the rapidly evolving requirements to participate effectively in the Knowledge Revolution. This is not a call for a massive redirection of our educational system to become a trade school or focused community college experience, solely concerned with instilling the skills required for gainful employment in the future. The challenge of growing technological unemployment may warrant more focus on this priority, but our broader educational goals should be reexamined and refocused, not discarded. As the Internet becomes more integrated into every fabric of our lives, the fundamental role of the three "R's" (reading, writing and arithmetic) needs to be reevaluated. And despite the protests from the Brakemen and our own misgivings of the loss of the human dimension in education (as discussed in Chapter Eighteen, "The Transformation of the Service Sector"), we need to embrace the role of AI and computers into our educational systems of the future.

Our problems in higher education are very different but no less challenging. The United States still has the finest institutions of higher learning in the world. Unfortunately parents all around the planet are well aware of this fact. The challenge of the twenty-first century will be to provide viable opportunities for our children to access and participate in this system *through* graduation.[216] This will require reinvigorating our

---

216 A harsh reality that must be addressed is the increasing trend for young Americans to start but fail to complete a higher education.

state-funded colleges and universities and funding federal programs of financial assistance such as the Pell Grant Program to reflect the reality of the current costs of a college education.

Finally, in our efforts to restore a sense of educational opportunity, we cannot overlook the struggle of students already burdened with crushing student debt incurred during the winter of our neglect of their plight. We need to institute plans to refinance (and in appropriate situations forgive) all or some portion of this debt. Without this relief, giving students with mountains of credit-score wrecking debt an opportunity to re-educate themselves for the high-tech jobs of the future is a hollow, if not cynical, promise.

V. We must get America back to work, performing meaningful jobs that benefit and strengthen our economy, not flipping burgers at fast-food outlets.

Better education, increased social mobility and reduced inequality may help to restore the ability and motivation of America to get back to work, but there also must be meaningful work to do. Stimulating the creation of more high-tech employment is certainly a part of this solution. To do this, we need to increase our commitment to funding basic research in technologies such as climate change, the environment, health, science, AI, energy, agriculture and water and sewage treatment. These investments can be made, in large part, through traditional conduits such as the National Institutes of Health (NIH), the National Institute of Science (NIS) and the Defense Advanced Research Projects Agency (DARPA). We should also find ways to increase funding for incentive prizes, innovation centers and early-stage investments in start-up technologies. The government infusion of funds in this process is essential because private investments have almost never supported significant early stage research in any new technology. By its very nature our capitalist system requires demonstrable evidence of a reasonable return on investment, or the investment is not made. This is not a criticism of the system; it is only a recognition that we should not expect the private sector to provide a solution to all of our problems or needs.

While these efforts are essential, this entire sector of the economy is currently too small to be able to grow quickly enough to meet the enormity of this challenge. As a result, we need to create publicly funded projects that provide not only meaningful work but also meaningful reinvestment in our future. There is bipartisan support for a massive investment in rebuilding the infrastructure of our nation. These programs can be administered through the states and will result rather quickly in the creation of many well-paying jobs in the construction industry. Given the current sad state of our infrastructure, this need will provide a relatively long-term source of employment. We should not, however, confuse government-funded employment (even in the context of private contractors building infrastructure at public expense) with long-term job creation.

Despite the adverse impact of new technologies on small business, some technologies have created a new class of small entrepreneurs. These start-up businesses are finding wonderful new opportunities to engage in global business through the Internet. We are also witnessing a resurgence in local and/or regional "organic" businesses such as locally grown agricultural produce, craft beers, etc. These efforts should be encouraged by reinvigorating the Small Business Administration and the myriad of federal, state and local economic development agencies to nurture these efforts.

VI. The appropriate role of government must be constantly reviewed, reconsidered and refined, not increased.

If we expect governmental intervention to wisely and effectively assist in a change of direction on our path to the Near Horizon, we must honestly reevaluate what government does well and what it does not. Governmental overregulation of private enterprise is an historic and politically volatile subject. The participants on both sides of this debate have by now staked their positions with an intransigence and mindless conviction that only a True Believer can appreciate. As a result, I am reluctant to suggest that we re-examine the extent of the damage that results from good intentions in this process. However, in an age of Radical Change, the role of the Brakemen will increasingly determine the rate and the direction of our progress to the future. The current reality (if you can step back from political persuasions on the subject) is that our governmental regulatory process has allowed many beneficial technologies and the applications they empower to become the hostage of the True Believers, whatever their politics. Whether the debate is over wind power on Cape Cod, nuclear waste disposal in Nevada, birth control and/or abortions, the trans-American pipeline, genetically modified food, Uber's disruption of the taxicab business, or Airbnb's intrusion into the hotel and housing industries, the agenda for America's future is being hijacked, often for months if not years, by a small minority of ardent, sometimes well-meaning True Believers. As Radical Change accelerates the process of new technologies transforming the way in which we live, this process will only become more constrictive. We see mounting evidence of this tension in the challenges facing promising new technologies such as drones, genetically engineered drugs, access to the Internet, and the ongoing enforcement of patent, copyright, licensing and other forms of regulations limiting the free flow of knowledge and the ATT it inspires.

As we emerge from the flat stage of exponential change, new uses of technology that disrupt the status quo will accelerate dramatically. It is my belief that most of the future applications of new technologies that destroy jobs *will not* require regulatory approval. Most of the technologies that create meaningful new jobs in the future *will* require such approvals. We need to be mindful of the consequences of this paradox or we will pay a heavy price for our inaction or undue tolerance of the mischief of the True Believers and the Brakemen in abusing this process.

VII. Because technology remains a tool, we need to shape how new technologies are developed safely and utilized for the benefit of the many, not the personal enrichment or empowerment of the few.

Training the human side of the challenge of technological unemployment is very important. However, we must recognize that this places unemployed workers on a very steep learning curve. In fact, left unchecked, the demands of the increasingly sophisticated nature of technological unemployment may exceed our capacity to retrain America. As a result, we need to reassess how, at least, some technologies can be developed that benefit from partnerships with workers' basic, innate human skills, not advanced knowledge or skills that will be very difficult for many workers to acquire. Incorporating advanced voice recognition, voice capability and AI into these technologies will enhance the possibilities of these partnerships. Why not offer an incentive prize for the first entity to develop an inexpensive computer program that will allow a sophisticated DNA clinical trial to be performed by someone with only a high school education? With the new, much smarter AI of the future, creating technologies that can instruct us as to how they are to be deployed is not as crazy as it may seem. Remember, once a technology learns how to accomplish a task, it never forgets, and it can pass this knowledge on to the next computer instantaneously and freely. This cannot be said of humans.

We must also redouble our efforts to develop the technologies of the future with safeguards to ensure (to the extent feasible) that they do not escape our control or are put to unintended, undesirable purposes. In our love affair and partnership with technology, we have allowed ourselves the understandable luxury of ignoring certain flaws in our partner's basic nature. As technologies become more powerful and able to act on their own volition, for example, stock market algorithms and drones, this will become a luxury we cannot afford. We are currently woefully unprepared to meet this challenge. We are not even prepared to meet the now well-known threat of identity theft, cyber attack on our electronic infrastructures or the massive intrusion on our personal freedoms and privacy that new technologies allow. Yet many experts[217] identified these potential abuses decades ago. We are now onto another generation of technologies in the fields of AI, DNA research, cyborg-like applications of technologies and drones and other forms of self-actuating technologies, yet we remain in a blissful state of denial of the ultimate dangers of these technologies.

Finally, as technologies create new disruptions in our traditional markets, we need to constantly reassess the appropriate role of government in this process. Governmental regulation of Uber and the like to ensure mandatory background checks for drivers is appropriate; continuing to support a monopoly in the taxicab industry is not. Paradoxically, the intervention of the Federal Trade Commission to regulate access to the Internet as a utility assured more open and less costly service for the majority of Americans. Allowing the operation of the free market by corporate giants such as Verizon would *not* have done so. New technologies will increasingly require a non-ideological approach to the appropriate role of government in order to best protect the public interest.

These principles are very general and are certainly not a complete set of values to utilize in plotting a new direction to the Near Horizon, but they are a start. I am not so politically naive as to put forth these principles without appreciating that they convey a very different set of core values than those that now define our current political arena, or as some would say, political stalemate. We could spend the next millennium bickering about the areas of our disagreement,[218] but the course of events, empowered by Radical Change, will not abate to allow us this indulgence. We must quickly come to realize that we have reached a point in history where the future of inaction is clear: two cities -- two nations -- without a dream to become united.

---

217 Science fiction writers such as George Orwell were actually first.
218 The Winners are rooting for this to happen -- the status quo is working just fine for them.

# Conclusion

## ONE PLANET, ONE EXPERIMENT[219]

We are all in this together -- all seven billion of us and growing fast. However, while the population is exploding, technology is shrinking the world faster than ever. Our fears of dire threats to humanity caused by ASI, such as those that were the subject of the movies *2001: A Space Odyssey*, *The Terminator*, *Robocop* and *Avengers: Age of Ultron*, create huge audiences based on scenarios of cataclysmic battles with ASI -- but they are not our real threat. The risk of the abuse or loss of control of an alien form of ASI in the future is real, not unlike the certainty that earth will be struck, yet again, by a giant meteorite of cosmic proportions or suffer a volcanic explosion that dwarfs the one that millions of years ago flattened what is now Yellowstone National Park. Like the dinosaur, there is little that humanity, with our current knowledge base, can do to thwart these risks, so I will accept them and tuck my grandchildren into bed with a clear conscience.

The nearer-term threats from Radical Change created by advancing technologies are fundamentally different, and they will come long before ASI may take control of the future of our world. These are the threats that will arise on our journey to the Near Horizon. Technology is the greatest tool that God has given us, but we get to choose how it will be used. One option includes choosing to do nothing and letting nature run her course. The mixed blessings of technology's great gifts and potentially greater perils will increase the future level of disagreement and resulting discourse and acrimony on these issues. But we cannot allow this uncertainty or discord to become an excuse for doing nothing on the basis that no one knows how it will all work out.

Despite all of its failings and notwithstanding our daily frustrations, America remains a wonderful place to live and work, raise our children, and fulfill our dreams. Most importantly, it remains the greatest place to leave for our children and grandchildren. This is, as they say, the bottom line. I have worked in Guatemala for many years. There is a saying there: "Es mas facile para entra al cielo que entra Los Estados Unidos" (It is easier to enter heaven than the United States). It may not feel like heaven, especially if you are unemployed and have suffered through a gridlocked government that failed to extend long-term unemployment benefits or create a meaningful living wage in a nation of unparalleled wealth. However, America still remains a land of great opportunity and abundance. Capitalism and technology have contributed greatly to this opportunity and to the abundance that we often take for granted. Our current economic problems are not the inevitable product of these forces, they are the result of how we have failed to manage and utilize the enormous power and opportunities that new technologies have created.

Technology can also take away what it has given. With the advent of Radical Change, the opportunities, where they exist, will become ever more enriching, but perhaps for only a very fortunate few. To avoid the serious consequences of failing to act, forewarned by this book, we will be required to use radical approaches, some of which have been failures in the past. But by doing nothing, the path we will follow seems clear. As Mario Cuomo and Tyler Cowen have stated, we may be on our way to creating a starkly divided people living in two cities or two nations. This is a clear insight into what our country may become, and it is not a disservice for Cuomo or Cowen to enunciate it. It is, however, a disservice to the moral aspirations and the heritage of our nation to settle for it. In this fatalistic prophesy, there is an unspoken message that this future is inevitable. This is not the way it has to be nor is it the "deal" we should leave for our children. Every generation in America has felt that it has struggled with the greatest forces of change in this country's history. Radical Change assures us and our children and grandchildren of the same challenge. But at the same time, it will give us the tools to do far better. Will we use this great abundance wisely and emerge more strongly united than ever before, or will we choose to allow the fittest to survive very, very well?

The Internet, Facebook, and Twitter all remind us of the truth and poignancy of six degrees of separation. We are all increasingly in this together. Lowering the lifeboats for the escape and safety of only some is still an option, but a very bad option. Our ride on the Cannonball Express will be very bumpy; it will go uphill and down and it will be filled with abundance and growing pains. It is a time for great moral leadership in a country nearly paralyzed by bitterly polarized partisan politics. It is a time to recall the advice of some great Conductors who have ridden with us in the past.

One such Conductor is former President John F. Kennedy. In today's sophisticated world, his legacy seems to emerge from a very innocent era. It was the age of Camelot, but, as is the case in all paradigm shifts, we can never go back to that simpler world. Certain truths, however, remain timeless, and today one immutable truth spoken by Kennedy at his inaugural address on January 20, 1961 may lie at the core of our ability as a nation to steer a different course to the Near Horizon: "Ask not what your country can do for you, but what you can do for your country." Simple words, delivered to a nation in a far simpler, more optimistic era -- but they may be more meaningful and poignant now than ever before.

The second great moral Conductor whose words and actions we should heed is Dr. Martin Luther King, Jr. On August 28, 1963, speaking on the steps of the Lincoln Memorial to over 250,000 people who had joined together for the March on Washington for Jobs and Freedom, Reverend King delivered one of the most powerful speeches in the history of American politics -- "I Have a Dream." It galvanized a movement and reminded many in the nation of their common heritage of arriving as immigrants with great hopes and aspirations that their efforts would be met with justice and equality.

As a nation, we had a dream long before Reverend King uttered these immortal words. Our dream is a bit tarnished now, but we have the tools to restore it to its previous promise. The immigrants who arrived at Ellis Island in the nineteenth and twentieth centuries had big dreams, hopes, and aspirations, but no illusions that America would provide them with a free lunch upon their arrival. I choose to be an optimist. It is not the spirit of the American working people that is tarnished; it is the American Dream itself that needs a shine. Radical Change and the technologies it will bring with it will create a great abundance for future generations if it is used wisely and distributed with a generosity motivated in part by self-interest. If we do this, upon our arrival at the Near Horizon we can find not just a "brave new world," but a great Cornucopia for most.

While writing this book, I was reminded of the gratitude we should feel and the lesson we should learn from our young men and women returning from the wars in Iraq and Afghanistan. They are not just reentering their homeland. They are reentering our society and our economy. Is America ready to greet them with open economic arms? There are many lessons these men and women can teach us. Their generals in Iraq and Afghanistan did not lead them into battle relying on polls to see where the enemy was weakest.[219] The commanders of their platoons did not treat them differently depending on whether they were Democrats or Republicans, members of the Tea Party or the Occupy Wall Street movement. Those who, in their civilian lives, were True Believers were expected to concentrate solely on the common goal rather than their fiercely held personal beliefs. The responsibilities each was given were not influenced by monetary contributions given to their leaders. But

---

219 Winston Churchill, "Nothing is more dangerous in wartime than to live in the temperamental atmosphere of a Gallup Poll...", Debate, House of Commons, September 30, 1941.

most important of all, every man and woman of the US Armed Forces has been taught to share and cherish one fundamental belief: "Leave no fallen comrade behind." We need a value system in the upcoming battle with advancing technologies as we determine the direction of our uncertain future. Why not this one?

We may be approaching a pivotal moment in history to choose our course between Cornucopia and Armageddon. The challenge is immense, but great minds have considered these hard choices before. One of the greatest, an intellect who thought a great deal about technology, left some brilliant insights as to both options.

If we proactively choose to chart a course to Cornucopia:

> The stakes are immense, the task colossal, the time is short. But we can hope, we must hope that man's own creation, man's own genius, will not destroy him ... there is no problem that human reason can propound which the human reason cannot reason out.[220]

Or shall we allow the power of the gathering force of Radical Change to plot a course that may lead us to Armageddon?

> I do not know how the Third World War will be fought, but I can tell you what they will use in the fourth -- rocks![221]

---

220 Albert Einstein, speaking on the horrors of the power of nuclear weapons, *New York Times Magazine*, June 22, 1946.

221 Albert Einstein, speaking on the advent of the nuclear arms race, in an interview with Alfred Werner, *Liberal Journalism*, May 1949.

# Epilogue

## PERSONAL REFLECTIONS

I began this book by stating that it was for our children and grand-children. I will end it with the hope that, despite the forces of Radical Change in the future, the essential qualities of their lives will remain the same as those cherished by prior generations. This thought reminded me of a poem written years ago to my middle daughter, Anna:

**Letter from a Father to Anna**
Do you remember the day lilies?

Those great orange blossoms that
grow along the driveway to our farm

Those days of play -- we fooled around with homemade
games in our field
filled with sheep
and birthday parties with squirt gun fights

Three sisters and yet those bright
day lilies always reminded me of you.

I wonder why?

Was it that your spirit and sense
of excitement were the natural
reflections of their annual displays?

You are grown now and no longer
play in our fields --
but the day lilies return each spring

Orange and brash and ever
spreading in their enthusiasm for life

To remind your mom and me of the days
with little children
who played and frolicked among the simple
pleasures of spring's promise
of the return of the day lilies!

Woodstock, Vermont, May 2005

# ABOUT THE AUTHOR

The author was born and raised in Alplaus, a small town outside of Schenectady, New York, the only child of second-generation Irish immigrants. He had the odd experience of attending a four-room school house with eight grades and with his mother as his teacher in grades one, two and four. Yes, Mom got promoted!

Mr. Sullivan went on to attend Saint Michael's College and the University of Virginia School of Law. Despite ski-bumming at Sugarbush and Killington, Vermont each winter during the school year, Mr. Sullivan graduated near the top of his class in both college and law school.

After a very close brush with the Vietnam War draft (his lottery number was "1"), he went on to accept a position in Boston at Ropes & Gray, at the time the largest and oldest law firm in Boston. However, it was the era of Kennedy's call to the new frontier, so Mr. Sullivan chose to leave Ropes & Gray (no one did that then) and pursue a career in public service working for the Boston Legal Assistance Project ("BLAP," as it was affectionately termed). After a few years, Mr. Sullivan left BLAP and fell back on what he did best, spending his days ski bumming, this time in Jackson Hole, Wyoming and Aspen, Colorado. Upon returning to Boston, Mr. Sullivan worked for the court-appointed receiver of the Boston Housing Authority, an agency that was so incompetent and politically corrupt that it was thrown into legal bankruptcy by the Housing Court of Boston. It had been in both moral and political bankruptcy for years.

One day an acquaintance called out of the blue and asked if Mr. Sullivan would be willing to take over his real estate practice as a partner in one of the top-tier law firms in Boston. Showing the impulsivity that marked his long legal career, Mr. Sullivan readily accepted the position -- "Of course, Rudy," he replied, "this is your lucky day, I was just thinking about changing jobs." Miraculously, there were no malpractice claims, and Mr. Sullivan stayed with the firm as it grew to over 180 lawyers, with offices in New York City, Hartford, Providence and London.

Mr. Sullivan practiced in the field of commercial real estate, representing clients as diverse as G.E. Capital, Fleet Bank, Citibank, MIT, the Children's Hospital of Boston, Oxfam, Jewish Community Housing for the Elderly, Inc. and B'nai B'rith Elderly Housing Corporation.

For many years, prior to his retirement, he spent the majority of his time representing MIT in the redevelopment of Kendall Square, Cambridge, Massachusetts. In the course of almost twenty years representing MIT, Kendall Square was transformed from a dangerous area of abandoned warehouses, debris-covered parking lots, seedy bars and gasoline stations into a world-class center of biotech, life science, computer science and telecommunications. It became the birthplace of many start-up innovation companies.

This experience did not, however, expose him to many new technologies. The closest he ever came to high tech was when one day, on his way to a meeting, he mistakenly stepped off the elevator on the wrong floor of Building 300 in Technology Square with a very distinguished older woman (wearing a very large official badge). Mr. Sullivan unexpectedly found himself in the US Army Nanotechnology Center at MIT. Two nice men holding sub-machine guns agreed he was on the wrong floor.

The only real qualification Mr. Sullivan has to write this book is that he has three beautiful daughters and three young grandchildren. He hopes that the lives of his children and grandchildren will be filled with security, fulfillment and, if not abundance, sufficiency. This wish motivated Mr. Sullivan to write this book in his retirement, when he and most of his colleagues thought he would be off playing golf. Someday this may still happen, especially if our journey to the Near Horizon goes well.